Praise for *The War*

CW01064443

"A rousing, revolutionary history of
ing class war! To liberate humanity, end exploitation and to prevent
planet from climate change, we need to organise and revolt to defend, extend
and deepen the commons. We can gain inspiration from this well written
and inspiring book."—DEREK WALL, author, *The Commons in History:
Culture, Conflict and Ecology*

"An impressive account of the *real* tragedy of the commons. Ian Angus
shows how enclosure shaped agrarian capitalism and created an overex-
ploited working class—and how working people fought back. *The War
Against the Commons* emphasizes that it is essential to overcome the rural-
urban divide to properly address the ecological crisis that threatens human
and non-human life in this century."—SABRINA FERNANDES, sociologist and ecosocialist activist; author, *Sintomas Mórbidos: A encruzil-
hada da esquerda brasileira* (Morbid Symptoms: The Crossroads of the
Brazilian Left)

"A potent antidote to the naturalization of capitalist property relations. *The
War Against the Commons* reveals the long history of struggle against the
expropriation of land and labor that is at the root of current social and ecological crises. This history is important, not only to better understand today's
world, but to better imagine the future we require—beyond capital's deadly,
imperial grip on the earth."—HANNAH HOLLEMAN, sociologist and
author, *Dust Bowls of Empire: Imperialism, Environmental Politics, and
the Injustice of "Green" Capitalism*

"An accessible and invaluable resource for activists seeking to understand
the rise of capitalism. Ian Angus details the heroic struggles of the Diggers
and others who resisted enclosure and the expropriation of the commons,
struggles that continue to inspire us today as we fight to overthrow this
system and restore our connection with nature in a society based on solidarity and cooperation."—SUSAN PRICE, founding member, Socialist
Alliance (Australia); co-editor, *Green Left*

"An impressive and accessible contribution on a vitally significant subject
of both historical and contemporary importance."—FRED MAGDOFF,
Emeritus Professor of Plant & Soil Science, University of Vermont. co-
author, *What Every Environmentalist Needs to Know About Capitalism*

"With characteristic verve and clarity, Ian Angus dissects the myth that capitalist agriculture rescued a hungry world. He shows that as the rich grabbed

common lands, poverty and inequality grew, first in England and then around the world. Since the loss of our shared heritage was key to the rise of capitalism, restoring the commons will be vital to creating greater equity." — JULIA ADENEY THOMAS, Associate Professor of History, University of Notre Dame; co-author, *The Anthropocene: A Multidisciplinary Approach*

"Both sparkling and profound, Ian Angus's study of peasant expropriation and resistance portrays five centuries of rural class struggle that laid the basis for today's movements for social and ecological liberation." —JOHN RIDDELL, editor, *The Communist International in Lenin's Time*

"Ian Angus has written a short, well crafted and scholarly history of early capitalism with special emphasis on the enclosures and their consequences." —HENRY HELLER, Professor of History at the University of Manitoba; author, *The Birth of Capitalism: A Twenty-First Century Perspective*

"The history of how peasants were dispossessed during the emergence of capitalism in England and Scotland really sheds light on the system that is responsible for today's ecological crises. Ian Angus's very readable history helps us to understand the world in which we live. Highly recommended!" —DAVID CAMFIELD, Associate Professor of Labour Studies & Sociology, University of Manitoba; author, *Future on Fire: Capitalism and the Politics of Climate Change*

"A rousing, revolutionary history of the enclosure of the commons as ongoing class war! To liberate humanity, end exploitation and to protect our planet from climate change, we need to organise and revolt to defend, extend and deepen the commons. We can gain inspiration from this well-written and inspiring book."—DEREK WALL, author, *The Commons in History: Culture, Conflict and Ecology*

"A clear, sweeping, well-informed narrative of the triumph of capitalism in Europe, and the destruction of humanity's *commonwealth* for the enrichment of the few. It is also the story of dogged resistance by dispossessed majorities for dignity and freedom, a story that challenges dogmatic understandings of 'progress.' There is much to learn here, for activists and scholars alike, about the possibility of a future in which the free development of each will be the condition for the free development of all."—PAUL LE BLANC, author, *From Marx to Gramsci: A Reader in Revolutionary Marxist Politics*, and *Lenin: Responding to Catastrophe, Forging Revolution*

The War Against the Commons

Dispossession and Resistance in the Making of Capitalism

by IAN ANGUS

MONTHLY REVIEW PRESS
New York

Library of Congress Cataloging-in-Publication data
available from the publisher.

ISBN 978-168590-016-8 paper
ISBN 978-168590-017-5 cloth

Typeset in Minion Pro

MONTHLY REVIEW PRESS | NEW YORK
www.monthlyreview.org

5 4 3 2 1

Contents

In memory of
JOHN MOLYNEUX
(1948–2022)

A socialist activist, writer and educator for more than five decades, John played a central role in initiating and coordinating the Global Ecosocialist Network, bringing together people and organizations on six continents from a wide range of socialist traditions. We honor his memory by fighting to defend and restore the commons.

Enclosure came, and trampled on the grave
Of labour's rights and left the poor a slave
And birds and trees and flowers without a name
All sighed when lawless law's enclosure came.

—JOHN CLARE, 1820

Introduction

Nature does not produce on the one hand owners of money or commodities, and on the other hand men possessing nothing but their
own labour-power. This relation has no basis in natural history, nor
does it have a social basis common to all periods of human history.
It is clearly the result of a past historical development, the product
of many economic revolutions, of the extinction of a whole series of
older formations of social production.

—KARL MARX[1]

FOR ALMOST ALL OF HUMAN existence, almost all of us were
self-provisioning. Together with our neighbors, we lived and
worked on the land, obtained and prepared our own food, and
made our own homes, tools and clothing. After our ancestors
invented agriculture, most of us lived in small communities where
the land was held and farmed in common, and most production
was consumed locally.

Today, almost all of us have to work for others. Our lives depend
on, and are largely defined by, our jobs. All the productive wealth
is owned by a tiny minority of individuals and corporations, and
most of us cannot eat unless we sell them our ability to work.

That's how capitalism works, and we are so used to it that it seems natural and obvious. Even sharp critics of injustice and inequality rarely question the division between owners and workers, employers and employees. It's just the way things are: some hard working and clever people have acquired property, and the rest of us are lucky to be able to work for them. It may not be fair, but you can't change human nature.

That argument ignores the fact that human beings evolved 300,000 years ago and capitalism arrived only a few hundred years ago. Even if we compare it only to the first great civilizations in Mesopotamia 6,000 years ago, capitalism is an infant. Some people worked for wages in some previous societies, but wage-labor has only become universal in the past few hundred years—and the change was forced on us by "the most merciless barbarism, and under the stimulus of the most infamous, the most sordid, the most petty and the most odious of passions."[2] Human nature, if there is such a thing, had little to do with it.

For wage-labor to triumph, there had to be large numbers of people for whom self-provisioning was no longer an option. The transition, which began in England in the 1400s, involved the elimination not only of shared use of the land, but of the common rights that had allowed even the poorest people access to essential means of subsistence. The right to hunt or fish for food, to gather wood and edible plants, to glean leftover grain in the fields after harvest, to pasture a cow or two on undeveloped land—those and more common rights were erased, replaced by the exclusive right of property owners to use Earth's wealth.

Through force and fraud, common land was privatized. Formerly shared fields were split into private plots bounded by fences and hedges, and commoners became laborers who could only survive by working for the owners. "Great masses of men . . . [were] suddenly and forcibly torn from their means of subsistence, and hurled onto the labour market as free, unprotected and rightless proletarians. The expropriation of the agricultural producer, of the peasant, from the soil is the basis of the whole process."[3]

Deprived of land, people whose forebears had worked the soil for millennia had to sell their labor to others and the separation of working people from the land that fed them became a permanent feature of the new social order. "The capital-relation presupposes a complete separation between the workers and the ownership of the conditions for the realization of their labour. As soon as capitalist production stands on its own feet, it not only maintains this separation but reproduces it on a constantly extending scale."[4]

Karl Marx discussed this separation in the section of *Capital* titled "So-Called Primitive Accumulation." In Appendix 1, I argue that the term "primitive accumulation" is misleading, and since Marx himself preferred "original expropriation," I will use that term in this book.

Original expropriation has taken different forms in different parts of the world, and it continues to this day, but this book focuses on the first and most complete case, the centuries-long war against the agricultural commons, known as *enclosure* in England and as the *clearances* in Scotland.

Before Marx, no one had researched the subject so thoroughly, or explained it so well. His account is still must-reading for anyone with the slightest interest in the origins of capitalism, but an enormous amount of new information has become available since then, and it would be very surprising if subsequent research hadn't cast new light on the subject. To cite just one example, the vitally important works of Gerrard Winstanley and the Diggers were not rediscovered and published until the 1880s, after Marx's death. The availability of a wealth of new evidence has prompted me to retell the history of original expropriation in England and Scotland in *The War Against the Commons*. I have placed particular emphasis on *resistance*—the long struggle of working people against expropriation and for control of their lives. Original expropriation was never a one-sided process; it was an arena of intense class struggle from the beginning.

THE PERIOD EXAMINED IN *The War Against the Commons* extends from the late 1400s to the mid-1800s, with a brief discussion of modern times in the final chapter.

Part One, Expulsion and resistance, 1450–1660, discusses the first great wave of enclosures and dispossessions, in the years when capitalism was taking form, leading up to the English Revolution of 1640–1660. It describes the "systematic theft of common property" (Marx's term) and the resistance it provoked, the emergence of a landless working class, and the state's efforts to impose work discipline by force. It concludes with a discussion of the revolutionary views of Gerrard Winstanley, whose call for a new society based on the commons was more sophisticated and radical than anything else written before the 1800s.

Part Two, Expansion and Consolidation, 1660–1860, discusses the second wave of enclosure, which was strengthened and financed by the forced labor of African slaves and the colonial plunder of India. Landowners and merchants used their control of the state to expropriate the remaining commoners. The poor were prevented from growing their own food and harshly punished if they dared to hunt for it. After 1760, Scotland too was transformed by the clearances that brutally expelled farmers and cottars in the Lowlands and Highlands.

Part Three, Consequences, discusses some results of centuries of expropriation. Chapter 10 responds to the often-made claim that enclosure increased production, reduced hunger, and enabled the Industrial Revolution. Chapter 11 shows that employers deliberately created hunger to ensure a supply of agricultural workers. Chapter 12 looks at ending the separation of town and country as a central feature of Marx and Engels's revolutionary program. Chapter 13 discusses the continuing importance of dispossession and resistance in modern times.

The first two appendices consider misconceptions about Marxism and the war against the commons. Appendix 1 examines what Marx meant by "so-called primitive accumulation," and why he thought "original expropriation" was a more correct term. Appendix 2 discusses Marx and Engels's views on the revolutionary potential of the Russian peasant communes that existed in their time. Appendix 3 is a manifesto issued by peasant organizations that are fighting enclosure and expropriation today. Finally, for reference, Appendix 4 is a timeline of key events discussed in this book.

THIS IS THE STORY OF AN essential part of the rise of capitalism—the forced separation of working people from the means of subsistence, especially the land itself, a separation achieved by robbery, violence, fraud, and worse. The expropriators used hunger to force the poor to work in their fields, mines, and factories—and the poor fought back with every weapon they had. It is a story written, as Marx said, in letters of blood and fire.

PART ONE

EXPULSION AND RESISTANCE

1480–1660

1

"Systematic Theft of Communal Property"

The ground of the parish is gotten up into a few men's hands, yea
sometimes into the tenure of one or two or three, whereby the rest
are compelled either to be hired servants unto the other or else to
beg their bread in misery from door to door.

—WILLIAM HARRISON, 1577[1]

In 1549, tens of thousands of English peasants fought, and thousands died, to halt and reverse the spread of capitalist farming
that was destroying their way of life. The largest action, known
as Kett's Rebellion, has been called "the greatest practical utopian
project of Tudor England and the greatest anticapitalist rising in
English history."[2]

On July 6, peasants from Wymondham, a market town in
Norfolk, set out across country to tear down hedges and fences
that divided formerly common land into private farms and pastures. As they walked, they were joined by farmers, farmworkers,
and artisans from other towns and villages. On July 12, as many
as 16,000 rebels set up camp on Mousehold Heath, near Norwich,
the second-largest city in England. They established a governing

council with representatives from each community, requisitioned food and other supplies from nearby landowners, and drew up a list of demands addressed to the king.

Over the next six weeks, they twice invaded and captured Norwich, rejected Royal pardons on the grounds that they had done nothing wrong, and defeated a force of 1,500 men sent from London to suppress them. They held out until late August, when they were attacked by some 4,000 professional soldiers, mostly German and Italian mercenaries, who were ordered by the Duke of Warwick to "take the company of rebels which they saw, not for men, but for brute beasts imbued with all cruelty."[3] Over 3,500 rebels were massacred, and their leaders were tortured and beheaded.

The Norwich uprising is the best documented and largest revolt in 1549, but what was long remembered as the *Commotion Time* involved camps, petitions, and mass assemblies in at least twenty-five counties, showing "unmistakable signs of coordination and planning right across lowland England."[4] The best surviving statement of their objectives is the 29 articles adopted at Mousehold Heath. They were listed in no particular order, but, as historian Andy Wood writes, "a strong logic underlay them."

> The demands drawn up at the Mousehold camp articulated a desire to limit the power of the gentry, exclude them from the world of the village, constrain rapid economic change, prevent the over-exploitation of communal resources, and remodel the values of the clergy. . . . Lords were to be excluded from common land and prevented from dealing in land. The Crown was asked to take over some of the powers exercised by lords, and to act as a neutral arbiter between lord and commoner. Rents were to be fixed at their 1485 level. In the most evocative phrase of the Norfolk complaints, the rebels required that the servile bondmen who still performed humiliating services upon the estates of the Duchy of Lancaster and the former estates of the Duke of Norfolk be freed: "We pray thatt all bonde men may be made Free, for god made all Free with his precious blode sheddyng."[5]

The scope and power of the rebellions of 1549 demonstrate, as nothing else can, the devastating impact of capitalism on the lives of the people who worked the land in early modern England. Marx called it "the systematic theft of communal property."[6]

Class and Commons before Capitalism

In medieval and early-modern England, most people obtained their essential needs directly from the land, a shared resource.

Commons-based farming systems were probably brought to England by Anglo-Saxon settlers after Roman rule ended. What we know for sure is that they were widespread, in various forms, when English feudalism was at its peak in the twelfth and thirteenth centuries. The land itself was held by landlords, directly or indirectly from the king. A minor gentry family might hold and live on just one manor—roughly equivalent to a township—while a top aristocrat, bishop, or monastery could hold dozens. The people who actually worked the land, often including a mix of unfree serfs and free peasants, paid rent and other fees in labor, produce, or (later) cash, and, in addition to the right to farm, had a variety of legal and traditional rights to use the manor's resources.

> Common rights were managed, divided, and redivided by the communities. These rights were predicated on maintaining relations and activities that contributed to the collective reproduction. No feudal lord had rights to the land exclusive of such customary rights of the commoners. Nor did they have the right to seize or engross the common fields as their own domain.[7]

Field systems varied a great deal, but usually a manor or township included both the landlord's farm (demesne) and land that was farmed by tenants who had lifelong rights to use it. Most histories only discuss open field systems, in which each family cultivated strips of land that were scattered through the arable fields so no one family had all the best soil, but there were other arrangements. In parts of southwestern England and Scotland, for example, farms on common arable land were often compact, not in strips, and were periodically redistributed among members of the commons community. This was called *runrig*; a similar arrangement in Ireland was called *rundale*.

Most communities also shared pasture for feeding cattle, sheep, and other animals, and in some cases forest, wetlands, and waterways. The right to use these common resources was not an occasional perk, but essential for survival in a society where hunting and gathering still provided many essentials of everyday life. Common woodland, for example, not only provided food (berries, nuts, greens, herbs, birds, small animals, and occasionally deer), but also firewood, a necessity for warmth and cooking, and other raw materials. Most villagers' houses were made of wood, as were their tables, benches, bowls and spoons, and farming necessities such as handles for ploughs, hoes, and scythes, wagons and wagon wheels, and much more.

Common forest rights were so important that when the barons forced King John to accept Magna Carta in 1215, they not only included clauses that protected forest rights from royal interference, but also made him sign the Great Charter of the Forest, which defined many common rights in detail.[8]

In her award-winning study of the commons-based communities, historian J. M. Neeson shows that common rights were particularly important to the very poor, who had little or no farmland.

> Waste gave them a variety of useful products, and the raw materials to make more. It also gave them the means of exchange with other commoners and so made them part of the network of exchange from which mutuality grew. More than this, common waste supported the economies of landed and cottage commoners too. It was often the terrain of women and children. And for everyone the common meant more than income.[9]

Though cooperative, open field villages were not communities of equals. Originally, all the holdings may have been about the same size, but in time considerable economic differentiation took place.[10] A few well-to-do tenants held land that produced enough to sell in local markets; others, probably a majority in most villages, had enough land to sustain their families with a small surplus in good years; and still others with much less land may have worked part-time for their better-off neighbors or for the landlord. "We can see this stratification right across the English counties in Domesday Book of 1086, where at least one-third of the peasant population were smallholders. By the end of the thirteenth century this proportion, in parts of southeastern England, was over a half."[11]

Marxist historian Rodney Hilton explains that the economic differences among medieval peasants were not yet *class* differences. "Poor smallholders and richer peasants were, in spite of the differences in their incomes, still part of the same social group, with a similar style of life, and differed from one to the other in the abundance rather than the quality of their possessions."[12] It wasn't until after the dissolution of feudalism in the 1400s that a layer of capitalist farmers developed.

The Tragedy That Wasn't

If we were to believe an influential article published in *Science* in 1968, shared, commons-based agriculture ought to have disappeared shortly after it was born.[13] "The Tragedy of the Commons" is one of the most-reprinted articles ever to appear in any scientific journal, and one of the most-quoted: a recent Google search found "about 1,950,000 results" for the phrase "tragedy of the commons."

The author, Garrett Hardin, a University of California professor who until then was best-known as the author of a biology textbook that argued for "control of breeding" of "genetically defective" people.[14] He had no training in or particular knowledge of social or agricultural history—his real goal was to prove that twentieth-century overpopulation was caused by "the commons in breeding"—but his argument quickly became, in the words of a World Bank Discussion Paper, "the dominant paradigm within which social scientists assess natural resource issues."[15] It has been used time and again to justify stealing Indigenous peoples' lands, privatizing health care and other social services, giving corporations "tradable permits" to pollute the air and water, and much more. Anthropologist G. N. Appell says it has been "embraced as a sacred text by scholars and professionals in the practice of designing futures for others and imposing their own economic and environmental rationality on other social systems of which they have incomplete understanding and knowledge."[16]

Hardin's argument was a just-so story about the commons in rural England. "Picture a pasture open to all," he wrote. A herdsmen who wants to maximize his income will calculate that the cost of additional grazing (reduced food for all animals, rapid soil depletion) will be divided among all, but he alone will get the benefit of having more cattle to sell. Inevitably, "the rational herdsman concludes that the only sensible course for him to pursue is to add another animal to his herd. And another; and another...." But every "rational herdsman" will do the same thing, so the commons will be overstocked and overgrazed until it supports no animals at all. "Freedom in a commons brings ruin to all."

Key to Hardin's argument is the unproven assertion that herdsmen always want to expand their herds and cannot be stopped from doing so. "It is to be expected that each herdsman will try to keep as many cattle as possible on the commons.... As a rational being, each herdsman seeks to maximize his gain." His conclusion was predetermined by his assumptions. "It is to be expected" that each herdsman will try to grow his herd without regard to consequences—and each one does exactly that. It's a circular argument that proves nothing.

The very fact that commons-based agriculture lasted for centuries disproves Hardin's assumptions. Where were the gain-maximizing rational herdsmen during all those years, and why did communities fiercely resist all attempts to eliminate common rights?

Self-Management

Remarkably, few of those who accepted Hardin's views as authoritative seem to have noticed that he provided no evidence to support his sweeping conclusions. He claimed that "tragedy" was inevitable, but he didn't show that it had happened even once.

Scholars who have studied commons-based agriculture draw very different conclusions. Political scientist Susan Cox, for example, concluded that "the traditional commons system is not an example of an inherently flawed land-use policy, as is widely supposed, but of a policy which succeeded admirably in its time."

> What existed in fact was not a "tragedy of the commons" but rather a triumph: . . . for hundreds of years—and perhaps thousands, although written records do not exist to prove the longer era—land was managed successfully by communities.[17]

Jeanette Neeson's study of manorial records from the 1700s showed that the common-field villagers, who met two or three times a year to decide matters of common interest, were fully aware of the need to regulate the flow of nutrients between livestock, crops, and soil.

> The effective regulation of common pasture was as significant for productivity levels as the introduction of fodder crops and the turning of tilled land back to pasture, perhaps more significant. Careful control allowed livestock numbers to grow, and, with them, the production of manure. . . . Field orders make it very clear that common-field villagers tried both to maintain the value of common use of pasture and also to feed the land.[18]

Village meetings selected "juries" of experienced farmers to investigate problems, and introduce permanent or temporary bylaws. Particular attention was paid to "stints"—limits on the number of animals allowed on the pasture, waste, and other common land.

"Introducing a stint protected the common by ensuring that it remained large enough to accommodate the number of beasts the tenants were entitled to. It also protected lesser commoners from the commercial activities of graziers and butchers."[19]

Juries also set rules for moving sheep from field to field to ensure even distribution of manure, and they organized the planting of turnips and other fodder plants in fallow fields, so that more animals could be fed and more manure produced. The jury in one of the manors that Neeson studied allowed tenants to pasture additional sheep if they sowed clover on their arable land. Long before scientists discovered nitrogen and nitrogen-fixing, these farmers knew that clover enriched the soil.[20]

And, given present-day concerns about the spread of disease in large animal feeding facilities, it is instructive to learn that commoners in the 1700s adopted regulations to isolate sick animals, stop hogs from fouling horse ponds, and prevent outside horses and cows from mixing with the villagers' herds. There were also strict controls on admitting bulls and rams to enter the commons for breeding, and juries "carefully regulated or forbade entry to the commons of inferior animals capable of inseminating sheep, cows or horses."[21]

Neeson concludes, "The common-field system was an effective, flexible and proven way to organize village agriculture. The common pastures were well governed, the value of a common right was well maintained."[22]

Commons-based agriculture survived for centuries precisely because it was organized and managed by people who were intimately involved with the land, the crops, and the community. Although it was not an egalitarian society, in some ways it prefigured what Karl Marx, referring to socialism, described as "the associated producers, govern[ing] the human metabolism with nature in a rational way."[23]

Class Struggles

That's not to say that agrarian society was tension-free. There were

almost constant struggles over how the wealth that peasants produced was distributed in the social hierarchy. The nobility and
other landlords sought higher rents, lower taxes, and limits on the
king's powers, while peasants resisted landlord encroachments
on their rights and fought for lower rents. Most such conflicts
were resolved by negotiation or appeals to courts, but some led to
pitched battles, as they did in 1215 when the barons forced King
John to sign Magna Carta, and in 1381 when thousands of peasants marched on London to demand an end to serfdom and the
execution of unpopular officials.

Historians have long debated the causes of feudalism's decline:
I won't attempt to resolve or even summarize those complex discussions here.[24] Suffice it to say that by the early 1400s in England,
the feudal aristocracy was much weakened. Peasant resistance
had effectively ended hereditary serfdom and forced landlords to
replace labor-service with fixed rents, while leaving common field
agriculture and many common rights in place. Marx described the
1400s and early 1500s, when peasants in England were winning
greater freedom and lower rents, as "a golden age for labor in the
process of becoming emancipated."[25]

But that was also a period when long-standing economic divisions within the peasantry were increasing. W. G. Hoskins described
the process in his classic history of life in a Midland village:

> During the fifteenth and sixteenth centuries there emerged at
> Wigston what may be called a peasant aristocracy, or, if this
> is too strong a phrase as yet, a class of capitalist peasants who
> owned substantially larger farms and capital resources than the
> general run of village farmers. This process was going on all over
> the Midlands during these years.[26]

Capitalist farmers were a small minority. Agricultural historian Mark Overton estimates that "in the early sixteenth century,
around 80 per cent of farmers were only growing enough food for
the needs of their family household." Of the remaining 20 percent,

few employed laborers and sought to accumulate more land and wealth. Nevertheless, by the 1500s two very different approaches to the land coexisted in many commons communities:

> The attitudes and behavior of farmers producing exclusively for their own needs were very different from those farmers trying to make a profit. They valued their produce in terms of what use it was to them rather than for its value for exchange in the market. . . . Larger, profit orientated, farmers were still constrained by soils and climate, and by local customs and traditions, but also had an eye to the market as to which crop and livestock combinations would make them most money.[27]

The rise of capitalist farming within, combined with powerful assaults on the commons from above, ultimately destroyed the traditional economy.

Sheep Devour People

Organized resistance and reduced population, following the Great Plague of the mid-1300s, allowed English peasants to win lower rents and greater freedom in the 1400s, but they didn't win every fight. Rather than cutting rents and easing conditions to attract tenants, some landlords forcibly evicted their smaller tenants and leased larger farms, at increased rents, to well-off farmers or commercial sheep graziers. Sheep required far less labor than grain, and the growing Flemish cloth industry was eager to buy English wool.

Local populations declined as a result, and many villages disappeared entirely. As Henry VIII's advisor Sir Thomas More famously wrote in 1516, sheep had "become so greedy and fierce that they devour human beings themselves. They devastate and depopulate fields, houses and towns."[28]

For more than a century, *enclosure* and *depopulation*—the words were almost always used together—were major social and political concerns for England's rulers. As early as 1483, Edward V's Lord Chancellor, John Russell, criticized "enclosures and emparking . . . [for] driving away of tenants and letting down of tenantries."[29] In the same decade, the priest and historian John Rous condemned enclosure and depopulation, and identified sixty-two villages and hamlets within twelve miles of his home in Warwickshire that were "either destroyed or shrunken," because "lovers or inducers of avarice" had "ignominiously and violently driven out the inhabitants." He called for "justice under heavy penalties" against the landlords responsible.[30]

Thirty years later, Thomas More condemned the same activity, in more detail:

> The tenants are ejected; and some are stripped of their belongings by trickery or brute force, or, wearied by constant harassment, are driven to sell them. One way or another, these wretched people—men, women, husbands, wives, orphans, widows, parents with little children and entire families (poor but numerous, since farming requires many hands)—are forced to move out. They leave the only homes familiar to them, and can find no place to go. Since they must leave at once without waiting for a proper buyer, they sell for a pittance all their household goods, which would not bring much in any case. When that little money is gone (and it's soon spent in wandering from place to place), what finally remains for them but to steal, and so be hanged—justly, no doubt—or to wander and beg? And yet if they go tramping, they are jailed as idle vagrants. They would be glad to work, but they can find no one who will hire them. There is no need for farm labor, in which they have been trained, when there is no land left to be planted. One herdsman or shepherd can look after a flock of beasts large enough to stock an area that used to require many hands to make it grow crops.[31]

Many accounts of the destruction of commons-based agriculture assume that that enclosure simply meant the consolidation of open-field strips into compact farms, and planting hedges or building fences to demark the now-private property. In fact, as the great social historian R. H. Tawney pointed out in his classic study of *The Agrarian Problem in the Sixteenth Century*, in medieval and early modern England the word enclosure "covered many different kinds of action and has a somewhat delusive appearance of simplicity."[32] Enclosure might refer to farmers trading strips of manor land to create more compact farms, or to a landlord preventing tenants and laborers from using common land, or to the violent expulsion of entire villages from land their families had worked for centuries. Or many other variations. In every case, the key issue was the loss of common rights.

Even in the Middle Ages, tenant farmers had traded or combined strips of land for local or personal reasons. That was *called* enclosure, but the spatial rearrangement of property as such didn't affect common rights or alter the local economy.[33] In the sixteenth century, opponents of enclosure were careful to exempt such activity from criticism. For example, the commissioners appointed to investigate illegal enclosure in 1549 received this instruction:

> You shall enquire what towns, villages, and hamlets have been decayed and laid down by enclosures into pastures, within the shire contained in your instructions, . . .
>
> But first, to declare unto you what is meant by the word enclosure. It is not taken where a man encloses and hedges his own proper ground, where no man has commons, for such enclosure is very beneficial to the commonwealth; it is a cause of great increase of wood: but it is meant thereby, when any man has taken away and enclosed any other men's commons, or has pulled down houses of husbandry, and converted the lands from tillage to pasture. This is the meaning of this word, and so we pray you to remember it.[34]

As Tawney wrote, "What damaged the smaller tenants, and produced the popular revolts against enclosure, was not merely

enclosing, but enclosing accompanied by either eviction and conversion to pasture, or by the monopolizing of common rights....
It is over the absorption of commons and the eviction of tenants
that agrarian warfare—the expression is not too modern or too
strong—is waged in the sixteenth century.[35]

An Unsuccessful Crusade

The Tudor monarchs who ruled England from 1485 to 1603 were
unable to halt the destruction of the commons and the spread of
agrarian capitalism, but they didn't fail for lack of trying. A general *Act Against Pulling Down of Towns* was enacted in 1489, just
four years after Henry VII came to power. Declaring that "in some
towns two hundred persons were occupied and lived by their
lawful labours [but] now two or three herdsmen work there and
the rest are fallen in idleness,"[36] the Act forbade conversion of
farms of twenty acres or more to pasture, and ordered landlords
to maintain the existing houses and buildings on all such farms.

Fourteen further anti-enclosure laws were enacted between
1515 and 1597. In the same period, commissions were repeatedly appointed to investigate and punish violators of those laws.
The fact that so many anti-enclosure laws were enacted shows
that while the Tudor government wanted to prevent enclosures
that reduced local populations, it was consistently unable to do
so. From the beginning, landlords simply disobeyed the laws. The
first Commission of Enquiry, appointed in 1517 by Henry VIII's
chief advisor, Thomas Wolsey, identified 1,361 illegal enclosures
that occurred after the 1489 Act was passed.[37] Undoubtedly more
were hidden from the investigators, and even more were omitted because landlords successfully argued that they were formally
legal. (The Statute of Merton, enacted in 1235, allowed landlords
to enclose common land, so long as sufficient remained to meet
customary tenants' rights; this provided a loophole for landlords
who defined "sufficient" as narrowly as possible.)

The central government had many reasons for opposing

depopulating enclosures. Paternalist feudal ideology played a role—those whose wealth and position depended on the labor of the poor were supposed to protect the poor in return. More practically, England had no standing army, so the king's wars were fought by peasant soldiers assembled and led by the nobility, but evicted tenants would not be available to fight. At the most basic level, fewer people working the land meant less money collected in taxes and tithes. And, as the rebellions of 1549 showed, enclosures contributed to social unrest, which the Tudors were determined to prevent.

Important as those issues were, for many landlords they were outweighed by their desire to maintain their income in a time of unprecedented inflation, driven by debasement of the currency and the influx, through Spain, of plundered New World silver. "During the price revolution of the period 1500–1640, in which agricultural prices rose by over 600 per cent, the only way for landlords to protect their income was to introduce new forms of tenure and rent and to invest in production for the market."[38]

Smaller gentry and well-off tenant farmers did the same, in many cases more quickly than the large landlords. The changes they made shifted income from small farmers and farmworkers to capitalist farmers, and deepened class divisions in the countryside.

> Throughout the sixteenth century the number of smaller lessees shrank, while large leaseholding, for which accumulated capital was a prerequisite, became increasingly important. The sixteenth century also saw the rise of the capitalist lessee who was prepared to invest capital in land and stock. The increasing divergence of agricultural prices and wages resulted in a "profit inflation" for capitalist farmers prepared and able to respond to market trends and who hired agricultural labor.[39]

As we've seen, the Tudor government repeatedly outlawed enclosures that removed tenant farmers from the land. They failed because they attacked *consequences* but not *causes*.

The special evil which they were intended to combat was depopulation caused by evictions. But evictions could be checked only by giving tenants security, which would have meant turning customary into legal titles, and fixing judicial rents for leaseholders and immovable fines for copyholders; in short, the sort of interference which the peasants and their champions demanded, but on which no Government depending on the support of the landed gentry would venture except upon an extraordinary emergency. In the absence of such an attempt to grapple directly with the fundamental fact that the peasants' insecurity made them liable to suffer whenever there was a change in the methods of agriculture, legislation designed merely to prevent those changes was almost certain to be evaded.[40]

On top of that, enforcement of the Tudors' anti-depopulation laws depended on justices of the peace, typically local gentry who, even if they weren't enclosers themselves, wouldn't betray neighbors and friends who were. Occasional commissions of enquiry were more effective—and so were hated by landlords—but their orders to remove enclosures and reinstate former tenants were rarely obeyed, and fines could be treated as a cost of doing business.

From Monks to Investors

The Tudors didn't just fail to halt the advance of capitalist agriculture, they unintentionally gave it a major boost. As Marx wrote, "The process of forcible expropriation of the people received a new and terrible impulse in the sixteenth century from the Reformation, and the consequent colossal spoliation of church property."[41]

Between 1536 and 1541, seeking to increase royal income, Henry VIII and his chief minister, Thomas Cromwell, disbanded nearly nine hundred monasteries and related institutions, retired their occupants, and confiscated their lands and income.

This was no small matter—together, the monasteries' estates comprised between a quarter and a third of all cultivated land in

England and Wales. If he had kept it, the existing rents and tithes would have tripled the king's annual income. But in 1543 Henry, a small-country king who wanted to be a European emperor, launched a pointless and very expensive war against Scotland and France, and paid for it by selling off the properties he had just acquired. When Henry died in 1547, only a third of the confiscated monastery property remained in royal hands; almost all that remained was sold later in the century, to finance Elizabeth's wars with Spain.[42]

The sale of so much land in a short time transformed the land market and reshaped classes. "More than any other act in the long history of the establishment of English private property," Peter Linebaugh writes, "it made the English land a commodity."[43] According to the noted Marxist historian Christopher Hill, "in the century and a quarter after 1530, more land was bought and sold in England than ever before."

> There was relatively cheap land to be bought by anyone who had capital to invest and social aspirations to satisfy. . . . By 1600 gentlemen, new and old, owned a far greater proportion of the land of England than in 1530—to the disadvantage of crown, aristocracy and peasantry alike.
>
> Those who acquired land in significant quantity became gentlemen, if they were not such already. . . . Gentlemen leased land—from the king, from bishops, from deans and chapters, from Oxford and Cambridge colleges—often in order to sub-let at a profit. Leases and reversions sometimes lay two deep. It was a form of investment. . . . The smaller gentry gained where big landlords lost, gained as tenants what others lost as lords.[44]

As early as 1515, there were complaints that farmland was being acquired by men not from the traditional landowning classes— "merchant adventurers, clothmakers, goldsmiths, butchers, tanners and other artificers who held sometimes ten to sixteen farms apiece."[45] When monastery land came available, owning or leasing multiple farms became even more attractive to urban merchants with money to spare. Some no doubt just wanted the prestige of a country estate, but others, used to profiting from their investments, moved to impose shorter leases and higher rents, and to make private profit from common land.

A popular ballad of the time expressed the change concisely:

> We have shut away all cloisters,
> But still we keep extortioners.
> We have taken their land for their abuse,
> But we have converted them to a worse use.[46]

Hysterical Exaggeration?

Early in the 1900s, conservative economist E. F. Gay—later the first president of the Harvard Business School—wrote that sixteenth-century accounts of enclosure were wildly exaggerated. Under the influence of "contemporary hysterics" and "the excited sixteenth-century imagination," a small number of depopulating enclosures were "magnified into a menacing social evil, a national calamity responsible for dearth and distress, and calling for drastic legislative remedy." Popular opposition reflected not widespread hardship, but "the ignorance and hide-bound conservatism of the English peasant," who combined "sturdy, admirable qualities with a large admixture of suspicion, cunning and deceit."[47]

Gay argued that the reports produced by two major commissions to investigate enclosures show that the percentage of enclosed land in the counties investigated was just 1.72 percent in 1517 and 2.46 percent in 1607. Those small numbers "warn against exaggeration of the actual extent of the movement, against an uncritical acceptance of the contemporary estimate both of the greatness and the evil of the first century and a half of the 'Agrarian Revolution.'"[48]

Gay's argument was accepted and repeated by right-wing historians eager to debunk anything resembling a materialist, class-struggle analysis of capitalism. The most prominent was

Cambridge University professor Geoffrey Elton, whose bestselling book *England Under the Tudors* dismissed critics of enclosure as "moralists and amateur economists" for whom landlords were convenient scapegoats. Despite the complaints of such "false prophets," enclosers were just good businessmen who "succeeded in sharing the advantages which the inflation offered to the enterprising and lucky." And even then, "the whole amount of enclosure was astonishingly small."[49]

The claim that enclosure was an imaginary problem is improbable, to say the least. R. H. Tawney's 1912 response to Gay applies with full force to Elton and his conservative co-thinkers:

> To suppose that contemporaries were mistaken as to the general nature of the movement is to accuse them of an imbecility which is really incredible. Governments do not go out of their way to offend powerful classes out of mere lightheartedness, nor do large bodies of men revolt because they have mistaken a ploughed field for a sheep pasture.[50]

The reports that Gay analyzed were far from complete. They didn't cover the whole country (only six counties in 1607), and their information came from local "jurors," who were easily intimidated by their landlords. Despite the dedication of the commissioners, it is virtually certain that their reports understated the number and extent of illegal enclosures.

And, as Tawney pointed out, enclosure as a percentage of *all* land doesn't tell us much about its economic and social impact— the real issue is how much *farmed and common* land was enclosed.

John Martin has reanalyzed Gay's figures for the most intensely farmed areas of England, the ten Midlands counties where 80 percent of all enclosures took place. He concludes that in those counties over 20 percent of cultivated land had been enclosed by 1607, and in two counties enclosed farms exceeded 40 percent. Contrary to Elton's claim, those are not "astonishingly small" figures—they support Martin's conclusion that "the enclosure movement must have had a fundamental impact upon the agrarian organization of the Midlands peasantry in this period."[51]

It's important to bear in mind that enclosure, as narrowly defined by Tudor legislation and enquiry commissions, was only part of the restructuring that was transforming rural life. W. G, Hoskins emphasizes this in *The Age of Plunder*:

> The importance of engrossing of farms by bigger men was possibly a greater social problem than the much more noisy controversy over enclosures, if only because it was more general. The enclosure problem was largely confined to the Midlands . . . but the engrossing of farms was going on all the time all over the country.[52]

George Yerby elaborates:

> Enclosure was one manifestation of a broader and less formal development that was working in exactly the same direction. The essential basis of the change, and of the new economic balance, was the consolidation of larger individual farms, and this could take place with or without the technical enclosure of the fields. This also serves to underline the force of commercialization as the leading trend in changes in the use and occupation of the land during this period, for the achievement of a substantial marketable surplus was the incentive to consolidate, and it did not always require the considerable expense of hedging.[53]

More large farms meant fewer small farms, and more people who had no choice but to work for others. The twin transformations of original expropriation—stolen land becoming capital and landless producers becoming wage workers—were well underway.

Turning Point

In the early 1500s, capitalist agriculture was new, and the landowning classes were generally critical of their peers who enclosed common land and evicted tenants. The sermons that defended traditional village society and condemned enclosure expressed views that were widely held in the aristocracy and gentry. "Private acquisitiveness was perceived not just as the enemy of the common people of the country-side. It threatened the whole commonwealth, by reducing the number of self-reliant and productive husbandmen and yeomen, who paid taxes, served as soldiers, relieved the poor, and generally provided the state and social order with its material and moral foundation."[54]

While anti-enclosure laws were drafted and introduced by the royal government, they were invariably approved by the House of Commons, which "almost by definition, represented the prospering section of the gentry."[55] But as the century progressed, growing numbers of landowners sought to break free from customary and state restrictions in order to "improve" their holdings. In 1601, Sir Walter Raleigh argued in Parliament that the government should "let every man use his ground to that which it is most fit for, and therein use his own discretion,"[56] and a large minority in the House of Commons agreed.

Christopher Hill writes that "we can trace the triumph of capitalism in agriculture by following the Commons' attitude towards enclosure":

> The famine year 1597 saw the last acts against depopulation; 1608 the first (limited) pro-enclosure act. . . . In 1621, in the depths of the depression, came the first general enclosure bill—opposed by some M.P.s who feared agrarian disturbances. In 1624 the statutes against enclosure were repealed. . . . No government after 1640 seriously tried either to prevent enclosures, or even to make money by fining enclosers.[57]

The early Stuart kings—James I (1603–1625) and Charles I (1625–1649)—played a contradictory role, reflecting their position as feudal monarchs in an increasingly capitalist country. They revived feudal taxes and prosecuted enclosing landlords in the name of preventing depopulation, but at the same time they raised their own tenants' rents and initiated large enclosure projects that dispossessed thousands of commoners.

Enclosure accelerated in the first half of the 1600s—to cite just three examples, 40 percent of Leicestershire manors, 18 percent of Durham's land area, and 90 percent of the Welsh lowlands were enclosed in those decades.[58] Even without formal enclosure, many small farmers lost their farms because they couldn't pay fast rising rents. "Rent rolls on estate after estate doubled, trebled, and quadrupled in a matter of decades," contributing to "a massive redistribution of income in favour of the landed class."

It was a golden age for landowners, but for small farmers and cottagers, "the third, fourth, and fifth decades of the seventeenth century witnessed extreme hardship in England and were probably among the most terrible years through which the country has ever passed.[59]

2

"Cormorants and Greedy Gulls"

I must needs threaten everlasting damnation unto them, whether they be gentlemen or whatsoever they be, which never cease to join house to house, and land to land, as though they alone ought to purchase and inhabit the earth.

—THOMAS CRANMER, ARCHBISHOP OF
CANTERBURY, 1550[1]

In the passage quoted above, the Archbishop of Canterbury paraphrased the Old Testament prophet Isaiah's denunciation of greedy landowners:

Woe to those who join house to house, who add field to field, until there is no more room, and you are made to dwell alone in the midst of the land.

The Lord of hosts has sworn in my hearing: "Surely many houses shall be desolate, large and beautiful houses, without inhabitant."[2]

Despite that clear biblical warning, joining house to house and land to land was already widespread when Cranmer spoke. In the following century, enclosure transformed English agriculture.

The privatization of land has been justly described as "perhaps the weirdest of all undertakings of our ancestors."[3] The transformation of common resources into private property involved not only new ways of using the land, but also, as both cause and effect, *new ways of thinking about it.* The idea that individuals could claim exclusive ownership of parts of nature on which all humans depend was very weird indeed. Contrary to the oft-expressed view that greed is inherent in human nature, the shift from commons-based to private profit-based farming was not accepted easily—in fact, it was denounced and resisted as an assault of the laws of God and the needs of humanity.

WHEN HENRY VIII DIED in 1547, he was succeeded by Edward VI, then only nine years old. For the next six years, actual political power rested with a regency council, headed by the Duke of Somerset until 1549, and by the Duke of Northumberland from late 1549 until Edward's death in 1553. Somerset and Northumberland were strong Protestants who wanted the English Church to move further from the Catholic doctrine and practices than Henry had allowed. To promote that, the law outlawing heresy was repealed and censorship was relaxed, beginning a period that has been called "the first great era in the history of English public discussion."[4]

Liberal Protestants took advantage of that opening to campaign vigorously, not only for religious reform, but against sin and corruption in society at large, particularly the erosion of traditional economic values. Their powerful condemnations of greedy landlords and merchants circulated both as books and sermons addressed to the wealthy, and as inexpensive pamphlets and broadsides that were sold in city streets.

They don't seem to have acted as an organized group, but their speeches and writings clearly reveal the presence of a strong current of anti-capitalist opinion in England in the mid-1500s. Because they focused on the *common weal*—common good—historians have labeled them the *commonwealth men.*

Graziers, Enclosers, and Rent-Raisers

R. H. Tawney's 1926 book *Religion and the Rise of Capitalism* is still the best account of the complex connections between social and religious criticism in Tudor England:

> It was an age in which the popular hatred of the encloser and the engrosser found a natural ally in religious sentiment, schooled, as it was, in a tradition which had taught that the greed of gain was a deadly sin, and that the plea of economic self-interest did not mitigate the verdict, but aggravated the offence.
>
> In England, as on the Continent, doctrinal radicalism marched hand in hand with social conservatism. The most scathing attack on social disorders came, not from the partisans of the old religion, but from divines on the left wing of the Protestant party, who saw in economic individualism but another expression of the laxity and licence which had degraded the purity of religion, and who understood by reformation a return to the moral austerity of the primitive Church, no less than to its government and doctrine.[5]

The great sin they condemned was covetousness—the desire to accumulate ever more wealth. Hugh Latimer, the most popular preacher of the day, condemned landlords' greed in general, and enclosure in particular, in a sermon preached before the King and other worthies.

> You landlords, you rent-raisers, I may say you step-lords, you unnatural lords, you have for your possessions yearly too much. For what here before went for twenty or forty pound by year (which is an honest portion to be had gratis in one lordship of another man's sweat and labour) now is let for fifty or an hundred pound by year. . . . Too much, which these rich men have, causes such dearth, that poor men, which live of their labour, cannot with the sweat of their face have a living. . . .

These graziers, enclosers and rent-raisers, are hinderers of the King's honour. For where as have been a great many households and inhabitants there is now but a shepherd and his dog.[6]

Those views found support in the country's top ruling circles. The *Book of Private Prayer*, prepared by Archbishop Cranmer and other officials of the established church in 1553, included a prayer "For Landlords":

We heartily pray Thee to send Thy Holy Spirit into the hearts of those that possess the grounds and pastures of the earth, that they remembering themselves to be Thy tenants may not rack nor stretch out the rents of their lands, nor yet take unreasonable fines. . . . Give them grace also . . . that they . . . may be content with that which is sufficient and not join house to house and land to land, to the impoverishment of others, but so behave themselves in letting out their lands, tenements and pastures that after this life they may be received into everlasting dwelling places.[7]

One of the most vehement critics of greed was the London-based printer and poet Robert Crowley, who offered this explanation for the 1549 peasant rebellions:

If I should demand of the poor man of the country what thing he thinks to be the cause of Sedition, I know his answer. He would tell me that the great farmers, the graziers, the rich butchers, the men of law, the merchants, the gentlemen, the knights, the lords, and I can not tell who; men that have no name because they are doers of all things that any gain hangs upon. Men without conscience. Men utterly devoid of God's fear. Yea, men that live as though there were no God at all! Men that would have all in their own hands; men that would leave nothing for others; men that would be alone on the earth; men that be never satisfied.

Cormorants, greedy gulls; yea, men that would eat up men, women, & children, are the causes of Sedition! They take our houses over our heads, they buy our lands out of our hands, they raise our rents, they levy great (yea unreasonable) fines, they enclose our commons! No custom, no law or statute can keep them from oppressing us in such sort, that we know not which way to turn so as to live.[8]

Condemning "lease mongers that cancel leases on land in order to lease it again for double or triple the rent," Crowley argued that landlords should "consider themselves to be but stewards, and not Lords over their possessions":

But so long as this persuasion sticks in their minds—"It is my own; who shall stop me from doing as I like with my own as I wish?"—it shall not be possible to have any redress at all. For if I may do with my own as I wish, then I may suffer my brother, his wife, and his children toil in the street, unless he will give me more rent for my house than he shall ever be able to pay. Then may I take his goods for that he owes me, and keep his body in prison, turning out his wife and children to perish, if God will not move some man's heart to pity them, and yet keep my coffers full of gold and silver.[9]

Back to the Feudal

Their criticism of the rich was sincere, but the commonwealth men were also "united in denouncing the rebels, whose sin could never be justified even if their grievances could."[10]

The Archbishop of Canterbury, whose denunciation of wealth accumulation is quoted at the beginning of this chapter, also, in the same sermon, condemned "unlawful assemblies and tumults," and people who "confound all things upsy down with seditious uproars and unquietness." "God in his scriptures expressly forbids all private revenging, and had made this order in commonwealths, that there should be kings and governors to whom he has willed all men to be subject and obedient."[11]

Speaking of the 1549 rebellions, Latimer declared that "all ireful, rebellious persons, all quarrelers and wranglers, all blood-shedders, do the will of the devil, and not God's will." Disobedience to one's superiors was a major sin, even if the superiors were themselves violating God's laws. "What laws soever they make as concerning outward things we ought to obey, and in no wise to rebel, although they be never so hard, noisome and hurtful."[12]

Immediately after condemning landlords as cormorants and greedy gulls, Crowley told the 1549 rebels that they had been misled by the devil: "To revenge wrongs is, in a subject, to take and usurp the office of a king, and, consequently, the office of God." The poor should suffer in silence, awaiting royal or divine intervention.

Like the "feudal socialists" that Marx and Engels criticized three centuries later in the *Communist Manifesto*, the commonwealth men were *literally* reactionary—they wanted to reverse history. "From the ills of present-day society this group draws the conclusion that feudal and patriarchal society should be restored because it was free from these ills."[13] As historian Michael Bush says, the commonwealth men "showed concern for the poor, but accepted the need for poverty":

> Without exception they subscribed to the traditional ideal of the state as a body politic in which every social group had its place, function and desert.... They pleaded with rulers to reform society, and proposed various means, but not by changing its structure. Their thinking was paternalistic and conservative. Although they censured the nobility, it was for malpractices, not for being ruling class.[14]

English Protestant reformers in the mid-1500s "inherited the social idea of medieval Christianity pretty much in its entirety," so their views were "especially antithetical to the acquisitive spirit that animated the emerging society of capitalism."[15]

Tawney writes that in the 1500s, "the new economic realities came into sharp collision with the social theory inherited from the Middle Ages."[16] What shocked and frightened the commonwealth men was not just poverty, but the growth of a worldview that repudiated "the principles by which alone, as it seemed, human society is distinguished from a pack of wolves."

> That creed was that the individual is absolute master of his own, and, within the limits set by positive law, may exploit it with a single eye to his pecuniary advantage, unrestrained by any obligation to postpone his own profit to the well-being of his neighbours, or to give account of his actions to a higher authority.

The wolf-pack creed they were fighting, as Tawney comments ironically, was "the theory of property which was later to be accepted by all civilized communities."[17]

A Losing Battle

The commonwealth men were eloquent and persuasive, but they were fighting a losing battle. The aristocrats who owned most of England's farmland could tolerate public criticism and ineffective laws, but not anything that actually threatened their wealth and power. They blamed the 1549 rebellions on the critics, and ousted the Duke of Somerset, the only member of the regency council who seemed to favor enforcing the anti-enclosure laws.

What remained of the commonwealth campaign collapsed after 1553, when the Catholic Mary Tudor became queen and launched a vicious reign of terror against Protestants. Some 300 "heretics," including Hugh Latimer and Thomas Cranmer, were burned at the stake, and hundreds more fled to Protestant countries on the continent.

Capitalist practices already had a strong foothold in the countryside in the 1540s, and they spread rapidly in the rest of the century, without regard to what Christian preachers might say. "Forms of economic behavior which had appeared novel and aberrant in the 1540s were becoming normalized virtually to the point of being taken for granted."[18]

For landowners who wanted to preserve their estates, that shift wasn't a choice. It was forced on them by changes beyond their control.

> Between the beginning of the sixteenth century and 1640, prices, particularly of foodstuffs, rose approximately sixfold. . . . [This] put an unusual premium on energy and adaptability and turned conservatism from a force making for stability into a quick way to economic disaster. Landed families which stuck to the old ways, left rents as they were, and continued to grant long leases soon found themselves trapped between static incomes and rising prices.[19]

As a result, the trends that Latimer and his co-thinkers opposed accelerated, and their vision of a reborn feudal paternalism was replaced in ruling class thought by what C. B. Macpherson calls "possessive individualism"—the view that society is a collection of market relations between people who have an absolute right to do as they wish with their property.[20] That view has remained central to all variants of capitalist ideology, down to the present.

But only the rich thought land privatization was a good idea. The poor continued to resist that weird undertaking.

—————— 3 ——————
.

Vagabonds, Migrants, and Forced Labor

Who built the seven gates of Thebes?
The books are filled with names of kings.
Was it the kings who hauled the craggy blocks of stone?
—BERTOLT BRECHT[1]

Much academic debate about the origin of *capitalism* has actually been about the origin of *capitalists*. Were they originally aristocrats, or gentry, or merchants, or successful farmers? Less attention has been paid to Brecht's penetrating question: *Who did the actual work?*

The answer is simple and of world-historic importance. Capitalism depends on the availability of large numbers of *non-capitalists* who are, as Marx said, "free in the double sense." Free to work for others because they are not legally tied to a landlord or master, and free to starve if they don't sell their labor-power, because they own no land or other means of production. "The possessor of labour-power, instead of being able to sell commodities in which his labour has been objectified . . . [is] compelled to offer for sale as a commodity that very labour-power which exists only in his living body."[2]

The social order that capital's apologists defend as inevitable and eternal is "the product of many economic revolutions, of the extinction of a whole series of older formations of social production."[3] Acceptance of the wages-system as a natural way to live and work did not happen easily.

Some commoners went directly from following a plough to full-time wage-labor, but as Christopher Hill has shown, "acceptance of wage labor was the last resort open to those who had lost their land, but many regarded it as little better than slavery."[4] Not only were wages low and working conditions abysmal, but the very idea of being subject to a boss and working under wage-discipline was universally detested. "Wage-laborers were deemed inferior in status to those who held the most minute fragment of land to farm for themselves," so "men fought desperately to avoid the abyss of wage-labor. . . . The apotheosis of freedom was the stultifying drudgery of those who had become cogs in someone else's machine."[5]

Dispossession

Some people worked for wages in feudal society, but it wasn't until after feudalism disintegrated that wage labor became generalized and the long-term growth of a property-less wage-working *class* began. It developed, directly and indirectly, from the destruction of the commons.

As we saw in chapter 1, there was significant economic differentiation in English villages long before the rise of capitalism. By the 1400s, in most communities there was a clear division between those whose farms were large enough to sustain their families and produce a surplus for the market, and the smallholders and cottagers who had to work full- or part-time for their better-off neighbors or the landlord.

Between the two groups was a surprisingly large category known as *servants in husbandry*—young people who lived with farm families to gain experience, until they could save enough to rent land and marry. They lived and ate with the farmer's family, often had the right to keep a few sheep or other animals, and usually received a small annual cash payment. "Between one-third and one-half of hired labor in early modern agriculture was supplied by servants in husbandry, and most early modern youths in rural England were servants in husbandry." At any time until about 1800, some 60 percent of men and women aged 15 to 24 were living-in as farm servants.[6]

In class terms, servants in husbandry were a transitional and temporary category, similar to apprentices or college students today. "Servants did not understand themselves, and were not understood by early modern society, to be part of a laboring class, youthful proletarians."[7] Many authors have interpreted an estimate from the late 1660s that more than half the population were servants to mean that most people were wage-laborers, but in fact, most servants could best be described as peasants-in-training. A substantial layer of people who had to sell their labor-power did exist in the late 1600s, but they were still a minority of the population.

In the 1400s and early 1500s, most enclosures involved the physical eviction of tenants, often entire villages. After about 1550, it was more usual for landlords to negotiate with their larger tenants to create bigger farms by dividing up the commons and undeveloped land. "It became typical for wealthier tenants to be offered compensation for the loss of common rights, while the landless poor, whose common rights were often much harder to sustain at law, gained little or nothing in return."[8]

Loss of common rights was catastrophic for smallholders and cottagers. The milk and cheese from two cows could generate as much income as full-time farm labor, and the animals' manure was fuel for the cottage or fertilizer for a garden. None of that was possible without access to pasture. Jane Humphries has shown that, before enclosure, in families where the men worked as day-laborers, the women and children worked on the commons, caring for animals, cutting turf and gathering wood for fuel and building, gathering berries, nuts and other wild foods, and gleaning leftover grain after harvest. "Since women and children were the primary exploiters of common rights, their loss led to changes in women's economic position within the family and more generally to increased dependence of whole families on wages and wage earners."[9]

At the same time, England was experiencing a baby boom— between 1520 and 1640, the population more than doubled, from about 2.4 million to over 5 million. That was still about a million fewer people than before the Black Death, but the self-provisioning system that formerly fed 6 million people no longer existed. Population growth, rising rents, and the trend toward larger farms were making it impossible for the poor to live on the land. The proportion of agricultural laborers who had no more than a cottage and garden jumped from 11 percent in 1560 to 40 percent after 1620.[10]

Forced Labor

Turning the dispossessed peasants of Tudor and Stuart England into reliable wage workers required not just economic pressure but state compulsion. "Throughout this period compulsion to labor stood in the background of the labor market. Tudor legislation provided compulsory work for the unemployed as well as making unemployment an offence punishable with characteristic brutality."[11]

The most comprehensive of those laws was the 1563 *Statute of Artificers*. Among its provisions:

- Unemployed men and women from 12 to 60 years old could be compelled to work on any farm that would hire them.
- Wages and hours for all types of work were set by local justices, who were drawn from the employing class. Anyone who offered or accepted higher wages was imprisoned.
- No one could leave a job without written permission from the employer; an unemployed worker without the required letter could be imprisoned and whipped.

The pioneering economic historian Thorold Rogers described the 1563 Statute as "the most powerful instrument ever devised for degrading and impoverishing the English worker."[12] R. H. Tawney compared its provisions to serfdom: "The wage-laborer … can hardly have seen much difference between the restrictions on his movement imposed by the Justices of the Peace and those laid on him by the manorial authorities, except indeed that the latter, being limited to the area of a single village, had been more easy to evade."[13]

But no matter what the law said, there were more workers than paying jobs, so many hit the roads in search of work. Such "masterless men" frightened the country's rulers even more than the unemployed who stayed home. Tudor authorities didn't recognize any such thing as structural unemployment. Able-bodied people without land or masters were obviously lazy idlers who had *chosen* not to work and were a threat to social peace. Like most governments then and now, they attacked symptoms, not causes, passing law after law to force "vagrants, vagabonds, beggars and rogues" to return to their home parishes and work.

A particularly vicious law, enacted in 1547, ordered that any vagrant who refused to accept any work offered be branded with a red-hot iron and literally enslaved for two years. His master was authorized to feed him on bread and water, put iron rings around his neck and legs, and "cause the said slave to work by beating, chaining or otherwise in such work and labor how vile so ever it be."[14] Vagabonds' children could be taken from their parents and apprenticed to anyone who would have them until they were 20 (girls) or 24 (boys).

Other vagrancy laws prescribed whipping through the streets until bloody, and death for repeat offenders. In 1576, every county was ordered to build houses of correction and incarcerate anyone who refused to work at whatever wages and conditions were offered.

As Marx wrote in *Capital*, "Thus were the agricultural folk first forcibly expropriated from the soil, driven from their homes, turned into vagabonds, then whipped, branded and tortured by grotesquely terroristic laws into accepting the discipline necessary for the system of wage labor."[15]

Migration and Emigration

In the 1500s and 1600s, much of England was still sparsely populated, so rather than live as landless laborers, many families traveled in search of available farmland:

> This surplus population moved from the more overcrowded areas to the regions of fen and marsh, heath and forest; moor and mountain, where there were extensive commons still, on which a cottager with a little or no land could make a living from the rights of common, by which he could pasture some animals on the common and take fuel and building materials; where there were still unoccupied waste lands, on which the poor could squat in little cabins and carve out small farms for themselves; and where there were industrial by-employments by which a cottager or small farmer could supplement his income. By this migration and from these resources of common rights, wastelands and industry, the small peasant survived and poor or landless peasants were saved from decline into wage-laborers or paupers.[16]

The largest number of migrants left England entirely, mostly for North America or the Caribbean. Net emigration in the century before 1640 was close to 600,000, and another 400,000 left by the end of the century—extraordinarily large numbers from a country whose mid-1600s population was barely 5 million. What's more, those are *net* figures—more left, but their numbers were partially offset by immigrants from Scotland, Wales, Ireland, and continental Europe.[17]

Most of the emigrants were young men, and about half paid for the dangerous ocean crossing by agreeing to be indentured servants for four or more years. That was a high price, but hundreds of thousands of landless peasants were willing to pay it. For some it was not a choice: English courts frequently sentenced vagrants and other criminals to indentured servitude in the New World.

Labor in the Metropolis

For many of the dispossessed, establishing new farms in England or overseas was not possible or, perhaps, desirable. The alternative was paid employment, and that was most easily found in London.

"Whereas the population of England less than doubled from 3.0 million to 5.1 million between 1550 and 1700, London quadrupled from 120,000 to 490,000,"—making it home to nearly 10 percent of the national population.[18] London normally had a high mortality rate, and repeated outbreaks of plague killed tens of thousands, so that growth could only have occurred if about 10,000 people moved there every year. Living conditions were terrible, but wages were higher than anywhere else, and hundreds of thousands of landless workers saw it as their best hope.

Most histories of London emphasize its role as a hub of global trade and empire. "Historians by and large hesitate to associate London with manufacturing. An industrial image somehow seems inappropriate."[19] That's understandable if "London" means only the walled capital-C City and the immediately surrounding parishes, where rich merchants lived and worked, and where guilds formed in medieval times still controlled most economic activity, but London was more than that. Most migrants lived in the eastern suburbs, which grew an astonishing 1,400 percent between 1560 and 1680. In those suburbs, and south of the Thames, there were so many industrial operations that historian A. L. Beier describes the metropolis as an "engine of manufacture." There were "water and corn mills on the rivers Lea and Thames; wharves and docks for repairing and fitting out ships between Shadwell and Limehouse; as well as lime-burning, brewing, bell-founding, brick and tile manufacture, wood- and metal-working."[20]

In the metropolis as a whole, industry was more important than commerce. Few records of the size and organization of industries have survived, but it appears from burial records that in the 1600s about 40 percent of the people in the metropolis worked in manufacturing, particularly clothing, building, metalwork, and leather work. Another 36 percent worked primarily in retail.[21]

Despite the growth of industry, few workers in London or elsewhere found long-term or secure jobs. Most wage-workers never experienced steady work or earned predictable incomes:

> Continuity in employment was not to be expected save among a minority of exceptionally skilled and valued employees. Most workers were engaged for the duration of a particular job, or in the case of seamen for a "run" or voyage, while general labor was usually hired on a daily basis. The bulk of the laboring population, both male and female, therefore constituted a large pool of partially employed labor, which was drawn upon selectively as need arose. . . . For some, periods of fairly regular employment were punctuated by lengthy bouts of idleness. For others, days of work were scattered intermittently across the year.[22]

London was by far the largest manufacturing center in England, but migrant workers also played key roles in industrial growth in smaller cities as well. Among others, Coventry (population 7,000) attracted spinners, weavers, and cloth finishers, and Birmingham (population 5,000) was an important center for cutlery and nail manufacture.[23]

Working at Sea

Many peasants who lived near coasts supplemented their diet and income by occasional fishing. For some, fishing became a full-time occupation.

Thousands of workers traveled to distant fishing grounds, where they worked for six or more months a year, catching, processing and preserving herring and cod. The Newfoundland fishery alone used more ships and employed more workers than the more famous Spanish treasure fleet that carried silver from Central and South America. The offshore bank-ships and onshore fishing-rooms were food factories, long before the Industrial Revolution, and the men who worked in them were among the first proletarians of the capitalist epoch.

In the 1600s, English ships and fishworkers became a dominant force in North Atlantic fishing. "The success of the North Sea and Newfoundland fisheries depended on merchants who had capital to invest in ships and other means of production, fishworkers who had to sell their labor power in order to live, and a production system based on a planned division of labor."[24]

The growth of long-distance fishing prefigured and contributed to the growth of a larger maritime working class. Mainstream economic histories of England in the 1500s and 1600s usually discuss the merchant companies that financed and organized trade with Russia, Scandinavia, the Ottoman Empire, India, and Africa, but few have much to say about the seamen whose labor made their trading voyages possible.

Historians Marcus Rediker and Peter Linebaugh have been remedying that neglect. In *Between the Devil and the Deep Blue Sea* and *The Many-Headed Hydra*, they document the growth of a working class on merchant and naval ships—"a setting in which large numbers of workers cooperated on complex and synchronized tasks, under slavish, hierarchical discipline in which human will was subordinated to mechanical equipment, all for a money wage. The work, cooperation and discipline of the ship made it a prototype of the factory."[25]

The capital that merchants invested in long-distance trade "necessarily set massive amounts of free wage labor in motion."

In the mid-sixteenth century, between 3,000 and 5,000 Englishmen plied the waves. But by 1750, after two centuries of intensive development, their number had ballooned to more than 60,000. Merchant shipping mobilized huge masses of men for shipboard labor. These workers entered new relationships both to capital—as one of the first generations of free waged laborers—and to each other—as collective laborers. . . . These cooperating hands did not own the tools or materials of production, and consequently they sold their skill and muscle in an international market for monetary wages. They were an absolutely indispensable part of the rise and growth of North Atlantic capitalism.[26]

The Elizabethan Leap

Despite migration and emigration, England's rural population grew substantially. The growth was accompanied by restructuring—the beginning of a long-term economic transition, away from farming to rural industry.

The rural population wholly engaged in agriculture fell from 76 per cent in 1520 to 70 per cent in 1600, and 60.5 per cent in 1670. The "rural non-agricultural population," a category which includes the inhabitants of small towns as well as those of industrial villages, rose from 18.5 per cent in 1520 to 22 per cent in 1600, and 26 per cent by 1670.[27]

Old rural industries prospered and new ones emerged as a result of what Marxist historian Andreas Malm calls the "Elizabethan leap"—the spectacular growth in the production of coal for industrial and domestic use, replacing wood and charcoal. "The years around 1560 marked the onset of a virtual coal fever, all major fields soon undergoing extensive development; over the coming century and a half, national output probably soared more than tenfold."[28] There were substantial coal mines in south Wales and Scotland, but the largest collieries were financed by groups of merchants and landowners in northeast England. Shipments down the east coast, from Newcastle to the fast-growing London market, rose from 50,000 tons a year in 1580 to 300,000 tons in 1640.

Large specialist workforces with an elaborate division of labor were employed in sinking, timbering and draining pits, the hewing, dragging, winding and sorting of coal and its transportation to riverside staithes, where it was stored ready for shipment downriver in keelboats to meet the collier fleets at the mouths of the Tyne and Wear. . . .

The overall growth of the industry meant that by 1650 coal was Britain's principal source of fuel, not only for domestic heating, but also for the smithies, forges, lime kilns, salt pans, breweries, soapworks, sugar refineries, dyeing vats, brick kilns and numerous other industrial processes which consumed perhaps a third of total output.[29]

By 1640, the English coal industry was producing three to four times as much coal as the rest of Europe; it employed more workers than all other kinds of English mining combined.[30] Some 12,000 to 15,000 workers labored directly in coal mining, and more worked in transportation and distribution—"those who produced the coal were greatly outnumbered by the carters, waggonmen, keelmen, seamen, lightermen, heavers, and coalmen who handled it on its way from pithead to hearth."[31]

Spinners and Weavers

The growth of coal mining and coal-based industries was impressive, but wool was by far the most important raw material, and clothmaking was the largest non-agricultural occupation.[32] Until the late 1400s most raw wool was produced for export, mainly to cloth makers in Flanders, but by the mid-1500s, almost all was spun and woven in England. By 1700 English textile production increased more than 500 percent, and cloth accounted for at least 80 percent of the country's exports.

Cloth had long been made by individual artisans for family use and for sale in local markets, but in the 1500s production came under the control of clothiers who delivered large quantities of wool to spinners, then collected the thread and delivered it to weavers. They specified what kinds of thread and cloth should be made, and shipped the product to the London merchants who controlled trade with Europe.

Clothmaking involved multiple tasks, including shearing, sorting, and cleaning the raw wool, separating and organizing the fibers by combing or carding, dyeing, spinning, and weaving. Spinning, done almost exclusively by women, was the most time-consuming and employed the most workers. The importance of women in spinning is illustrated by the fact that in the 1500s, the word *spinster* came to mean a single woman, and *distaff* (the staff that held wool or flax during spinning) referred to the female side of a family line.

Working backward from the amount of cloth produced for export and domestic use, historian Craig Muldew estimates that at least 225,000 women worked as spinners in 1590; 342,000 in 1640; and 496,000 in 1700. These estimates assume that all the spinning was done by married women, who would have to do other household work as well. Some would have been done by single women, so the actual number of working spinners was probably somewhat smaller, but nevertheless, "spinning was by far the largest industrial occupation in early modern England."[33]

Roughly speaking, it took ten spinners working full-time to produce enough thread to keep one weaver and an assistant working full time. Weavers were almost all men: some were employed in workshops with a few other weavers, but most worked in their homes. By the early 1600s, it was not unusual for a single capitalist to employ hundreds of cottage workers, and some clothiers employed as many as a thousand, all paid on a piecework basis. For capitalists, putting-out was an effective means of mobilizing many workers in a complex division of labor while retaining control and minimizing capital investment. Cottagers were a wonderfully flexible workforce, easily discarded when the market contracted, which it often did.

Some spinners and weavers were successful peasants who

supplemented their income with part-time wage-labor, but a growing number received most of their income in wages and topped that up with the produce of small plots of land and the commons. As Marxist historian Brian Manning points out, in the 1600s increasing numbers had no land—they "were very poor at the best of times, but during the periodic depressions of trade and mass unemployment they came close to starving."[34] A class division was developing, between the yeomen (small farmers) and a rural proletariat.

> The critical divide lay in the borderland in which small holders or "cottage-famers" with a little land and common rights, but partly dependent on wages earned in agriculture or industry, shaded into landless cottagers wholly dependent on wages. In the background to the revolution the number of the latter was growing.[35]

In traditional handicraft production, the artisan purchased wool or flax from a farmer, decided what to make, and sold the finished product in a market or to an itinerant merchant. In the putting out system, a capitalist provided the raw material, dictated the type, quantity, and quality of product to be produced, owned the product from beginning to end, and controlled payment. The producers were no longer independent artisans engaged in petty commodity production, they were employees in a system of capitalist manufacture.

"Free, unprotected and rightless"

A new class of wage-laborers was born in England when "great masses of men [were] suddenly and forcibly torn from their means of subsistence, and hurled onto the labor-market as free, unprotected and rightless proletarians."[36]

With those words, and in his entire account of "so-called primitive accumulation," Marx was describing the long arc of capitalist development, not an overnight change. It was sudden for those who lost their land, but the social transformation took centuries. In the early 1700s, two hundred years after Thomas More condemned enclosures and depopulation in *Utopia*, about a third of England and almost all of Scotland was still unenclosed, and most people still lived and worked on the land. It took another great wave of assaults on commons and commoners, after 1750, to complete the transition to industrial capitalism.

The century before the Civil War broke out in 1642 was a time of transition, a time when, to paraphrase Gramsci, the old order was dying while the new order was struggling to be born. An important part of that transition was the exclusion of uncounted commoners from the land, and the consequent birth of a new class of wage-laborers. None of the industries described in this chapter could have survived a day without them.

Over time, and with many detours and reverses, the dispossessed became proletarians.

Looking back, that transition appears inevitable, but it did not seem so to commoners at the time. They furiously resisted the privatizations that forced them off the land and into wage-labor. Mass opposition to the destruction of the commons was widespread, and some argued eloquently for a commons-based alternative to both feudalism and capitalism.

4

"Here Were We Born and Here We Will Die"

A great number of rude and ignorant people in certain shires of England, [had] done great and most perilous and heinous disorder, and had riotously assembled themselves, plucked down men's hedges, disparked their parks, and taken upon them the king's power and sword.

—ROYAL PROCLAMATION, JUNE 14, 1549[1]

In 1542, Henry VIII gave his friend and privy councillor Sir William Herbert the buildings and lands of Wilton Abbey, a dissolved monastery near Salisbury. Herbert expelled the monastery's tenants and had the buildings torn down, erasing an entire village. In their place he built a large mansion and fenced off the surrounding lands as a private deer-hunting park.

In May 1549, local officials alerted London that people who had long used that land as common pasture were tearing down Herbert's fences:

There is a great number of the commons up about Salisbury in Wiltshire, and they have plucked down Sir William Herbert's park that is about his new house, and diverse other parks and commons that be enclosed in that county, but harm they do to [nobody]. They say they will obey the King's master and my lord Protector with all the counsel, but they say they will not have their commons and their grounds to be enclosed and so taken from them.

Herbert responded by organizing an armed gang of two hundred men, "who by his order attacked the commons and slaughtered them like wolves among sheep."[2]

The attack on Wilton Abbey was one of many enclosure riots in the late 1540s that culminated in the rebellions of 1549, discussed in chapter 1. There had been peasant uprisings in England in the Middle Ages, most notably in 1381, but most were local and short-lived. As Engels wrote of the German peasantry, their conditions of life militated against coordinated rebellion. "They were scattered over large areas, and this made every agreement between them extremely difficult; the old habit of submission inherited by generation from generation, lack of practice in the use of arms in many regions, and the varying degree of exploitation depending on the personality of the lord, all combined to keep the peasant quiet."[3]

Enclosure of common land, a direct assault on the peasants' centuries-old way of life, upset the old habit of submission. In continental Europe, enclosure played a key role in provoking the great peasant war of 1524–25. In Swabia, a peasant assembly declared: "We are aggrieved by the appropriation by individuals of meadows which at one time belonged to a community. These we will take again into our own hands."[4]

In England, protests against enclosure were reported as early as 1480, and became frequent after 1530. "Hundreds of riots protesting enclosures of commons and wastes, drainage of fens and disafforestation . . . reverberated across the century or so between 1530 and 1640."[5]

Most of the events that Tudor and Stuart authorities called "riots" were actually disciplined community actions to prevent or reverse enclosure, often by pulling down fences or uprooting the hedges that landlords planted to separate enclosed land.

> The point in breaking hedges was to allow cattle to graze on the land, but by filling in the ditches and digging up roots those involved in enclosure protest made it difficult and costly for enclosers to re-enclose quickly. That hedges were not only dug up but also burnt and buried draws attention to both the considerable time and effort which was invested in hedge-breaking and to the symbolic or ritualistic aspects of enclosure opposition. ... Other forms of direct action against enclosure included impounding or rescuing livestock, the continued gathering of previously common resources such as firewood, trespassing in parks and warrens, and even ploughing up land which had been converted to pasture or warrens.[6]

The forms of anti-enclosure action varied, from midnight raids to public confrontations "with the participants, often including a high proportion of women, marching to drums, singing, parading or burning effigies of their enemies, and celebrating with cakes and ale."[7] (I'm reminded of Lenin's description of revolutions as festivals of the oppressed and exploited.) Villagers were very aware of their rights—it was joked that some farmers read Thomas de Lyttleton's *Treatise on Tenures* while ploughing—so physical assaults on fences and hedges were often accompanied by petitions and legal action.

A frequent focus of enclosure was the privatization of previously unallocated land that provided pasture, wood, peat, game, and more. For cottagers who had no more than a small house and an acre or two of poor quality land, access to those resources was a matter of life and death. "Commons and common rights, so far from being merely a luxury or a convenience, were really an integral and indispensable part of the system of agriculture, a lynch-pin, the removal of which brought the whole structure of village society tumbling down."[8]

Coal Wars

In the last decades of the 1500s, farmers in northern England faced a new threat to their livelihoods, the rapid expansion of coal mining, which landlords found was more profitable than renting farmland. Thousands who were made landless by enclosure ultimately found work in the new mines, but the creation of those mines required the dispossession of farmers and farmworkers. The search for coal seams left pits and waste that endangered livestock; actual mines destroyed pasture and arable land and polluted streams, making farming impossible.

The prospect of mining profits led to a different kind of enclosure, the expropriation of mineral rights under common land. "Wherever coal-mining became important, it stimulated the movement towards curtailing the rights of customary tenants and even of small freeholders, and towards the enclosure of portions of the wastes." In the landlords' view, it wasn't enough just to fence off the mining area, "not only must the tenants be prevented from digging themselves, they must be stripped of their power to refuse access to minerals under their holdings, or to demand excessive compensation."[9]

As a result, economic historian John Nef writes, tenant farmers "lived in constant fear of the discovery of coal under their land," and attempts to establish new mines were often met by sabotage and violence. "Many were the obscure battles fought with pitchfork against pick and shovel to prevent what all tenants united in branding as a mighty abuse." Fences were torn down, pits filled in, buildings burned, and coal was carried off. In Lancashire, the enclosures surrounding one large mine were torn down sixteen times by freeholders who claimed "freedom of pasture." In Derbyshire in 1606, a landlord complained that twenty-three men "armed with pitchforks, bows and arrows, guns and other weapons" had threatened to kill everyone involved if mining continued on the manor.[10]

In these and many other battles, commoners heroically fought to preserve their land and rights, but they were unable to stop the growth of a highly profitable industry that was supported physically by the state and legally by the courts. Coal capital defeated the commons.

Revolt in the Midlands

Enclosure riots in the 1600s were generally larger, more frequent, and more organized than in previous years. Most were local and lasted only a few days, but several were large enough to be considered regional uprisings, "the result of social and economic grievances of such intensity that they took expression in violent outbreaks of what can only be called class hatred for the wealthy."[11]

The Midland Revolt broke out in April 1607 and continued into June. A subsequent royal commission found that landlords in the area had enclosed over 27,000 acres, destroyed over 350 farms, and evicted some 1,500 people in eighteen villages.[12]

The rebels described themselves as "diggers" and "levellers," labels later used by radicals during the Civil War of 1642–1649, and they claimed to be led by "Captain Pouch," who supposedly had magical powers.[13] Martin Empson describes the revolt in his history of rural class struggle, *Kill All the Gentlemen*:

> Events in 1607 involved thousands of peasants beginning in Northamptonshire at the very start of May and spreading to Warwickshire and Leicestershire. Mass protests took place, involving 3,000 at Hilmorton in Warwickshire and 5,000 at Cotesback in Leicestershire. In a declaration produced during the revolt, *The Diggers of Warwickshire to all other Diggers*, the authors write that they would prefer to "manfully die, then hereafter to be pined to death for want of that which those devouring, encroachers do serve their fat hogs and sheep withal."[14]

These were well-planned actions, not spontaneous riots. Cottagers from multiple villages met in advance to discuss where and when to assemble, arranged transportation, and provided tools, meals, and places to sleep for the rebels who would spend days tearing down fences, uprooting hedges and filling in ditches. Local militias could not stop them—indeed, "many members of the militia themselves became involved in the rising, either actively or by voting with their feet and failing to attend the muster."[15]

The movement was only stopped when mounted vigilantes, hired by local landlords, attacked protesters near the town of Newton, killing more than fifty and injuring many more. The leaders of the rising were publicly hanged and quartered, and their bodies were displayed in towns throughout the region.

Fighting for the Forests

The Western Rising was less organized, but it lasted much longer, from 1626 to 1632. The rebels' focus was "disafforestation"— Charles I's privatization of royal forests in which thousands of farmers and cottagers had common rights. (Most royal "forests" were only lightly wooded—the term referred to areas that were subject to restrictive Forest Laws.) The government appointed commissions to survey the land, propose how to divide it up, and negotiate compensation for tenants. The largest portions were leased to investors, mainly the king's friends and supporters, who in turn rented enclosed parcels to large farmers.[16]

Generally speaking, the forest enclosures seem to have allotted fair shares to people who could prove that they had common rights, but those who had never had formal leases, or couldn't prove that they had, were excluded from the negotiations and expelled from the land they had worked on all their lives.

For at least six years, landless workers and cottagers fought to prevent or reverse enclosures in Dorset, Wiltshire, Gloucestershire, and other areas where the Crown was selling off public forests.

The response of the inhabitants of each forest was to riot almost as soon as the post-disafforestation enclosure had begun. These riots were broadly similar in aim and character, directed toward the restoration of the open forest and involving destruction of the enclosing hedges, ditches, and fences and, in a few cases, pulling down houses inhabited by the agents of the enclosers, and assaults on their workmen.[17]

Declaring "Here were we born and here we will die," as many as 3,000 men and women took part in each action against forest enclosures. Historian Buchanan Sharp's study of court records shows that the majority of those arrested for anti-enclosure rioting identified themselves not as husbandmen (farmers) but as artisans, particularly weavers and other cloth workers, who depended on the commons to supplement their wages. "It could be argued that there were two types of forest inhabitants, those with land who went to law to protect their rights, and those with little or no land who rioted to protect their interests."[18]

Fen Tigers: "An open fen forever"

The longest continuing fight against enclosure took place in eastern England, in the Fens, the lush wetlands that covered over 1,400 square miles in Lincolnshire and adjacent counties. Most Fennish farmers worked small plots of arable land, generally under forty acres, and made extensive use of common areas for grazing, hunting, fishing, and gathering. Even landless laborers typically had a cow or two on the common. As R. H. Tawney writes, for potential developers these were "economic arrangements and a manner of existence unintelligible to civilized men."

> They depicted the fens as a swamp, useful only when, through drainage, it should have ceased to exist, and their inhabitants as a population sub-human in its lawlessness, poverty, and squalor. Piety and profits demanded, it was felt, the reclamation of both.[19]

Replying to such abuse, an anti-enclosure pamphlet complained that "the undertakers have always vilified the Fens, and have misinformed many Parliament men, that all the Fens is a mere quagmire, and that it is a level hurtfully surrounded, and of little or no value: but those which live in the Fens, and are neighbours to it, know the contrary." Farmers in the Fens, the authors wrote, raised large numbers of horses, cattle, and sheep, and sold butter and cheese to the navy and fodder to nearby farmers. They emphasized the presence of "many thousand Cottagers, which live on our Fens, which otherwise must go a begging."[20]

Beginning in the 1620s, developers allied with the king sought to drain and enclose the Fens to create "new land" that could be sold to investors and then rented to large farmers. The drainage projects would dispossess thousands of peasants whose lives depended on the region's rich natural resources. The result was almost constant conflict, as groups, some calling themselves Fen Tigers after a local species of wildcat, fought to prevent or sabotage drainage projects. The rebels had widespread popular support, as can be seen in historian James Boyce's description of an attempt to arrest opponents of draining a 10,000-acre common marsh, in the Cambridgeshire village of Soham, in 1632:

The constables charged with arresting the four Soham resistance leaders so delayed entering the village that they were later charged for not putting the warrant into effect. When they finally sought to do so, an estimated 200 people poured onto the streets armed with forks, staves and stones. The next day a justice ordered 60 men to support the constables in executing the warrant but over 100 townspeople still stood defiant, warning that "if any laid hands of any of them, they would kill or be killed." When one of the four was finally arrested, the constables were attacked and several people were injured. A justice arrived in Soham on 11 June with about 120 men and made a further arrest before the justice's men were again "beaten off, the rest never offering to aid them." Another of the four leaders, Anne Dobbs, was eventually caught and imprisoned in Cambridge

Castle but on 14 June 1633, the fight was resumed when about 70 people filled in six division ditches meant to form part of an enclosure. Twenty offenders were identified, of whom fourteen were women.[21]

Militant and often violent protests challenged every drainage project. As elsewhere in England, Fenland rioters uprooted hedges, filled ditches and destroyed fences, but here they also destroyed pumping equipment, broke open dikes, and attacked drainage workers, many of whom had been brought from the Netherlands. "By the time of the civil war the whole fenland was in a state of open rebellion."[22]

In February 1643 in Axholme, for example, commoners armed with muskets opened floodgates at high tide, drowning over six thousand acres of recently drained and enclosed land, and then closed the gates to prevent the water from flowing out at low tide. Armed commoners held the position for ten weeks, threatening to shoot anyone who attempted to let the water out.[23]

As an MP before the Civil War, Oliver Cromwell had opposed Charles I's drainage plans, so the Fennish reasonably expected the republican government to support them, but he and Parliament swung to the right after the king's execution. An act of 1649 renewed approval for draining the Fens, and in the 1650s Cromwell several times sent troops to put down opposition. Nevertheless, the Fenland resistance continued through the Commonwealth years and after the Restoration of the monarchy.

In the last decades of the 1600s, projectors successfully drained the large area known as the Great Level, but in most of the rest of the Fens they were defeated. Resistance to enclosure was particularly strong in the Holland Fen, which covered 22,000 acres in southern Lincolnshire. After arrests in April 1642, thousands of commoners freed the prisoners, and then destroyed drainage works worth £60,000, declaring that "they would lose their lives before they would desist." The developers complained to the House of Lords that the commoners had established "a general confederacy" which enforced its own laws. By the end of the spring the rebels had driven the developers out, and they were kept out for many years.[24] Over a century later, in 1769, when one John Yerburgh attempted to enclose land in Holland Fen, local commoners continued a long tradition by firing shots at his house and leaving a letter to explain why they had done so:

> John Yar Brah this is to let you know that as you have used the utmost of your power to persuade your neighbours and knaves like your self to cheat the poor of their right, except a reformation is heard of in the neighbourhood that [is] but the beginning of sorrow.
>
> From your friend and well wisher to liberty, and [for] an open fen for ever![25]

As Boyce writes, the commoners' two-century war in defense of the Fens explodes Garrett Hardin's "tragedy of the commons" myth:

> The problem with the "tragedy of the commons" hypothesis is that the history of the Fens (and countless other commons) shows it to have been a well-managed country that provided sustainable resources for thousands of years. In 1700, the Fens was not the depleted, over-hunted, over-fished, over-grazed environment that Hardin's theory suggested it should be. This was because use of resources was embedded in communal relationships that did not merely police how people behaved but guided how they lived. The Fens were sustainably managed because the Fennish were not just motivated by their own material gain. Hardin was wrong about the commons because he was wrong about the commoners.[26]

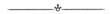

The Diggers of Warwickshire to All Other Diggers

Adopted by participants in the 1607 Midland Revolt:

Loving friends and subjects all under one renowned Prince, for whom we pray long to continue in his most royal estate to the subverting of all those subjects of what degree so ever that have or would deprive his most true hearted communality both from life and living.

We as members of the whole do feel the smart of these encroaching tyrants, which would grind our flesh upon the whetstone of poverty, and make our loyal hearts to faint with breathing, so that they may dwell by themselves in the midst of their herds of fat wethers.

It is not unknown unto your selves the reason why these merciless men do resist with force against our good intents.

It is not for the good of our most gracious sovereign, whom we pray God that long he may reign amongst us, neither for the benefit of the communality but only for their own private gain, for there is none of them but do taste the sweetness of our wants.

They have depopulated and overthrown whole towns, and made thereof sheep pastures nothing profitable for our commonwealth.

For the common fields being laid open would yield us much commodity, besides the increase of corn, on which stands our life.

But if it should please God to withdraw his blessing in not prospering the fruits of the earth but one year (which God forbid) there would a worse and more fearful dearth happen than did in King Edward the Second's time when people were forced to eat cat's and dog's flesh, and women to eat their own children.

Much more we could give you to understand, but we are persuaded that you yourselves feel a part of our grievances, and therefore need not open the matter any plainer.

But if you happen to show your force and might against us, we for our parts neither respect life nor living; for better it were in such case we manfully die, than hereafter to be pined to death for want of that which these devouring encroachers do serve their fat hogs and sheep withal.

For God hath bestowed upon us most bountiful and innumerable blessings and the chiefest is our most gracious and religious King, who doth and will glory in the flourishing estate of his communality.

And so we leave you, commending you to the sure hold and safeguard of the mighty Jehovah, both now and evermore.

From Hampton field in haste, we rest as poor delvers and day labourers for the good of the Commonwealth till death.

5

"A Common Treasury for All"

Was the earth made for to preserve a few covetous, proud men, to live at ease, and for them to bag and barn up the treasures of the earth from others that they might beg or starve in a fruitful land, or was it made to preserve all her children?

—GERRARD WINSTANLEY, 1649[1]

From 1629 to 1640, Charles I tried to rule as an absolute monarch, refusing to call Parliament and unilaterally imposing taxes that were widely viewed as oppressive and illegal. When his need for more money finally forced him to call Parliament, the House of Commons refused to approve new taxes unless he agreed to restrictions on his powers. Civil war broke out in 1642, leading to victory for Parliament and the king's execution in 1649, followed by adoption of *An Act declaring England to be a Commonwealth*. For the next eleven years, England was a republic.

Many histories of the English Civil War treat it as purely a conflict *within* the ruling elite: indeed, in some accounts it seems "as if the other 97 per cent of the population did not exist or did not matter."[2] But as Brian Manning shows in *The English People and the English Revolution*, poor peasants, wage laborers, and small producers were not just followers and foot soldiers—they were conscious participants whose actions influenced and often determined the course of events. The fight for the commons was an important part of the English Revolution:

> Between the assembling of the Long Parliament in 1640 and the outbreak of the civil war in 1642 there was a rising tide of protest and riot in the countryside. This was directed chiefly against the enclosures of commons, wastes and fens, and the invasions of common rights by the king, members of the royal family, courtiers, bishops and great aristocrats.[3]

Between 1640 and 1644 there were anti-enclosure riots in more than half of England's counties, especially in the Midlands and north. In July 1641, the House of Lords, composed of the wealthiest landowners, complained that "violent breaking into possessions and enclosures, in riotous and tumultuous manner, in several parts of this kingdom," was happening "more frequently . . . since this Parliament began than formerly." They ordered local authorities to ensure "that no enclosure or possession shall be violently, and in a tumultuous manner, disturbed or taken away from any man,"[4] but their orders had little effect. "Constables not only repeatedly failed to perform their duties against neighbours engaged in the forcible recovery of their commons, but were also sometimes to be found in the ranks of the rioters themselves."[5]

The commoners hated the landowners' government and weren't reluctant to say so. When an order against anti-enclosure riots was read in a church in Wiltshire in April 1643, for example, a parishioner stood and "most contemptuously and in dishonor of the Parliament and their authority said that he cared not for their orders and the Parliament might have kept them and wiped their arses with them."[6] In 1645, anti-enclosure protesters in Epworth, Lincolnshire, replied to a similar order: "They did not care a fart for the order which was made by the lords in Parliament and published in the churches, and, that notwithstanding that order, they would pull down all the rest of the houses in the level that were built upon those improvements which were drained, and destroy all the enclosures."[7]

Peasant uprisings were widespread during the English Revolution, but, as Brian Manning points out, they were disconnected from the revolution's main course:

> Many peasants opposed to enclosures rioted against those who held and profited from the enclosed lands whether they were royalists or parliamentarians, and their war was against enclosures and loss of common rights rather than against king or parliament. Other peasants supported parliament in the civil war in the expectation that would help them, but found in the 1650s that the new regimes endorsed enclosure and erosion of common rights.[8]

Both houses of Parliament repeatedly condemned anti-enclosure riots, and no anti-enclosure measures were adopted during the Civil War or by the republican regime in the 1650s. The last attempt to regulate (not prevent) enclosure occurred in 1656, in a bill that was rejected on first reading: the Speaker said "he never liked any Bill that touched upon property," and another MP called it "the most mischievous Bill that ever was offered to this House."[9]

Like the royal government it replaced, the republican government in the 1650s raised revenue by selling off royal forests and supported the drainage and enclosure of the fens. It eliminated the remaining feudal restrictions and charges on landowners, but left the insecure tenures of farmers and cottagers unchanged. "Thus landlords secured their own estates in absolute ownership, and ensured that copyholders remained evictable."[10]

That outcome might have been avoided, if the rural anti-enclosure protesters and the mass urban radical movement known as the Levellers had joined forces. For a brief period, such an alliance seemed possible. In July 1647, in *An Appeal from the degenerate Representative Body of the Commons assembled at Westminster*, the imprisoned Leveller leader Richard Overton demanded that "all grounds which anciently lay in common for the poor, and are now impropriate, inclosed, and fenced in, may forthwith (in whose hands soever they are) be cast out, and laid open again to the free and common use and benefit of the poor."[11] And in September 1648, *The humble Petition of Thousands of well-affected persons*, written by Leveller leaders, listed twenty-seven radical measures that Parliament ought to have implemented, including "That you would have laid open all late Inclosures of Fens, and other Commons, or have enclosed them only or chiefly to the benefit of the poor."[12] (The word "late" may be significant—it meant "recent," and so may have been a step back from Overton's call for reopening "all grounds which anciently lay in common.")

Reversing existing enclosures would have given current relief, but would not have prevented landlords from evicting tenants in future. With that in mind, *A new engagement, or, Manifesto*, published in 1648, proposed that tenants be allowed to buy their land outright.

Unfortunately, the Levellers didn't carry through. Their most important manifesto, the May 1649 *Agreement of the People*, said nothing at all about enclosures or tenures, and there is no evidence that the Levellers' London-based leadership made any practical moves to link up with the anti-enclosure protests. "They did enough for the tenants' cause to provoke Cromwell and the gentry to crush them, but not enough to mobilise the villages as their resolute allies."[13]

Diggers

In 1649, at the peak of the revolution and while Cromwell was moving against the Levellers, another revolutionary movement emerged, espousing a far more radical program. The Diggers didn't just oppose enclosures, they sought a commons-based revolution.

On April 1, 1649, about two dozen men and women began farming undeveloped common land on St. George's Hill, about twenty miles southwest of London. Their goal was to "work in righteousness and lay the foundation of making the earth a common treasury for all, both rich and poor, that everyone that is born in the land may be fed by the earth his mother that brought him forth, according to the reason that rules in the creation."[14]

The Diggers' manifesto was written by Gerrard Winstanley, who has been described as "the foremost radical socialist English thinker and activist of the early modern period and one of the significant radical social thinkers of any time."[15] When he led the occupation of St. George's Hill, England was facing nationwide political, social, and economic crises. Seven years of destructive civil war had climaxed with the king's execution in January 1649. Three years of disastrously bad harvests and virulent livestock disease had bankrupted many farmers and caused widespread hunger. From 1646 to 1650, prices increased nearly 50 percent: "Poorly housed, ill-clothed, and badly fed, the poor suffered not only from the lack of work but also from the shortages and rises in prices of foodstuffs, which became more serious as stocks were exhausted in the late winter and the spring of 1649."[16]

Rural workers in Northamptonshire described the intolerable conditions that led them to join Winstanley's movement:

> We have spent all we have; our trading is decayed; our wives and children cry for bread; our lives are a burden to us, divers of us having 5, 6, 7, 8, 9 in family, and we cannot get bread for one of them by our labor. Rich men's hearts are hardened; they will not give us if we beg at their doors. If we steal, the Law will end our lives. Divers of the poor are starved to death already; and it were better for us that are living to die by the Sword than by the Famine.[17]

These were not naïve back-to-the-land dreamers; they were lifelong laborers and cottagers who knew how to farm and were prepared for hard work. On St. George's Hill—which they called George's Hill because they didn't believe in saints—they first dug a garden for parsnips, carrots, and beans, then burned off the cover vegetation on about ten acres so it could be ploughed for wheat and barley. They built rough huts for themselves and pens for a few cattle, and invited others to join them, promising that everyone who helped farm the common land would share its produce. If farming skills alone had been sufficient, their cooperative community would have succeeded. But it was not to be.

By mid-August, magistrates and mobs had driven the Diggers away from St, George's Hill, and by the following April a second commune on Little Heath in nearby Cobham was dispersed by the army and hired thugs. Digger communities elsewhere in central and south England were also broken up by August 1650.

With the benefit of hindsight, it is clear that they had made two strategic miscalculations. On one hand, they overestimated their ability to win mass support through the power of their ideas and example. They expected to be joined by thousands of poor workers who would share the labor and the produce. They did grow, especially in Cobham, and digger camps formed in at least ten other places, but their movement never included more than a few hundred active participants.

At the same time, they underestimated the determination of landlords to maintain control of common land, even undeveloped and barren areas. The gentry and yeoman farmers weren't just uninterested in sharing the land, they were downright hostile. Local magistrates, themselves landowners, indicted Diggers for trespass and unlawful assembly, and imposed fines that no poor person could pay. Mobs organized by landowners tore down and burned the Diggers' modest homes, trampled their crops, and physically attacked men, women, and children. When the Diggers finally abandoned Little Heath, Winstanley claimed a moral victory, but physically they were defeated.

Not only defeated, but written out of history. There is some evidence that Winstanley's ideas influenced Quaker thought in the 1650s, and some radicals read his pamphlets in the 1700s, but his ideas had little lasting influence. Samuel Gardiner's ten-volume history of the period, published in 1883–84, dismissed the Diggers in a single sentence. Marx and Engels, who read and admired the work of their socialist predecessors from Thomas Müntzer to Saint-Simon, Fourier, and Robert Owen, were apparently unaware of Winstanley and the movement he led. The Diggers aren't mentioned in Engels's classic account *Socialism: Utopian and Scientific*.

Winstanley was rescued from obscurity in 1895 by Eduard Bernstein, a leader of Germany's Social Democratic Party and editor of its official newspaper. He is infamous in socialist history for rejecting revolution in favor of incremental reform, but he was still an orthodox Marxist when he wrote *Sozialismus und Demokratie in der großen englischen Revolution* (Socialism and Democracy in the Great English Revolution). The English translation, published in 1930, is misleadingly titled *Cromwell and Communism*.

Bernstein was the first of many to describe Winstanley as a socialist ahead of his age, and his chapters on the Diggers included the first published account of Winstanley's final book, *The Law of Freedom in a Platform*, "which is well worth being rescued from the total oblivion to which it has hitherto been consigned."

> He represents the most advanced ideas of his time; in his Utopia we find coalesced all the popular aspirations engendered and fertilized by the Revolution. It would be more than absurd to criticize, from our modern standpoint, his positive proposals, or to stress their imperfections and inexpediency. They are to be explained in the light of the economic structure of society as he found it. We would fain admire the acumen and sound judgment exhibited by this simple man of the people, and his insight into the connection existing between the social conditions of his time and the causes of the evils which he assails.[18]

True Levellers?

"Levellers" and "Diggers" were derogatory labels first applied to participants in the 1607 Midlands Revolt—*levellers* because they tore down fences and hedges, *diggers* because they were poor farmers who worked the soil. In the 1640s, conservatives referred to radical democrats as Levellers, and the name stuck. The Levellers were by far the largest and most influential radical current in the English Revolution.

It is often claimed that in 1649 the Diggers called themselves True Levellers, but that term was used only once, in the title of Winstanley's April 1649 pamphlet, *The True Levellers Standard Advanced*. It does not appear elsewhere in that pamphlet or in any of his other works. The second edition of the pamphlet, published in the summer, was retitled *A Declaration to the Powers of England.*

It is likely that the "True Levellers" title was chosen by the printer, in an attempt to boost sales at a time when the Levellers were facing severe state repression. What it actually did was cause confusion. Royalists used it to smear the Levellers as communists, and Leveller leaders vehemently disavowed any connection with the revolutionaries on St. George's Hill. Winstanley certainly read and borrowed from Leveller literature, but he was called, and proudly called himself, a Digger.

"If Thou Dost Not Act, Thou Dost Nothing"

We know little about Gerrard Winstanley's early life. He was born in 1609, the son of a cloth merchant in Wigan. Judging by the quality and content of his writing, he received a good education and read widely. From 1630 to 1638 he was an apprentice in London, but his own cloth business failed in 1642, a victim of the economic downturn brought on by the Civil War. For the next five or six years he grazed other people's cattle and worked as a day laborer in Cobham.

Until then he was, as he put it, "a blind professor and strict goer to church, as they call it, and a hearer of sermons . . . [who] believed as the learned clergy believed,"[19] but the religious debates and turmoil of the time affected him deeply. He developed anti-clerical and heretical views and rejected all forms of organized religion—"For all your particular churches are like the enclosures of land which hedges in some to be heirs of life, and hedges out others; one saying Christ is here with them; another saying no, but he is there with them."[20]

His first theological writings, published after April 1648, were much like other mystical works of the time, but by the end of the year he was espousing an analysis of social problems that was far in advance of any other seventeenth-century thinker. Using the word Reason for God, he asked:

> Did the light of Reason make the earth for some men to engross up into bags and barns, that others might be oppressed with poverty? Did the light of Reason make this law, that if one man have not such abundance of the earth as to give to others he borrowed of; that he that did lend should imprison the other, and starve his body in a close room? Did the light of Reason make this law, that some part of mankind should kill and hang another part of mankind that could not walk in their steps?[21]

He answered that inequality and oppression were not made by Reason but by "covetousness, the murdering God of this world." That would soon change:

> When this universal law of equity rises up in every man and woman, then none shall lay claim to any creature, and say, this is mine, and that is yours, this is my work, that is yours; but every one shall put to their hands to till the earth, and bring up cattle, and the blessing of the earth shall be common to all; when a man hath need of any corn or cattle, take from the next storehouse he meets with.
>
> There shall be no buying nor selling, no fairs nor markets, but the whole earth shall be a common treasury for every man.[22]

These ideas were so unlike anything he had heard or read elsewhere that he attributed them to a vision.

My heart was filled with sweet thoughts, and many things were revealed to me which I never read in books, nor heard from the mouth of any flesh, and when I began to speak of them, some people could not bear my words, and amongst those revelations this was one: that the earth shall be made a common treasury of livelihood to whole mankind, without respect of persons; and I had a voice within me bade me declare it all abroad, which I did obey, for I declared it by word of mouth wheresoever I came.[23]

Whatever the source of those revelations, they changed the direction of his thought and life. By early in 1649, he was calling for a revolutionary alternative based on the commons, and he didn't just write and talk about it. Like Karl Marx two centuries later, Winstanley believed that it was not enough to interpret the world, it had to be changed.

Yet my mind was not at rest, because nothing was acted, and thoughts run in me that words and writings were all nothing and must die, for action is the life of all, and if thou dost not act, thou dost nothing. Within a little time I was made obedient to the word in that particular likewise; for I took my spade and went and broke the ground upon George Hill in Surrey, thereby declaring freedom to the creation, and that the earth must be set free from entanglements of lords and landlords, and that it shall become a common treasury to all, as it was first made and given to the sons of men.[24]

General Strike

Winstanley estimated that a third or more of the land in England was unused, but "children starve for want," because "the lords of the manors will not suffer the poor to manure it." By farming that land, the poor could feed themselves, without attacking the landowners' property rights:

Let the gentry have their enclosures free from all Norman enslaving entanglements whatsoever, and let the common people
have their commons and waste lands set free to them from
all Norman enslaving lords of manors, that so both elder and
younger brother, as we spring successively one from another,
may live free and quiet one by one and with another, not bur-
dening one another in this land of our nativity.[25]

That paragraph should have been labeled *true but misleading*,
because if Winstanley's full program had been implemented, the
landowners would have had to work their land alone. Arguing that
it was sinful to pay rent or work for others, he called on the poor to
withdraw their services and stop enriching the ruling class:

> Therefore you dust of the earth, that are trod under foot, you
> poor people, that make both scholars and rich men your oppres-
> sors by your labours, take notice of your privilege. The law of
> righteousness is now declared.
>
> If you labour the earth, and work for others that live at ease, and
> follow the ways of the flesh by your labours, eating the bread which
> you get by the sweat of your brows, not their own: know this, that
> the hand of the Lord shall break out upon every such hireling
> labourer and you shall perish with the covetous rich men.[26]

As Christopher Hill says, "The Digger colony on St. George's
Hill was intended to be the first stage of a sort of general strike
against wage-labour."[27] Brian Manning elaborates:

> The landlords would be unable to rent land to farmers who did
> not have the labour to cultivate it. Large estates would cease to
> be economically viable, enclosures would cease, and every big
> proprietor—gentry and yeoman—would be reduced to living off
> only such land as he could tend with his own and his family's
> labour. The assumption was that then they would be constrained
> to give up their properties to Digger communities. . . .

By this strategy the manorial system would have collapsed and the nobility and gentry would have been deprived of a great deal of their wealth and power. The combination of a labour strike and a rent strike would have accomplished an economic and social revolution.[28]

The Digger poet Robert Coster wrote that if rents weren't paid and laborers didn't work, then "the Lords of Manors, and other Gentlemen who covet after so much Land, could not let it out by parcels, but must be constrained to keep it in their own hands, then would they want those great bags of money (which do maintain pride, idleness, and fullness of bread) which are carried into them by their tenants."[29]

The Diggers claimed the right to farm not just manorial commons, but all formerly royal land and all land that had been seized from the church and royalists at the end of the Civil War.[30]

The Law of Freedom

All but one of Winstanley's books and pamphlets were published between April 1648 and April 1650. He wrote most of another in the autumn of 1649, but set it aside to participate in the Cobham commune's fight for survival. After the defeat of the digging project, he fell silent for more than a year, but in the autumn of 1651 he returned to the unfinished book, possibly inspired by Parliament's final military victory over the royalists. "I was stirred up to give it a resurrection, and to pick up as many of my scattered papers as I could find, and to compile them into this method."[31]

The Law of Freedom in a Platform: or, True Magistracy Restored, published in February 1652, was his most ambitious book. It is often described as his blueprint for an ideal society, but it is better understood as a description of a *transitional society* in which reconstruction is well underway, but society still has to protect itself against threats that could reinstate an oppressive regime. The society Winstanley describes is ruled by a commonwealth government that "*in time* will be the restorer of long lost freedoms to the creation, and delights to plant righteousness over the face of the whole earth."[32]

When the Diggers occupied George Hill, they expected quick and universal acceptance of their program. The revolutionary turmoil then shaking England, especially the execution of the king, showed that the spirit of Reason was rising in the hearts of commoners, that the law of righteousness would soon prevail. As Christopher Hill puts it, once the communes were established, "Winstanley then expected the state, in Marxist phrase, to wither away immediately."[33] Experience was a hard teacher:

> As the experience of the colony soon taught him, Winstanley had underestimated the institutional power of the Beast, and had equally underestimated the hold of the Serpent over the minds of men. What he must have found most upsetting of all was the hostility of many local tenants to the Diggers. . . . Clearly a period of education was needed before Christ arose in a sufficient number of sons and daughters to overthrow kingly power.[34]

The Law of Freedom is framed as an appeal to the head of the army, Oliver Cromwell, but it is unlikely that Winstanley believed Cromwell would support the changes he proposes. The early 1650s were a time of intense public discussion of government and law reform, and the Digger was inserting himself into those debates, to win a hearing and perhaps some partial reforms. The latter possibility is implied by his suggestion that Cromwell could accept some of his ideas and reject others—"suck out the honey and cast away the weeds."[35]

Contrary to modern critics who say he had abandoned his ideals, his appeal for state support was not new. Winstanley's strategy for change had always included both direct action to create working communes and appeals to the army and Parliament to "let the common people have their commons and waste lands set free to them from all Norman enslaving lords of manors."[36] As

Darren Webb of Sheffield Utopia argues, "for Winstanley, the earth was to be made a common treasury for all through action from below *and* from above."[37] What we see in *The Law of Freedom* is not a change of principle, but a shift from agitation to propaganda, from immediate seizure of common land to arguing for a longer-term and nationwide transition.

An Incomplete Revolution

The Law of Freedom gets straight to the point: in a prefatory letter to Cromwell, Winstanley congratulates the general for defeating the royalists, but insists that more remains to be done. The war could not have been won without the support of common people who fought in the army, paid war taxes, and billeted soldiers. Now Cromwell must either "set the land free to the oppressed Commoners, who assisted you," or leave the land and the king's laws unchanged. If he takes the second course, he will lose his honor and "lay the foundation of greater Slavery."[38]

Other radicals blamed England's problems on individuals and institutions—the king, his councillors, or the monarchy as an institution. Winstanley's more sophisticated analysis focused on what he called *kingly power,* meaning oppressive class rule in general, not just the crimes of a particular individual or political arrangement. For him, executing the king was only a first step toward freedom:

Kingly power is like a great spread tree, if you lop the head or top-bow, and let the other branches and root stand, it will grow again and recover fresher strength. . . . That top-bow is lopped off the tree of tyranny, and kingly power in that one particular is cast out; but alas oppression is a great tree still, and keeps off the sun of freedom from the poor commons still.[39]

Now Cromwell must cut down the rest of the tree. "You do not see the end of your work, unless the kingly law and power be removed as well as his person."[40] Even if Cromwell did not act, revolution was inevitable: "The spirit of the whole creation (who is God) is about the reformation of the world, and he will go forward in his work."[41]

The common people had been promised freedom when they agreed to fight the monarchy in 1643 and when they signed loyalty oaths in 1650, but the promise had been broken.

> For is not this a common speech among the people, We have parted with our estates, we have lost our friends in the wars, which we willingly gave up, because freedom was promised us; and now in the end we have new task-masters, and our old burdens increased: and though all sorts of people have taken an engagement to cast out kingly power, yet kingly power remains in power still in the hands of those who have no more right to the earth than our selves.[42]

Introducing an early version of the labor theory of value, Winstanley denies that it is necessary or natural for one man to be richer than another.

> No man can be rich, but he must be rich either by his own labors, or by the labors of other men helping him. If a man have no help from his neighbor, he shall never gather an estate of hundreds and thousands a year. If other men help him to work, then are those riches his neighbors, as well as his; for they be the fruit of other men's labors as well as his own.[43]

To live, people must have food, so by monopolizing the land, the rich are restricting the right to live to those who can pay. In a prescient passage, Winstanley says that those who demand payment for using land would also, if they could, charge for all the necessities of life.

> Surely then, oppressing lords of manors, exacting landlords, and

tithe-takers, may as well say, their brethren shall not breathe in the air, nor enjoy warmth in their bodies, nor have the moist waters to fall upon them in showers, unless they will pay them rent for it: as to say, their brethren shall not work upon earth, nor eat the fruits thereof, unless they will hire that liberty of them. For he that takes upon him to restrain his brother from the liberty of the one, may upon the same ground restrain him from the liberty of all four; viz. fire, water, earth, and air.

A man had better to have had no body, than to have no food for it; therefore this restraining of the earth from brethren by brethren, is oppression and bondage; but the free enjoyment thereof is true freedom.[44]

And in a passage that presages a materialist understanding of the psychological effects of alienation, he writes that the "outward bondage" of enforced separation from the land doesn't just cause physical ills: "I am assured that if it be rightly searched into, the inward bondages of the mind, as covetousness, pride, hypocrisy, envy, sorrow, fears, desperation, and madness, are all occasioned by the outward bondage, that one sort of people lay upon another."[45]

Winstanley proposed to remove the outward bondage, but it would take time and effort to heal the inward bondages of the mind that are barriers to true freedom for all. For him, C. B. Macpherson writes, the road to freedom "lay in free common access to the land . . . for that was the only way to assure freedom from exploitation of man by man."[46]

"Relieve the Oppressed Ones"

Under a law passed in 1641, a new Parliament was supposed to be called and elected at least once every three years, but when *The Law of Freedom* was published in 1652 there had been no elections for twelve years. The common people, Winstanley wrote, were "more offended by an hereditary Parliament than we were oppressed by an hereditary king."[47] Like the Levellers, Winstanley favored annual Parliaments, but he wanted representatives who would further the revolution: "their eye and care must be principally to relieve the oppressed ones." In addition to representing England in dealings with other countries, Parliament should:

- "Give out orders for the free planting and reaping of the commonwealth's land [by] all who have been oppressed." In addition to manorial commons, royal lands and land seized from royalists after the Civil War, Winstanley now insisted that the commonwealth's land should include all the church land that was confiscated by Henry VIII in the 1530s, a huge increase from the Diggers' previous demands. "And when the land is once freed from the oppressors power and laws, a parliament is to keep it so, and not suffer it by their consent to have it bought or sold, and so entangled in bondage upon a new account."

- "Abolish all old laws and customs, which have been the strength of the oppressor, and to prepare, and then to enact new laws for the ease and freedom of the people, but yet not without the peoples knowledge." Winstanley proposed sixty-two "short and pithy laws" to replace all existing laws—not as a finished legal code, but as suggestions that should only be enacted with "the consent, not of men interested in the old oppressing laws and customs, as kings used to do, but of them who have been oppressed."

- Remove any burdens "which have hindered or do hinder the oppressed people from the enjoyment of their birthrights." Winstanley particularly argues for recovering public land that had been sold "without a general consent of the people," a reference to land the king sold to raise funds before the Civil War. More generally, Parliament should punish anyone who used their position or wealth to oppress the poor.[48]

These measures, especially the first, laid the basis for a *commonwealth,* a social order based on sharing land, labor, and goods. Of course he never used the word, but his program was profoundly anti-capitalist. Private ownership of land, wage-labor and buying or selling would all be banned. Unlike the Levellers, whose vision of freedom was purely political, for Winstanley, "true commonwealth's freedom lies in the free enjoyment of the earth."[49] Freedom was not individual, but communal and cooperative.

Every family would work in the fields "at seed time to plow, dig, and plant, and at harvest time to reap the fruits of the earth." Farm work would be organized and supervised by an Overseer, who, like all officers at every level in Winstanley's system of government, was elected by universal manhood suffrage, was unpaid and could only hold office for one year, "to prevent the creeping in of oppression into the commonwealth again."[50]

Everyone would work the land and at a trade, and their products would be distributed for free from shops or public storehouses. "As every one works to advance the common stock, so every one shall have a free use of any commodity in the storehouse, for his pleasure and comfortable livelihood, without buying and selling, or restraint from any."[51] He doesn't say "from each according to his abilities, to each according to his needs," but the thought is certainly there.

Long before mainstream economists described the "free rider" problem, Winstanley realized that during the transition some might take without giving. In the commonwealth, anyone who refused to work "and yet will feed and clothe himself with other men's labor," or who took more than his family needed from the common stock, was liable to punishments ranging from public shaming to whipping to a year of forced labor.[52] Judges could reduce or cancel sentences if offenders changed their ways, "for it is amendment not destruction that commonwealth's law requires."[53]

"Amendment not destruction" was the basis of the penalties for violating most of the laws that Winstanley hoped the new parliament would pass, but actions that tended to restore kingly bondage could not be forgiven. In his view, anyone who tried to buy or sell land or its products should be executed as a traitor, as should anyone who practiced law for gain, or who used religion to acquire land or wealth.

It is noteworthy that he recommended the death penalty for rape, on the grounds that "it is robbery of a woman's bodily freedom."[54] This was at a time when rape was commonly treated as a crime against the husband's property, not against women's right to control their bodies. Winstanley was no feminist, as allowing only men to vote and supporting patriarchal households show, but overall, Sarah Apetrei writes, his "discussion of gender relations ... points in a direction that is as interesting, and as radical, as anything conceived in the seventeenth century."[55]

That's true of all of Winstanley's work. As James Holstun argues in his study of class struggle in the English revolution, "the Diggers produced the most important seventeenth-century critique of this transformation *from the point of view of its victims*."

> Responding to the misery and dislocation born of enclosure, the Diggers turn not to the paternalists' mythical past, not to the improvers' enriched vision of an oppressive present, but to the revolutionary praxis of an egalitarian future.[56]

Only Winstanley and his Digger comrades identified private ownership of the land as the cause of exploitation and poverty, and only they fought for an entirely different system in which the land would be a *universal commons,* and the people who work the land would rule. They weren't waiting for salvation in heaven: as the final line of *The Diggers' Song* says, their goal was *glory here.*

WINSTANLEY AND OTHERS WHO FOUGHT for democracy and land "rose with the English Revolution and went down with its decline."[57] The defeats of the Levellers and Diggers in 1649–50 were decisive victories for the conservative wing of the parliamentary cause: it was one thing to overthrow and execute a king, and quite another to allow the poor rights to the land they worked. In the conservatives' view, defended by General Ireton in the famous Putney Debates in 1647, property was "the most fundamental part of the constitution of the Kingdom, which if you take away, you take all away," by which they meant the property of the rich.[58]

In the 1650s, Parliament freed large landowners from their remaining feudal duties but refused to limit enclosures and explicitly left poor farmers' insecure tenures in place. "Tithes and an Established Church remained, the legal system was largely unreformed, power was not devolved to the local communities, and the common and waste lands were not taken over by the poor."[59]

In the last decades of the 1600s, large landowners and merchants won decisive control of the English state. In the 1700s, they would use that power to continue the dispossession of commoners and consolidate their absolute ownership of the land. In Christopher Hill's words, "the common people were defeated no less decisively than was the crown."[60]

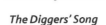

The Diggers' Song

Sung to the tune of a traditional song, the lyrics have been attributed,
without evidence, to Gerrard Winstanley. There are several recorded ver-
sions online, including by Chumbawama at https://www.youtube.com/
watch?v=OA4FTIz2Zrw.

You noble Diggers all, stand up now, stand up now,
You noble Diggers all, stand up now,
The waste land to maintain, seeing Cavaliers by name
Your digging does disdain, and persons all defame.
    Stand up now, stand up now.

Your houses they pull down, stand up now, stand up now,
Your houses they pull down, stand up now.
Your houses they pull down, to fright poor men in town,
But the gentry must come down, and the poor shall wear the crown.
    Stand up now, Diggers all.

With spades and hoes and ploughs, stand up now, stand up now,
With spades and hoes and ploughs, stand up now,
Your freedom to uphold, seeing Cavaliers are bold
To kill you if they could, and rights from you to hold.
    Stand up now, Diggers all.

Their self-will is their law, stand up now, stand up now,
Their self-will is their law, stand up now.
Since tyranny came in, they count it now no sin
To make a gaol a gin, to starve poor men therein.
    Stand up now, stand up now.

The gentry are all round, stand up now, stand up now,
The gentry are all round, stand up now.
The gentry are all round, on each side they are found,
This wisdom's so profound, to cheat us of our ground.
    Stand up now, stand up now.

The lawyers they conjoin, stand up now, stand up now,
The lawyers they conjoin, stand up now.

To arrest you they advise, such fury they devise,
The devil in them lies, and hath blinded both their eyes.
    Stand up now, stand up now.

The clergy they come in, stand up now, stand up now,
The clergy they come in, stand up now.
The clergy they come in, and say it is a sin
That we should now begin, our freedom for to win.
    Stand up now, Diggers all.

The tithes they yet will have, stand up now, stand up now,
The tithes they yet will have, stand up now.
The tithes they yet will have, and lawyers their fees crave,
And this they say is brave, to make the poor their slave.
    Stand up now, Diggers all.

'Gainst lawyers and 'gainst priests, stand up now, stand up now,
'Gainst lawyers and 'gainst priests, stand up now.
For tyrants they are both, even flat against their oath,
To grant us they are loath, free meat and drink and cloth.
    Stand up now, Diggers all.

The club is all their law, stand up now, stand up now,
The club is all their law, stand up now.
The club is all their law, to keep poor men in awe,
But they no vision saw, to maintain such a law.
    Stand up now, Diggers all.

The Cavaliers are foes, stand up now, stand up now,
The Cavaliers are foes, stand up now.
The Cavaliers are foes, themselves they do disclose
By verses not in prose, to please the singing boys.
    Stand up now, Diggers all.

To conquer them by love, come in now, come in now,
To conquer them by love, come in now,
To conquer them by love, as it does you behove,
For he is King above, no power is like to love.
    Glory here, Diggers all.

PART TWO

EXPANSION AND CONSOLIDATION

1660–1860

6

Empire and Expropriation

The discovery of gold and silver in America, the extirpation, enslavement and entombment in mines of the indigenous population of that continent, the beginnings of the conquest and looting of India, and the conversion of Africa into a preserve for the commercial hunting of blackskins, are all things which characterize the dawn of the era of capitalist production.

—KARL MARX[1]

Most accounts of the enclosure movement in Britain present it as a purely domestic matter, but it could not have happened so quickly or thoroughly without the imperial wealth that slave traders, plantation owners, and colonial profiteers invested in British estates. In Marx's words, "The treasures captured outside Europe by undisguised looting, enslavement, and murder, floated back to the mother-country and were there turned into capital."[2]

A full account of England's empire is beyond the scope of this book, but it is important to understand that the aristocrats and gentry who waged the war on the commons included many whose wealth originated overseas. The two main sources of that expropriated wealth in the 1700s were the slave trade and plantation slavery in the Caribbean, and colonial plunder in India.

IN THE 1700s, THE WORLD was increasingly divided between the imperial powers of Western Europe and the countries that the Europeans viewed as a "sacrifice zone for the sake of their own development."

> No loss of human life, no amount of suffering, no degree of degradation was too much so long as the economic interests of colonial companies and states were served. The inequity was justified by dehumanising those with black and brown skin—by repeatedly asserting that they were not quite as human as white people, and that therefore their suffering did not matter.[3]

In the sixteenth and seventeenth centuries, England was a minor player among the European powers competing for overseas conquests. By most measures it was outranked by France, Spain, Portugal, and the Netherlands, countries that had far more ships and were reaping far greater rewards from the Americas and Asia. But by the end of the 1700s, Britain ruled the largest empire the world has ever seen.

Human Trafficking and Plantation Slavery

The first modern study of the key role that slavery played in British economic development was Eric Williams's brilliant *Capitalism and Slavery*, published in 1944. Despite many attempts by conservative historians to discredit the "Williams Thesis," his central argument is indisputable: "The West Indian islands became the hub of the British Empire, of immense importance to the grandeur and prosperity of England. It was the Negro slaves who made these sugar colonies the most precious colonies ever recorded in the annals of imperialism."[4]

Defenders of British imperialism like to brag that Britain outlawed the slave trade in 1807, but that's like praising a serial killer because he eventually retired. The ban came after centuries in which British investors had grown rich as human traffickers, and it did nothing for the 700,000 Africans who remained enslaved in Britain's Caribbean colonies. Britain's vaunted humanitarianism is belied by the British army's slaughter of rebellious slaves in Guyana—seventeen years *after* the slave trade was declared illegal.

Over four centuries, some 12.5 million Africans were shipped across the Atlantic in conditions so horrendous that 1.5 million died on route. Another 1.5 million died after less than a year of labor in the New World. The European slave trade started as small coastal operations by Portuguese bandits in the 1400s, and became very big business, growing from 370,000 people in the 1500s to 1,870,000 million in the 1600s to over 6,100,000 in the 1700s, when English ships carried over 40 percent of the total. As historian Joseph Inokori has shown, the eighteenth-century British slave trade was dominated by a few large merchant companies, and "the best firms earned upwards of 50 percent on their investments, well above the normal profits of an easy trade."[5]

While the slave trade itself was profitable, it was the combination of human trafficking and slave plantations in the Caribbean that really promoted economic growth in England. In the sugar plantations on Barbados, Jamaica, Nevis, Antigua, and other islands, hundreds of thousands of Africans planted, tended, and harvested sugarcane, and then—because cane rots quickly after harvesting—worked round the clock in the mills where it was ground and boiled to make raw sugar and molasses:

> Divorced from the rhythm of natural seasons, or even the cycles of labor and rest incorporated within the church calendar, the experience of labor on the sugar plantation was monotonous and relentless, a continuous staged cycle of cutting, crushing, boiling, curing, cutting, crushing, boiling, curing. The sugar plantation realized the very modern drudgery of industrial efficiency. The plantation was a machine.[6]

Slaves were cheap, so plantation owners literally worked them to death. "In the century and a half before the abolition of the

British transatlantic slave trade in 1808, some 2.7 million captive Africans were brought to the British West Indies. Yet by 1808, the total British Caribbean slave population was barely a third that number—about 775,000. . . . Slaves died faster than they could reproduce."[7]

Millions of African lives were expropriated to enrich plantation owners and sugar merchants. That genocidal policy was precisely why Adam Smith could write: "The profits of a sugar-plantation in any of our West Indian colonies are generally much greater than those of any other cultivation that is known either in Europe or America."[8] As the Archbishop of Canterbury said in a 2007 sermon, Britain's historic prosperity—that is, the prosperity of Britain's ruling elite—"was built in large part on this atrocity."[9]

Robin Blackburn estimates that in 1770 the so-called triangular trade—guns and textiles from Britain to Africa, slaves from Africa to the West Indies, sugar from the West Indies to Britain—accounted for between 21 and 35 percent of Britain's gross fixed capital formation.[10] Economic power and political power went hand in hand: in the second half of the eighteenth century, about fifty Members of Parliament had connections to Caribbean plantations. Known as the "West Indian Interest," they consistently voted against proposals to weaken or abolish the plantation slavery system.[11]

When slavery was finally abolished in the British Empire in 1834, the government paid 20 million pounds, the largest state payout for any purpose until 2008, to compensate 46,000 West Indian slave owners, half of them resident in Britain, for the loss of their property. The slaves received nothing.

Looting India

As Mike Davis writes in *Late Victorian Holocausts*, "If the history of India were to be condensed into a single fact, it is this: there was no increase in India's per capita income from 1757 to 1947."[12] The eighteenth century saw the beginning of the large-scale plunder of India by the East India Company, and the acquisition of country estates by Company employees who returned to England laden with stolen riches. As prominent Whig politician and novelist Horace Walpole wrote in 1772, those *nabobs*—a disparaging term derived from *nawab*, meaning viceroy—were known for their unparalleled greed and brutality in India and their conspicuous consumption in Britain:

> They starved millions in India by monopolies and plunder, and almost raised a famine at home by the luxury occasioned by their opulence, and by that opulence, raising the price of everything, till the poor could not afford to purchase bread. Conquest, usurpation, wealth, luxury, famine.[13]

Since 1600, the East India Company had operated global trading networks, carrying spices, tea, textiles, and slaves between Britain, Persia, India, China, Indonesia, and the West Indies. It changed direction in 1757, when the Company's private army, headed by Robert Clive, took advantage of the decline of the Mughal empire to seize control of Bengal, India's richest province, after a battle at Plassey (Palashi) near Calcutta:

> More of a commercial transaction than a real battle, Plassey was followed by the systematic looting of Bengal's treasury. In a powerful symbol of the transfer of wealth that had begun, the Company loaded the treasury's gold and silver onto a fleet of over a hundred boats and sent them downriver to Calcutta. In one stroke, Clive had netted £2.5 million for the Company and £234,000 for himself. Today this would be equivalent to a £232 million corporate windfall and a cool £22 million success fee for Clive. Historical convention views Plassey as the first step in the creation of the British Empire in India. It is perhaps better understood as the East India Company's most successful business deal.[14]

Clive's triumphant takeover effectively enabled the Company

to divert Bengal's surplus from the courts of the Mughal emperor and the provincial nawab to the mansions and country estates of Britain.[15]

An eyewitness wrote that under Company rule, "the country was depopulated by every species of public distress.... In the space of six years, half the great cities of an opulent kingdom were rendered desolate; the most fertile fields in the world laid waste; and five millions of harmless and industrious people were either expelled or destroyed."[16]

The Company became the de facto government of Bengal. It took over tax collection, raised tax rates, and enforced payment by force. Farmers who had formerly paid a percentage of the crop were now taxed on the amount of land they farmed, and full payment was demanded in cash, even if the crop failed. To obtain cash, farmers had to reduce or eliminate the main subsistence crop, rice, and switch to export crops such as cotton and mulberries. As taxes increased, less rice could be set aside for bad years, so there was no cushion when bad years came. Poor harvests in 1768 and 1769 were followed in 1770 by total failure and one of the worst famines in history. As many as 10 million people died, a third of Bengal's population.

For the Company and its agents, that catastrophe was another opportunity for profit. As a Company employee reported, "As soon as the dryness of the season foretold the approaching dearness of rice, our gentlemen in the Company's service, particularly those whose stations gave them the best opportunities, were as early as possible in buying up all they could lay hold of." They held on to the rice while thousands were dying in the streets, then sold it to local merchants for hundreds of times their cost. "One of our writers at the Durbar, who was interested therein, not esteemed to be worth 1,000 rupees last year, has sent down it is said £60,000 to be remitted home this year."[17]

While individual agents profiteered, the Company mobilized its private army to ensure that tax revenues stayed high:

Platoons of sepoys [Indian soldiers] were marched out into the countryside to enforce payment, where they erected gibbets in prominent places to hang those who resisted the tax collection. Even starving families were expected to pay up; there were no remissions authorised on humanitarian grounds. . . .

The only rice they stockpiled was for the use of the sepoys of their own army; there was no question of cuts to the military budget, even as a fifth of Bengal was starving to death.[18]

At the height of the famine, Company executives sent over a million pounds sterling to London. Pleased that tax revenues remained high, the Company's shareholders voted themselves an unprecedented 12.5 percent dividend.[19]

Famine profiteering was only one aspect of the Company's long-term export of Indian wealth to Britain. Central to the drain, as economist Utsa Patnaik has shown, was the Company's dual role as tax collector and merchant: it collected taxes in India, then used that money to buy textiles, opium, tea, and other commodities. The products the Company sold in Europe and elsewhere essentially cost it nothing.

Since the peasants and artisans were the main contributors to the total tax revenue, this meant they were not actually paid; all that happened was that the relevant part of their tax merely changed its form from cash to goods for export. This direct linking of the fiscal system with the trade system is the essence of drain in colonies where the producers were not slaves but nominally free petty producers, namely tax-paying peasants and artisans.[20]

From 1765 until the year the Company lost its monopoly in 1836, the drain was about £270 million. Invested at 5 percent, that would have yielded £30 billion in 1947, the year India won independence—more than the combined GDP of the United Kingdom, the United States, and Canada. Rather than contribute to India's economic growth, those profits enriched the Company.

As the French ambassador to England wrote in 1768, "There are few kings in Europe richer than the Directors of the English East India Company."[21]

It is not surprising that one of the first Hindi words to be adopted into English was *loot*.

Empire and Estates

"The period of enclosure and agricultural improvement," historian Corinne Fowler writes, "was also the period of empire and slavery. Commodifying land and commodifying people went hand in hand."[22]

In 1962, Marxist economist Ernest Mandel added up what was then known of the wealth that European countries extracted from Africa, the Americas, and Asia before the nineteenth century. "The total amount comes to over a billion pounds sterling, or more than all the capital of all the industrial enterprises operated by steam which existed in Europe around 1800!"[23] A more recent study by Utsa Patnaik finds that by 1801 the combined annual transfer of wealth from the West Indies and India to Britain equalled 86 percent of Britain's entire capital formation from domestic saving.[24]

These figures powerfully illustrate the importance of slavery and colonialism in financing the Industrial Revolution: without global expropriation, industrial capitalism could not have developed so quickly and thoroughly. That does not mean, however, that individual plantation owners and nabobs rushed to invest their wealth in coal mines and factories. On the contrary, most had gone to the West Indies or India to earn or steal enough to purchase or restore a country estate in Britain and many did exactly that. The money they spent on conspicuous consumption contributed indirectly to British industrial growth.

A majority of the owners of slave plantations in the British Caribbean colonies lived, as Stephanie Barczewski writes in her history of English country mansions, "the lifestyles of country gentlemen," in British country mansions—"very large, very powerful, very physical symbol[s] of the wealth that the Empire could generate."[25] A West Indies absentee could count on a steady flow of income from his slaves' labor, and his ownership of an English landed estate ensured his position in the ruling elite:

> The wealth of the West Indians [absentee owners of Caribbean plantations] became proverbial. Communities of opulent West Indians were to be found in London and Bristol. . . . The public schools of Eton, Westminster, Harrow, and Winchester were full of the sons of West Indians. The carriages of the planters were so numerous, that, when they gathered, Londoners complained that the streets were for some distance blocked. . . . A West Indian heiress was a desirable plum.[26]

Most nabobs, in contrast, didn't own land in India that would produce continuing income. Most of those who returned to England had saved enough to support a middle-class life, but a minority, particularly those who were high in the Company hierarchy, had taken full advantage of every opportunity to obtain bribes, divert company revenue, and run private businesses on the side. P. J. Marshall calculates that in the last decades of the 1700s, Company servants sent about £500,000 a year to relatives or agents in England. That was 3.5 percent of Britain's national income in 1770, an astounding amount for a small group of men.[27]

After accumulating fortunes in cash or cash equivalents, often diamonds, successful Company men who returned to Britain converted their wealth into land and influence. Robert Clive took home £276,000 in 1760 and another £239,000 in 1767—one of the largest personal fortunes in Europe at the time. He bought several large estates, an Irish peerage, and a seat in the House of Commons, where he joined about a hundred other MPs who had connections to India and the East India Company.

Country homes—usually immense mansions—absorbed a great deal of imperial wealth, in what Raymond Williams describes as "the extraordinary phase of extension, rebuilding and enlarging, which occurred in the eighteenth century."[28] When Lord Shelburne said, in 1778, that "there were scarcely ten miles together throughout the country where the house and estate of a rich West Indian was not to be seen,"[29] he was exaggerating, but the remark shows that the connection between slavery and the formation of great estates was obvious to contemporaries.

Historians have recently begun studying that connection, using the records of the government commission that paid compensation to slave owners when slavery was abolished in 1834. A report published in 2020 by the National Trust, which owns some two hundred historic houses, reveals that twenty-nine of its properties were directly connected to individuals who received compensation, and about a third had colonial connections.[30]

Also in 2020, Community Land Scotland published a groundbreaking study of the involvement of slave owners in the Highland Clearances, in which thousands of people were evicted to create sheep farms and private hunting preserves. It has long been known that many former clan chiefs sold property in the Highlands between 1810 and 1860. The new study shows that over a third of the land in the western Highlands and Islands "was sold into the hands of people directly or indirectly enriched by slavery," and that "at least 1,834,708 acres of the west Highlands and Islands—more than half of the area's total landmass, and approaching ten percent of the total landmass of Scotland—has been owned by families that have benefitted significantly from slavery."

> In the nineteenth century, some of the worst examples of clearance can be found on the estates of members of the new slavery elite. . . . The total number cleared by the new slavery elite . . . is highly unlikely to be less than 5,000. After the actions of traditional clan families implicated in slavery are taken into account this figure will be very much higher, almost certainly into the tens of thousands.[31]

Those incomplete figures, covering just part of the Highlands, clearly demonstrate that imperial plunder and the clearances were closely connected. The brutally expropriated labor of Africans and Indians made possible the expulsion of English and Scottish workers from their land. In Marx's words, "the veiled slavery of the wage-labourers in Europe needed the unqualified slavery of the New World as its pedestal."[32]

7

"A Plain Enough Case of Class Robbery"

Have the agricultural population received a farthing's compensation for the 3,511,770 acres of common land which between 1801 and 1831 were stolen from them and presented to the landlords by the landlords through the agency of Parliament?

—KARL MARX[1]

In 1688–89, England's aristocracy and gentry supported the overthrow of James II, who had tried to rule without Parliament. The accession of William III effectively completed the landowners' fight for political dominance.

Throughout the long eighteenth century—from the misnamed Glorious Revolution in 1689 to the misnamed Great Reform Act in 1832—the British state was controlled by "great agrarian magnates, privileged merchant capitalists, and their hangers on, who manipulated the organs of the State in their own private interests."[2] The very rich ruled Parliament through their unchallenged domination of the House of Lords, their effective control of the executive, and their strong influence on the slightly less-rich members of the House of Commons. The lower House was elected, but only about 3 percent of the population (all male) could vote, and high property qualifications ensured that only the wealthy could be candidates.

In E. P. Thompson's words, "The British state, all eighteenth-century legislators agreed, existed to preserve the property and, incidentally, the lives and liberties, of the propertied."[3]

But to preserve property rights, and to manage the complexities of buying, selling, mortgaging, and inheriting property, the landlords needed an institutional framework—a system of laws and legal procedures—that all obeyed. Previous generations of landowners had consolidated and expanded their holdings by force, often in the face of state opposition, but now they used legal means to take over millions of acres in England and millions more in Scotland, actively aided by an enthusiastically pro-capitalist state. The laws it established and enforced didn't have to be fair—they certainly were not—but to maintain social stability, they had to be respected.

In the first half of the eighteenth century, much of the action was what has been called piecemeal enclosure. Rather than enclose entire manors at once—an expensive proceeding—landlords tended to consolidate their holdings gradually, by refusing to renew leases, foreclosing on tenants who fell behind in their rent, buying out freeholders, or simply by bullying tenants into leaving.

One of the most popular stage plays in the seventeenth and eighteenth centuries was Philip Massinger's *A New Way to Pay Old Debts*. First performed in 1625, it featured a wealthy villain named Sir Giles Overreach, who was based on a notoriously corrupt government official, Sir Giles Mompesson. To illustrate his vicious character, Massinger had him explain his plan to acquire land from a poorer neighbor whose refusal to sell had prevented Overreach from completely enclosing the district:

I'll therefore buy some cottage near his manor,
Which done, I'll make my men break ope his fences,
Ride o'er his standing corn, and in the night
Set fire on his barns, or break his cattle's legs :

These trespasses draw on suits, and suits' expenses,
Which I can spare, but will soon beggar him. . . .

Then, with the favour of my man of law,
I will pretend some title: want will force him
To put it to arbitrement [arbitration]; then, if he sell
For half the value, he shall have ready money,
And I possess his land.

Such practices, repeated many times over, led to "a major concentration of landownership in the hands of a limited class of very large landlords, at the expense both of the lesser gentry and the peasants."[4] Most landlords didn't farm the land themselves—they combined the small farms into larger units that commanded higher rents. The number of large farms worked by hired labor increased, and the number of small family-operated farms declined.

A Den of Thieves

By the mid-1700s, as Marx writes, "the law itself becomes now the instrument by which the people's land is stolen. . . . The Parliamentary form of the robbery is that of 'Bills for Inclosure of Commons.'"[5]

When successful, piecemeal consolidation led to negotiations between the landlord and the remaining landholders to divide the common land and extinguish common rights, but the law required unanimous agreement of all tenants, including the smallest. Some manors were undoubtedly enclosed by force, but for most landlords the need for legal certainty about their property made that course impractical.

Fortunately (for landlords), Parliament could and did override the unanimity requirement. As the Scottish radical democrat John Oswald said in 1790, "The Houses of Lords and Commons have never lost sight of the main end of their institution, the accumulation and perpetuation of property." He described visiting the House of Commons when an Enclosure Bill was being discussed:

Having left England at a very early age, and being engaged in a life too active to permit political enquiries, I had, like other young men, taken it for granted that the British Constitution was the very model of legislative wisdom. I therefore listened with much pleasure to the decorous preamble of the bill, which professed to have for its sole object the improvement of agriculture; and I imagined to myself, that the House of Commons were going to divide the common lands among the poor.

But what was my astonishment and my indignation, when, by the after-clauses of the bill, I found that the poor and indigent were to be driven from the commons; and that the land which before was common to all, was now to become the exclusive property of the rich! The honourable House of Commons vanished from my sight; and I saw in its stead a den of thieves, plotting in their midnight conspiracies the murder of the innocent, and the ruin of the fatherless and the widow![6]

There was no formal rule until the 1800s, but Parliament would usually approve enclosure agreements that had been signed by the holders of three-quarters of the land *by value*, which almost always allowed the landlord and a few others to impose enclosure on a much larger number of small farmers and cottagers. As the pioneering social historians J. L. and Barbara Hammond later commented, "The suffrages were not counted but weighed."[7]

Many parliamentary enclosure acts in the early 1700s simply confirmed previous agreements, but landlords quickly realized that although it was more expensive, the parliamentary road was faster and more certain than ad hoc consolidation. Between 1730 and 1840, more than four thousand enclosure acts were passed, affecting over six million acres—about one-quarter of all cultivated land. The social impact was greater than that suggests, because over 80 percent of parliamentary enclosures took place in two periods of intense activity. The first, in the 1760s and 1770s, was characterized by widespread conversion of arable land to pasture; the second, during the wars with France between 1793 and 1815, mainly involved the privatization of undeveloped common land, to take advantage of high wartime food prices. At peak, in the early 1800s, Parliament passed more than a hundred private enclosure acts a year. By 1830, almost all open field farms and most common land had been enclosed.

To begin the process, the landlord, usually in association with the tithe-owner and a few large tenants, submitted a petition and a draft bill to Parliament. (Tithes were mandatory payments to support the Established Church. In many cases, the payments actually went to landowners who had acquired former Church property.) After two routine readings, the House of Commons referred the bill to a committee which heard witnesses and reported back with a recommendation to accept or reject. After approval by the House of Commons and the House of Lords, it received royal assent and became law.

That whole process was heavily weighted in favor of the landlord. Until 1774, there was no requirement for him to let anyone know that enclosure was being considered, so often "those whose land was to be enclosed knew nothing whatever of transactions in which they were rather intimately concerned, until they were virtually completed."[8]

Challenging a bill required resources that few commoners had. Enclosure itself had become a profitable business for the lawyers and lobbyists who wrote the petitions and bills, obtained signatures, shepherded the bill through Parliament, coached witnesses, represented the petitioners at committee meetings, and greased the appropriate palms in the notoriously corrupt government bureaucracy.

Dividing the Land

Getting a private enclosure act passed was only the beginning: the land still had to be divided and allocated, and landlords and capitalist farmers took property very seriously indeed. To ensure that the interests of property were respected, decisions were made by an independent commission, usually three people: one named by the landlord, one by the tithe-owner, and one by other large landholders. Patronage played a big role: commissioners were well paid, and any who hoped to be recommended for future enclosures would be careful to represent their patrons' interests.

Usually the act specified that a certain proportion of the land would be automatically assigned to the lord of the manor and the tithe-owner, and some land had to be set aside for new roads so farmers could reach their farms without crossing others' property. After these and other deductions, each proprietor was supposed to receive land equal to the combined value of the land and rights he owned before the act. It would be more than a year, and was often three or four years, before the commissioners' awards were announced. Only then could the owners begin building roads, erecting fences, planting hedges, and building new farm buildings.

Parliamentary enclosure awards were rarely challenged, which suggests that most commissioners followed the law, but that did not mean the process was fair. In fact, as the Hammonds pointed out, it was never about fairness, it was about *property*, and the winners were those who already had the most:

> Two classes were ignored . . . two classes to whom enclosure meant not a greater or less degree of wealth, but actual ruin. These were such cottagers as enjoyed their rights of common in virtue of renting cottages to which such rights were attached, and those cottagers and squatters who either had no strict legal right, or whose rights were difficult of proof. Neither of these classes was treated even outwardly and formally as having any claim to be consulted.[9]

As well as consolidating land, enclosure eliminated common rights. After the award, "landless commoners could no longer feed pigs, geese and poultry on commons, lanes and roadsides; they could no longer gather fuel; in the fens they lost their fishing and fowling; in forest villages they could no longer hire a common right for their cattle, unless the commons remained open."[10] In some cases, cottagers received a few acres in exchange for loss of common rights, but because they were charged a disproportionate share of the enclosure costs, including the expensive work of fencing and hedging, many had to sell their rights. And because enclosure acts also terminated existing leases, small tenants often had to abandon farming when landlords doubled or tripled rents.

Two conservative twentieth-century historians called Parliamentary enclosure "perfectly proper," because the law was obeyed and property rights were protected. E. P. Thompson replied that they were ignoring the real issue—"a redefinition of the nature of agrarian property itself."

> In village after village, enclosure destroyed the scratch-as-scratch-can subsistence economy of the poor. The cottager without legal proof of rights was rarely compensated. The cottager who was able to establish his claim was left with a parcel of land inadequate for subsistence and a disproportionate share of the very high enclosure cost.
>
> Enclosure (when all the sophistications are allowed for) was a plain enough case of class robbery, played according to fair rules of property and law laid down by a parliament of property-owners and lawyers. . . .
>
> What was "perfectly proper" in terms of capitalist property-relations involved, none the less, a rupture of the traditional integument of village custom and of right: and the social violence of enclosure consisted precisely in the drastic, total imposition upon the village of capitalist property-definitions.[11]

Parliamentary enclosure completed the long transition from peasant-based agriculture to the peculiarly English form of agrarian capitalism, in which independent peasant farmers were squeezed out, large tenant farmers became capitalists, and manors were consolidated into huge estates. By the early 1800s, a three-tier social structure was firmly in place: "a few thousand landowners, leasing out their land to some tens of thousands of tenant farmers, who in turn operated it with the labour of some hundreds of thousands of farm-labourers."[12]

Resistance

In theory, anyone who opposed a particular enclosure bill could submit a counter-petition and testify before the parliamentary committee, but that seldom happened. Some historians have suggested that was because there was little dissatisfaction, others that England's peasants were so demoralized by past defeats that they accepted harmful changes without a fight. Both views are contradicted by Parliament's decision, in 1769, to decree exile for seven years as the punishment for damaging or destroying "fences made or to be made for inclosing lands by virtue of acts of parliament."[13] Clearly, the MPs did not believe that commoners were passively accepting Parliamentary enclosure.

What's surprising is not that few commoners submitted counter-petitions, but that some did. The time and difficulty of travelling to London to testify, and the cost of legal assistance, were major barriers to participation, and, as the commoners knew, counter-petitions from the poor rarely succeeded. In most cases they didn't even try, not because they were too ignorant or frightened, but because Parliament was controlled by the class that was trying to take their land. "Commoners were up against a Parliament of enclosers and they knew it."[14]

But that did not mean capitulating without struggle. As Jeanette Neeson has shown, there was substantial local resistance to enclosure acts, primarily in the form of "stubborn non-compliance, foot-dragging and mischief." Villagers routinely refused to cooperate with surveys, lied about the boundaries of their holdings, and intimidated surveyors. In some cases, the Commission's surveys and reports were stolen. And when such means failed, some took direct action.

After the defeat of their parliamentary counter-petition the West Haddon commoners, with help from nearby villages, had burned £1,500 worth of posts and rails; when the Wilbarston local counter-petition failed, three hundred men and women tried to prevent the fencing of the common; and when the Raunds parliamentary counter-petition was dismissed petitioners also became rioters: led by the village women and some shoemakers they pulled down fences, dismantled gates, lit huge bonfires and celebrated long into the night....

The two principal landowners of neighbouring Guilsborough had suffered theft and arson even before their fences had gone up: Richard Clarke's brakes were burnt, and with them went the gate to his home close, some posts and their rails from his hayrick, and seventy perches of hedging from his fields. Ten days later justice John Bateman lost four gates and their locks. In the following year, opponents of Hardingstone's enclosure began a systematic campaign of fence-breaking and tree-barking. They kept up their raids for years, destroying live hedges, throwing down posts and rails, digging up sand in the roads.[15]

When the Earl of Uxbridge fenced 3,500 acres of common land and built warrens for 15,000 rabbits, commoners complained that they had lost grazing land for their sheep, and that the rabbits were destroying their crops. In 1753, after losing their lawsuit on a technicality, some three hundred peasants and laborers invaded the enclosed land and spent two weeks destroying burrows and killing thousands of rabbits. It was a brave act of rebellion, but the earl responded by evicting cottagers and tearing their homes down, and then spent heavily to win a lawsuit against his tenants. A judge in the Court of King's Bench ruled that a commoner could not "destroy the estate of the lord, in order to preserve his own small right of common." That decision became a widely cited precedent, for extinguishing the traditional rights of the poor.

As Marx wrote, Parliamentary Enclosure Acts were "decrees by which the landowners grant themselves the people's land as private property, decrees of expropriation of the people."[16] Non-compliance, sabotage, and arson inconvenienced the enclosers but couldn't defeat them. Despite the commoners' resistance, the wealthy landowners and their state prevailed.

> Capitalist modes transmuted offices, rights and perquisites into round monetary sums, which could be bought and sold like any other property. Or, rather, the offices and rights of the great were transmuted in this way—those of the Rangers, bishops, manorial lords. The rights and claims of the poor, if inquired into at all, received more perfunctory compensation, smeared over with condescension and poisoned with charity. Very often they were simply redefined as crimes: poaching, wood-theft, trespass.[17]

———————✤———————

Thomas Spence: *The End of Oppression*

At the time of the French Revolution, Thomas Spence (1750–1814) was one of the best-known thinkers and activists in the left wing of the radical democratic movement in Britain. In 1775, outraged by the injustice of Parliamentary enclosures in Yorkshire, he began arguing for what came to be called Spence's Plan, common ownership of all land governed by a decentralized elected government based on parishes.

In this excerpt from The End of Oppression *(1795), Spence replies to a young man who asks, when most people favor implementing the Plan, what will be "the most easy method of doing so, and with least bloodshed"?*

In a country so prepared, let us suppose a few thousands of hearty determined fellows well armed and appointed with officers, and having a committee of honest, firm, and intelligent men to act as a provisionary government, and to direct their actions to the proper object.

If this committee published a manifesto or proclamation, directing the people in every parish to take, on receipt thereof, immediate possession of the whole landed property within their district, appointing a committee to take charge of the same, in the name and for the use of the inhabitants; and that every landholder should immediately, on pain of confiscation and imprisonment, deliver to the said parochial committee, all writings and documents relating to their estates, that they might immediately be burnt; and that they should likewise disgorge at the same time into the hands of the said committee, the last payments received from their tenants, in order to create a parochial fund for immediate use, without calling upon the exhausted people.

If this proclamation was generally attended to, the business was settled at once; but if the aristocracy arose to contend the matter, let the people be firm and desperate, destroying them root and branch, and strengthening their hands by the rich confiscations.

Thus the war would be carried on at the expense of the wealthy enemy, and the soldiers of liberty beside the hope of sharing in the future felicity of the country, being well paid, would be steady and bold.

And wherever the lands were taken possession of by the people, (which by all means should be as early accomplished as possible) the grand resource of the aristocracy, the rents, would be cut off, which would soon reduce them to reason, and they would become as harmless as other men. . . .

The good effects of such a change, would be more exhilarating and reviving to the hunger-bitten and despairing children of oppression, than a benign and sudden Spring to the frost-bitten Earth, after a long and severe Winter.

Only think of the many millions of rents that are now paid to those self-created nephews of god almighty, the landed interest, which is literally paid for nothing but to create masters. I say only think of all this money, circulating among the people, and there promoting industry and happiness, and all the arts and callings useful in society; would not the change be unspeakable?

This would neither be a barren revolution of mere unproductive rights, such as many contend for, nor yet a glut of sudden and temporary wealth as if acquired by conquest; but a continual flow of permanent wealth established by a system of truth and justice, and guaranteed by the interest of every man, woman, and child in the nation.

The government also of such a people could no longer be oppressive. The democratic parishes would take care how they suffered their money to be lavished away upon state speculations. And their senators, who could not be men of landed property, would be found to be much more honest and true to the services of their constituents than our now-a-days so much boasted gentlemen of independent fortunes.

When a people create landlords, they create a numerous host of hereditary tyrants and oppressors, who not content with their lordly revenues of rents, seize also upon the government, and parcel it out among themselves, and take as enormous salaries for the places they occupy therein, as if they were poor men; so that the rents which the foolish people foolishly pay for nothing, and the poor dull ass the public, become thus loaded, as it were, with two pair of paniers.

So then, whoever will be so silly good-natured and over-generous as to pay rents to a set of individuals, must not be surprised, if their masters by all ways and means and pretences should keep them to it, and give scope sufficient to their liberal propensities.

8

"The Lords and Lairds May Drive Us Out"

To concentrate the estates, small holdings had first to be abolished, thousands of tenants had to be driven from their native soil and a few shepherds in charge of millions of sheep to be installed in their place. Thus, by successive transformations, landed property in Scotland has resulted in men being driven out by sheep.

—KARL MARX[1]

There is a crude version of Marxism that says all societies go through the same stages of change and growth. That wasn't Marx's view, and it has frequently been contradicted by history. Some societies decay, collapse, or stagnate, while others leap over so-called stages, trading stone axes for rifles and spears for ploughs, as it were. Explaining the complex mix of feudalism and advanced capitalism in pre-revolutionary Russia, Leon Trotsky dubbed this phenomenon *uneven and combined development*:

A backward country assimilates the material and intellectual conquests of the advanced countries. But this does not mean that it follows them slavishly, reproduces all the stages of their past. . . . The privilege of historic backwardness—and such a privilege exists—permits, or rather compels, the adoption of whatever is ready in advance of any specified date, skipping a whole series of intermediate stages.[2]

In the case of Scotland, one of the most backward countries in Europe in 1700, the very existence of capitalist England both enabled and compelled shortcuts. Its feudal rulers quickly learned from, emulated, and in many ways surpassed their southern neighbors. "The technical methods and class structures that had taken centuries to develop in England could be applied immediately in Scotland, in their most advanced form."[3] Between 1750 and 1800, Scottish landlords carried out "one of the most spectacularly successful transitions to capitalist agriculture in the historical record."[4]

In 1707, the Parliaments of England and Scotland voted to become a single country, Great Britain. Scotland received seats in Parliament in London, financial assistance, and free trade with England. The agreement left Scotland's existing feudal structures and laws intact, creating an unstable mash-up of two incompatible social systems in one state. The arrangement was opposed from within by the Jacobite lairds and nobles who were unwilling or unable to adapt. (*Jacobite* is from Jacobus, the Latin equivalent of James: they supported the deposed Stuart King James II and his descendants.) Over the next four decades, those forces repeatedly rebelled, seeking to turn back the clock.

The last Jacobite uprising was defeated in 1746 in the bloody Battle of Culloden, "the final battle in the British bourgeois revolution."[5] After the English commander, the Duke of Cumberland, carried out the brutal reprisals that earned him the label "Butcher," Britain's rulers confiscated rebels' lands and imposed laws that destroyed the social basis of the lairds' and clan chiefs' power. To save their wealth and position, Scotland's traditional rulers had to become capitalist landlords.

All those who had hoped to avoid committing themselves to 'commercial society' found themselves without alternatives. Landowners who had hoped to subsist through feudal superexploitation of the peasantry or, at best, by supplementing their feudal rent through the sale of coal or timber, now found that they had no option but to enter the marketplace, or to fail in competition with their more commercially orientated rivals.[6]

In England, the development of agrarian capitalism was unplanned: it proceeded in fits and starts over several centuries, with each landlord responding to economic and social pressures as he saw fit. Only in retrospect was it clear that the combined effect was what Marx called original expropriation, the conversion of land into capital and the creation of a class of landless wage-workers.

In Scotland, by contrast, "the process was systematically theorized in advance of implementation."[7] From the beginning, landowners had access to an extensive English literature on agricultural improvement, and the benefits of "commercial society" were promoted by Adam Smith and other theorists of the Scottish Enlightenment. Landlords seeking to protect their wealth had no shortage of advisors, including men who hired themselves out as "improvers," promising great increases in revenue. At the beginning of the 1700s, few farms in Scotland practiced even elementary crop rotation; by the early 1800s, English agriculturalists were traveling north to learn from some of the most technologically sophisticated farms in Europe.

The transition to capitalist agriculture happened differently in Scotland's two major geographic regions, the relatively flat Lowlands in the south and the rocky, mountainous Highlands in the north. In 1700, "Scottish agriculture was remarkable only in one respect: the rural class structure within which it took place corresponded to the classic feudal model more closely than that of any other state west of Poland."[8]

By about 1830, capitalist agriculture prevailed in both regions, but with significant differences. Lowland farming was generally either arable or combined arable/livestock, and the class structure was similar to England's three-tier configuration. The Highlands were dominated by huge sheep farms, operated by a few large tenants and worked by a small number of laborers. In both, a large proportion of the traditional peasantry had been removed from the land.

Enclosures to establish large capitalist farms first occurred in the southwest, in Galloway, an area long dominated by cattle raising. By no coincidence, that was also the site of Scotland's first anti-enclosure uprising.

The Galloway Levellers

In 1667, the landlord-dominated parliaments in England and Scotland created new markets for themselves by banning the import of Irish cattle. In response, landlords in Galloway began evicting small farmers to make room for fenced grazing fields where cattle could be fattened before being driven south to English markets. A visitor described one of these "cattle parks" in 1682:

> Sir David Dunbar of Baldoon has a park, about two miles and an half in length and a mile and an half in breadth; the greatest part whereof is rich and deep valley ground, and yields excellent grass. . . . This park can keep in it, winter and summer, about a thousand beasts, part whereof he buys from the country, and grazes there all winter, the other part whereof is his own breed; for he has nearly two hundred milch kine [milk cows], which for the most have calves yearly.[9]

The union of England and Scotland in 1707 eliminated import and export duties, making the trade of Galloway cattle for English cash even more attractive, and evictions increased. A visitor in 1721 wrote that "the inhabitants of Galloway are much lessened since the custom of inclosing their grounds took place, for there are certainly above 20,000 acres laid waste on that account."[10]

In 1724, the "the Poor Distressed Tenants of Galloway" decided "to assemble in a body together," in response to tenants being driven out in order to inclose the ground, their grievous cries who did not know where to put their heads or what to do with their stocks, together with the fear of others of us who expect the same fate in a short time, did alarm us so that we thought it our duty by the laws of God and self-preservation to do whatever we could to show the world not only our own distressed state but the dangerous consequences of inclosing the lands and turning out the inhabitants.[11]

When sixteen families were evicted to expand cattle parks in May 1723, rumors spread that the landlords were planning hundreds more evictions. After an initial meeting at the annual summer fair in Kelton, tenant farmers spent the winter gathering signatures for a document in which they promised to support each other in opposing enclosures, and planning direct actions against enclosures. Beginning in March 1724, teams of tenants and cottars (cottagers) led by captains from each parish would converge on a cattle park, carrying long poles to lever up and topple the stone dykes (fences) that surrounded it. They called themselves Levellers, not in reference to the left-wing party in England's Civil War, but because, like the anti-enclosure rebels in the Midlands in 1607, they *leveled* the fences that divided their land. An eyewitness described an action in May 1724:

On Sunday 10th instant they caused public proclamation to be made at doors of eight Parish Churches, ordering all men and women upward of 15 to repair to the Main of Bomby.

I saw them yesterday between the hours of 8 and 12 in the morning coming in bodies from all quarters . . . making in all a body upwards of 2000, half of which were armed with good effective firelocks upwards of 400, and pitchforks and clubs; the other half being the workmen had long poles for prizing up the seams of the dykes for quick despatch.

About 12 of the clock Mr Basil Hamilton's servants with about two or three of this town, advanced to them in order to make a Treaty. They were quickly enclosed, dismounted and taken prisoner, and instead of coming to any agreement they were with much difficulty dismissed. The mob fired three shots upon them in retreat then gave the word 'Down with the Dykes' upon which they fell vigorously to work to Mr Hamilton's large dyke, for the space of three hours they levelled to the ground seven miles of stone dyke in length.[12]

Galloway landlords who also owned cattle farms in Ireland, a short sea-journey away, were widely suspected of smuggling Irish-raised cattle into their Scottish parks. Animals that were believed to have come from Ulster were slaughtered or maimed during the protests.

The Levellers also conducted an effective propaganda campaign. Pamphlets, manifestos, and appeals for support were widely distributed, as were notices of forthcoming actions. This call to action, for example, was posted on church doors in three parishes:

Therefore in order to prevent such a chain of miseries as are likely to be the consequences of this unhappy parking we earnestly entreat the assistance and aid of you the loyal parish of Borgue in order to suppress these calamities and that we may either live or die in this land of our nativity. We beg your assistance which will tend to your own advantage in order to which we desire you to meet at David Low's in Woodhead of Tongland where we expect the concurrence of Tongland and Twynholm upon Tuesday morning an hour after the sun rise which will gratify us and oblige yourselves.[13]

Verses like these, from the *Lamentation of the People of Galloway by the Pairking Lairds*, by Leveller poet James Charters, were circulated in manuscript, printed as broadsheets, and sung or recited when poor people gathered:

A generation like to this
Did never man behold,
I mean over great and mighty men
Who covetous are of gold.

Solomon could not well approve
The practice of their lives
To oppress and to keep down the poor,
Their actions cut like knives.

Among great men where shall ye find
A godly man like Job,
He made the widow's heart to sing
But our lairds make them sob.

It is the duty of great men
The poor folks to defend,
But worldly interest moves our lairds,
Their mind another end.

The lords and lairds may drive us out
From mailings where we dwell
The poor man says: "Where shall we go?"
The rich says: "Go to Hell."[14]

As late as August 1726, a man in Kirkcudbright was jailed just for owning a copy of that poem.

Support for the Levellers went beyond farmers and cottars. When the Church of Scotland ordered its ministers to denounce levelling as a mortal sin, many in Galloway refused to do so, and at least one was formally charged with participating in dyke-breaking. Soldiers sent to arrest protesters sometimes took no action, or allowed arrested men to escape on the way to jail. A supporter in Edinburgh, using the pen-name Philadelphus, published a twenty-page pamphlet titled *Opinion of Sir Thomas More,*

Lord High Chancellor of England concerning enclosures, in an answer to a letter from Galloway. He quoted Thomas More's 1516 book *Utopia*, and an English anti-enclosure pamphlet from 1646, to support his assertion that "no man must do that in his own property or possessions as may hurt another man."[15] The Lord Advocate tried unsuccessfully to identify the author and suppress the pamphlet.

About 37,000 people lived in Galloway, so armed gatherings of two thousand or more, and an unknown number of less active supporters, showed that local opposition to enclosure was far stronger, and more determined, than the local gentry could handle. Terrified, they appealed for assistance, and six troops of British dragoons were sent. In multiple confrontations, most rebels avoided arrest by disappearing into the hills and vales they knew well, but the uprising was suppressed by October. Judges, most of whom were local landlords, imposed sentences of imprisonment, deportation, and high fines. Little is known about the eventual fates of individual Levellers, but it is likely that many joined the growing exodus of Scottish peasants to the Americas.

Clearance by Stealth in the Lowlands

In 1700 about 1,200,000 people lived in Scotland. Of those, fewer than 2,000 owned over 90 percent of the land, and about 200 very large landlords—150 in the Lowlands, 50 in the Highlands—owned most of that. The land owners' wealth depended on tenant farmers, most of whom paid a third or more of each year's crop in rent and had to perform compulsory labor of various kinds. Many tenants owed military service as well—in a country that was frequently wracked by wars and internal conflict, clan chiefs who owned more land could raise bigger armies.

Peasants were subject to their landlord's court, where they could be tried and sentenced for virtually any crime short of treason, with no right of appeal. This "heritable jurisdiction," in which the landlord's agents were the police, prosecutors, and judges, played a key role in maintaining the lords' power and enforcing obedience. Leases were short and could be terminated on forty days' notice.

The Scottish equivalent of common-field farming was *runrig*, in which each tenant held a share of the arable land—usually twenty or thirty acres each—but the actual strips (rigs) were periodically redistributed, so no one had permanent use of the best land. Essential tasks, such as ploughing, harvesting, peat-cutting, and thatching, were done collectively. Most villages were surrounded by commons or waste, which was shared for pasture and foraging.[16] Like the open field system in England, runrig was not communal ownership—it was *collective right to use the land.*

Below tenants in the social hierarchy were *cottars*, who had a few acres and a dwelling, provided by a tenant farmer on a customary basis in return for seasonal labor. As sub-tenants, their possession of land depended on local customs, and if the tenant lost his lease, the cottars were usually removed as well. "In the final analysis, indeed, they might be more accurately described as 'labourers' who had a patch of land rather than 'possessors.'"[17]

Scottish courts did not recognize traditional or common rights, so landlords could impose changes pretty much at will, and tenants had no right of appeal. The actual course of change varied, depending on local conditions, but some measures were implemented almost everywhere in the Lowlands between 1750 and 1800. Cash rent replaced payment in kind; multiple tenancies and runrig were abolished; small holdings were combined into larger farms; common lands were privatized; and written leases required tenants to implement crop rotations, manuring, and other practices that increased production.

The most willing and able tenants were rewarded with longer leases and more land—land which was taken from others who were considered in a less favourable light. In this way an embryonic capitalist tenant-farmer class began to emerge—a social grouping which had a huge stake in making the changes successful.[18]

Adjusted for inflation, farm rents rose about 1500 percent between 1660 and 1815, with most of the increase occurring in the late 1700s.[19]

In most cases, the professional managers who actually planned and implemented the changes proceeded cautiously, keeping costs down and minimizing resistance. "The general pattern of tenant reduction, movement to compact holdings and larger farms, was a gradual, step-wise process which might often take several decades to accomplish."[20] Short leases could be terminated one at a time, and tenants who couldn't pay higher rents could be removed as required, allowing gradual consolidation of larger farms. This allowed the manager to experiment and see results before going ahead, spreading costs over time, and reducing the danger of organized resistance.

The process has been called "clearance by stealth and attrition." It took place legally and quietly, "but in the end had the same long-term effect as the dramatic episodes of collective eviction: many fewer people at the end of the process with a stake in the land."[21] (Until the 1840s, the evictions were usually called *removals*, but *clearances* then became the usual term for the displacement of occupiers by landlords.)

Hardest hit were the cottars, who made up about half of the rural population in 1750. The land they had occupied was incorporated into the new large farms, and the common land they had depended on was enclosed. Their houses were demolished and the stone was used to make the dykes that divided enclosed fields. In just a few decades, a class whose labor was essential to the old order was erased.

Cottar families, the dominant social formation in the countryside before c.1750, had been entirely stripped out of the system by the early nineteenth century. Wage-earning married servants, hired for a year, and single male and female servants contracted for six months, now comprised the vast majority of the farm labour force. There had always been some landless servants in the fermetouns [farming villages] but their numbers now swelled into a great rural army which outnumbered all other workers.[22]

Enclosure and Industry

In England, where capitalist agriculture developed well before capitalist industry, enclosure created large numbers of landless workers. In Scotland, the clearances took place at *the same time* as the early Industrial Revolution, and many landlords also became industrial entrepreneurs, so the birth of an agrarian proletariat was more tightly connected to the development of an industrial proletariat.

The new large farms required large numbers of laborers at harvest time, so some landlords built model villages to encourage evicted tenants not to move to cities or emigrate. Rents were low, but part-time farm work didn't pay enough to support a family. "It was quickly realised that the plans for laying down villages would be no use at all for stemming emigration out of the estate unless the kind of opportunity that the Industrial Revolution was presenting to emigrants to the towns could itself be reproduced in the villages."[23] Rather than simply renting to former tenants, landlords preferred and even advertised for workers with industrial skills, whether or not they were local. Villages that attracted skilled artisans became preferred locations for putting-out industries, especially textiles: In 1780 there were about 25,000 handloom weavers producing cotton, linen, and wool cloth in Scotland; by 1810 there were 78,000.[24] As in England, these home-based workers were not independent artisans, they were wage-workers in a system of capitalist manufacture.

In industry as well as agriculture, Scottish development quickly caught up with England's, without having to go through the same stages. Many landlords invested their increased agricultural income in industry, either indirectly, through institutions such as the British Linen Bank, or directly, by building small factories—especially distilleries, which provided a local market for the estates' grain—and revenue-generating infrastructure such as turnpike (toll) roads and canals.

The most important industrial projects were cotton mills that used the water-powered spinning machines first deployed in England in 1774 by industrialist-inventor Richard Arkwright. Just two years later, water-powered cotton mills opened in Scotland, in Penicuik, Midlothian, and Rothesay, Bute. They were small by later standards, but far more productive than hand-spinning— each mill produced enough yarn to keep thirty hand-loom weavers working full-time.

A decade later, the Duke of Atholl, who owned a huge estate near Perth, partnered with Arkwright to build the much larger Stanley Mill on the Tay River. It soon employed about 350 workers, including many children, who lived in a planned village on the duke's land. Family members who didn't work in the mill may have been weavers, using yarn from the mill, or farm workers. The duke received profits from the mill and rents from the village, and his farmer tenants had easy access to labor at harvest time.

Other landlords whose land included fast flowing rivers followed suit—over a hundred similar mills were built by the end of the century. Imports of raw cotton, grown by slaves in the West Indies and the United States, rose from half a million pounds a year in the early 1780s to over seven million pounds a year in the early 1800s.[25] Scotland had become "the second heartland of cotton, only one step behind Lancashire."[26]

Industrial development and growing cities provided employment for many evicted tenants in the Lowlands, but farther north things were different.

The Ross-shire Insurrection

For many years, 1792 was remembered throughout Gaelic Scotland as *Bliadhna nan Caorach*—the Year of the Sheep.[27] The poor celebrated it as the time they fought back against the introduction of vast herds of sheep that were stealing pasture from their cattle. "The eruption was volcanic and there was especial alarm among the lairds that the north would become contaminated with radicalism imported from the south," at a time when radical movements inspired by the French Revolution were growing throughout Britain.[28]

In eastern Ross-shire, in the borderland between Lowlands and Highlands, peasants had long pastured small herds of cattle on the hills. In 1791, Sir Hector Munro, who had made his fortune in India and spent a great deal of it acquiring land, evicted thirty-seven families from his estate and rented their land and grazing rights to a former army officer, Captain Allen Cameron, who stocked the land with several thousand sheep and ordered the remaining farmers to keep their cattle away. Over the next year there were frequent conflicts, particularly because Cameron ordered his workers to seize any cow or ox that strayed onto the land they now held, and then charged the owner a fee to return it.

The issue came to a head in June 1792, when Cameron impounded all of the cattle at once for supposed trespass, and about fifty villagers, including some from a nearby community, marched on Cameron's farm in Strathrusdale to forcibly free their animals. The villagers were not armed, but Cameron, backed by all of his workers, met them carrying a loaded shotgun and a long knife, promising to shoot them like birds and have the survivors sent to Australia. The villagers' leader, Big Wallace, disarmed him, bent the gun's barrel and took the knife as a souvenir. Cameron's employees fled, the villagers roughed him up, and the cattle were liberated.

The matter might have ended there, but when Cameron brought charges against the villagers, they decided to end the conflict by permanently removing the sheep. On Sunday July 29, delegates read a proclamation in local churches, demanding reduced rents, more land reserved for wheat to bring down the cost of bread, and an end to enclosure of pasture. On July 31, in a carefully planned and organized operation, some two hundred people from several communities began rounding up sheep, including the Camerons' flock, and driving them to Strathrusdale. By August 4 they had assembled an estimated 10,000 sheep and began moving them south. The plan was to drive them across the Beauly River, into Inverness-shire, and there release them in open country.

The rebels were well organized but politically naïve. They seem to have believed that if the sheep were gone the problem would be gone too. They didn't reckon with the landowners' determination to protect their property and class interests. During the eight days it took to collect sheep in multiple parishes, the estate owners organized a posse of their tenants and soldiers from nearby Fort George. Early in the morning on August 5, when most of the insurgents were home sleeping, the forces of order attacked the fifty or so men who were watching the sheep overnight. Outnumbered and unarmed, the villagers dispersed into the hills.

Everyone from miles around knew the men who had taken part, but no witnesses came forward, so the sheriff was able to arrest only fifteen. Eight, including Big Wallace, were charged with assaulting Cameron, but because he had threatened them with a gun, the jury concluded that they acted in self-defense and found them not guilty. Seven were accused of "advising, exciting, and instigating of persons riotously and feloniously to invade, seize upon, and drive away the property of . . . our Lieges, especially by lawless and seditious proclamations made at . . . the churches or places of worship where the inhabitants are convened upon a Sunday."[29] Five received relatively minor sentences, but two, Hugh Breck Mackenzie and John Aird, were apparently considered the ringleaders, because they were sentenced to seven years' transportation (exile) to Australia. Before the sentence could be carried out they escaped—it was rumored that the jailers deliberately left the doors open—and despite a £5 reward, they were never captured.

Although the Year of the Sheep was long an inspiration to opponents of the clearances, it was a defeat. Historian Eric Richards sums up the long-term consequences:

Just as the Galloway disturbances of 1722–24 signified the

first and last determined resistance to enclosure in southern Scotland, so the Ross-shire rebellion in 1792 provided its northern counterpart. The defeat of the resistance to sheep farming was comprehensive; co-ordinated obstruction of the sheep farmers was thoroughly broken and never again was there a chance for the old Highland society to hold back the invasion of the sheep. The last stronghold, the northern Highlands, was breached.[30]

Clearing the Highlands

Feudalism in the Highlands took the form of clans that supposedly owned the land as one big family, and farmers believed their right to use the land was guaranteed by their kinship to the clan chief and their willingness to support him in battle. As Neil Davidson comments, "The chiefs were prepared to encourage this belief as long as they needed the presence of fighting men on their territory, but, as was to become all too apparent after 1746, a right which subsists on the sufferance of the powerful is no right at all."[31] In the late 1700s, clan chiefs claimed personal ownership of the land and began expelling their supposed kin. "Customary relationships between clan elites and followers swiftly disintegrated as the entire fabric of society was recast in response to the new rigour of landlord demand, ideological fashion and, above all, the overwhelming force of market pressures emanating from the south."[32]

The Ross-shire Insurrection taught the clan chiefs that halfway measures were dangerous. Sir Hector Munro's mistake wasn't evicting tenants, but not evicting *all* of them. So long as any remained, conflict was inevitable. The graziers who wanted to lease sheep farms drew the same conclusion: they wanted thousands of acres, entirely free of potential troublemakers. The result, between 1800 and 1850, was the forced removal of tens of thousands of peasants from land that their families had farmed for generations.

Across the north, landlords' agents "cleared the crofts of men, women and children, using police and soldiers where necessary."[33]

Small farmers' leases were terminated *en masse*, to make room for sheep. In 1811 there were about 250,000 sheep in the Highlands; by the 1840s there were close to a million. Evicted tenants who didn't immediately emigrate to the Lowlands or North America were relocated to tiny holdings on the coast.

The most notorious Highland Clearances were those carried out by the Duchess of Sutherland, who removed as many as 10,000 tenants between 1807 and 1821. To ensure that evicted tenants left quickly and didn't return, her factor (agent) Patrick Sellar and his gang burned their houses, often before they could remove their belongings. An eyewitness, Donald McLeod, later described what had happened in two parishes on the Sutherland estate:

In the month of March, 1814, a great number of the inhabitants of the parishes of Farr and Kildonan were summoned to give up their farms at the May term following, and, in order to ensure and hasten their removal with their cattle, in a few days after, the greatest part of the heath pasture was set fire to and burnt, by order of Mr. Sellar, the factor, who had taken these lands for himself. . . .

As the lands were now in the hands of the factor himself, and were to be occupied as sheep-farms, and as the people made no resistance, they expected at least some indulgence, in the way of permission to occupy their houses and other buildings till they could gradually remove, and meanwhile look after their growing crops. Their consternation, was, therefore, the greater when, immediately after the May term day, and about two months after they had received summonses of removal, a commencement was made to pull down and set fire to the houses over their heads!

The old people, women, and others, then began to try to preserve the timber which they were entitled to consider as their own. But the devastators proceeded with the greatest celerity, demolishing all before them, and when they had overthrown the houses in a large tract of country, they ultimately set fire to the wreck. So that timber, furniture, and every other article that could not be instantly removed, was consumed by fire, or otherwise utterly destroyed.

These proceedings were carried on with the greatest rapidity as well as with most reckless cruelty. The cries of the victims, the confusion, the despair and horror painted on the countenances of the one party, and the exulting ferocity of the other, beggar all description. In these scenes Mr. Sellar was present, and apparently, (as was sworn by several witnesses at his subsequent trial,) ordering and directing the whole.

Many deaths ensued from alarm, from fatigue, and cold; the people being instantly deprived of shelter, and left to the mercy of the elements. Some old men took to the Woods and precipices, wandering about in a state approaching to, or of, absolute insanity, and several of them, in this situation, lived only a few days. Pregnant women were taken with premature labour, and several children did not long survive their sufferings.[34]

Public outrage forced the authorities to charge Sellar with culpable homicide, but despite a mass of eyewitness testimony, it took less than fifteen minutes for a jury of landowners and their employees to acquit him. He is still remembered as a symbol and perpetrator of the crime against humanity known as the Clearances.

Tenants who were relocated to the coast were expected to pay rent and deliver a profit by collecting and burning kelp, a source of chemicals used by the glass and soap industries. It was hard and dirty work, but it provided some income until the long war with France ended in 1815, and the Highland kelp industry collapsed in face of European competition. That, combined with a general postwar depression, forced many former clan chiefs to sell land. About two-thirds of the estates in the four Highland counties changed hands by mid-century.

The new owners, many of whom paid for the land with the money they received as compensation when West Indies slavery was abolished in 1834, quickly discovered that there was little profit in renting land to sheep farmers and poverty-stricken crofters. They initiated a new wave of clearances, this time to create deer forests (so-called despite the absence of trees) where wealthy men from the south, Europe, and overseas paid large fees for the privilege of killing deer that had been imported from Europe. By 1884, private deer-hunting preserves covered ten percent of Scotland, an area larger than Wales.

Scottish journalist Robert Somers, whose work Marx quoted in *Capital,* described the situation in the Highlands in 1848:

> It is curious, though painful to trace the perversity with which the Highland people are pursued from bad to worse, and from worse to worse again. In the first place, sheep were introduced into glens which had been the seats of communities of small farmers; and the latter were driven to seek subsistence on coarser and more sterile tracks of soil. Now deer are supplanting sheep; and these are once more dispossessing the small tenants, who will necessarily be driven down upon still coarser land and to more grinding penury. . . .
>
> Sufferings have been inflicted in the Highlands scarcely less severe than those occasioned by the policy of the Norman kings. Deer have received extended ranges, while men have been hunted within a narrower and still narrower circle.... One after one, the liberties of the people have been cloven down. To kill a fish in the stream, or a wild beast upon the hills, is a transportable offence. . . .
>
> Even to travel through the fenceless forests is a crime; and paths, which have linked hamlets with hamlets for ages past, have been shut and barred. These oppressions are daily on the increase; and if pushed much further, it is obvious that the sufferings of the people will reach a pitch when action will be the plainest duty and the most sacred instinct.[35]

Crofters fought back throughout the 1800s, physically assaulting sheriffs, tearing up eviction notices, and on some occasions battling police and soldiers, but the clearances continued, peaking in the 1850s:

> Over the two decades from 1841 to 1861 many west Highland parishes experienced an unparalleled fall in population, primarily caused by large-scale emigration. . . .
>
> Coercion was employed widely and systematically. . . . The mechanism employed to ensure that they went came to be described as "compulsory emigration." Families were offered the bleak choice between outright eviction or removal together with assistance to take ship across the Atlantic with costs of passage covered by proprietors.[36]

The Highlands are now one of the most thinly populated regions in Europe.

Land Leviathans

Peasants who thought that loyalty to their clan would guarantee their hereditary rights were disillusioned when clan chiefs began evicting their followers to increase their personal wealth. In short order, the fifty clan chiefs who claimed ownership of the Highlands converted themselves into profit-focused capitalist landlords. As the Romantic poet Robert Southey wrote in 1819, referencing a voracious biblical sea monster, they were *Land Leviathans*—"Their only object is to increase their revenue, and they care not by what means this is accomplished. . . . They dispeople whole tracks to convert them into sheep-farms."[37]

The Land Leviathans were no longer a distinct Highland ruling class. They were tightly connected, socially, culturally, and financially, to their capitalist counterparts in the Lowlands and the rest of Britain. "By the eighteenth century's end any lingering traces of a patriarchal outlook had been strictly subordinated to the pursuit of profit. And Highland 'chieftains' were firmly set on the road to becoming the landed and anglicized gentlemen that they have ever since remained."[38]

Aristocratic marriages, in which capital accumulation was more important than affection, played a big role in creating the great Anglo-Scottish fortunes. The most noteworthy example was Elizabeth Gordon, chief of Clan Sutherland, later named Duchess of Sutherland. She was known for her business acumen, and that was probably a factor in her marriage to one of the richest men in England, the Marquess of Stafford. Although she had far more land (1,000,000 versus 30,000 acres), he was richer because, in addition to very productive farmland, he owned the famous Bridgewater Canal, built in the 1760s to link Liverpool and Manchester and other industrializing centers in Lancashire. They vacationed in the Highlands, but spent most of their time in English mansions, including one that was said to be the largest and most luxurious palace in London. The Stafford fortune financed the infamous Sutherland Clearances, which the Duchess ordered, and which solidified their place as the richest couple in Britain.

The Sutherlands were an extreme case, but combinations of English and Scottish capital were not unusual. "Through the years of the Clearances, external capital flowed into the Highlands as never before. Much of this capital had been generated in the Lowlands, in England and in the colonies, some brought home by expatriates returning with the booty of empire."[39]

The Sutherland Clearances took place almost exactly three hundred years after Thomas More wrote his famous attack on enclosures that led to sheep devouring people. Sheep also devoured people in the nineteenth century, but in contrast to More's time, the Highland enclosures took place *after* Scotland's feudal landowners had been turned into or been replaced by capitalists who controlled the state and were already investing in industry. This wasn't a new social order struggling to be born, it was mature capitalism in the age of industry and colonialism.

Like the Parliamentary enclosures in England, the Highland

Clearances were class robbery plain and simple. They destroyed the Highlanders' way of life solely to enrich people who were already wealthy.

--- **9** ---

Poaching and the Bloody Code

Piracy, highway robbery, smuggling and poaching were all strate-gies developed by the impoverished to survive without submitting to the discipline of full time wage labour increasingly being imposed by the advance of capitalism. . . . Resistance by means of poaching was an aspect of class struggle between peasants and landowners.

—BRIAN MANNING[1]

In 1845, in *The Condition of the Working Class in England*, Frederick Engels described the Game Laws as an "especially barbaric cruelty against the working class."

The labourer lays snares, or shoots here and there a piece of game. It does not injure the landlord as a matter of fact, for he has a vast superfluity, and it brings the poacher a meal for himself and his starving family. But if he is caught he goes to jail, and for a second offence receives at the least seven years transportation. From the severity of these laws arise the frequent bloody conflicts with the gamekeepers, which lead to a number of murders every year. . . . Such is the moderate price at which the landed aristocracy purchases the noble sport of shooting.[2]

The poaching battles that Engels described continued centuries of class warfare in the English countryside. Nearly five hundred years earlier, thousands of peasants had marched on London, protesting serfdom, taxes, and poverty. A contemporary witness identified one of their most important demands—*the right to hunt for food*:

> The rebels petitioned the king that all preserves of water, parks, and woods should be made common to all so that throughout the kingdom the poor as well as the rich should be free to take game in water, fish ponds, woods and forests as well as to hunt hares in the fields—and to do these and many other things without impediment.[3]

This identifies a form of enclosure that isn't often discussed as such—the rich preventing the poor from hunting. In the 1070s, William the Conqueror began the creation of vast royal forests in which only he and his friends could hunt: by the twelfth century, up to a third of England, including all of some counties, was subject to the Forest Laws. At the time of the 1381 Peasants' Revolt, England's rulers had been enclosing wildlife for their private hunting pleasure for more than three centuries.

Not content with crushing the Peasants' Revolt and executing its leaders, England's elite made hunting even more dangerous for the poor, by outlawing not just hunting in certain places, but *hunting by the poor anywhere*. After condemning commoners who hunted and engaged in seditious talk when they ought to be in church, a 1390 act ordered:

> No manner of artificer, labourer, nor any other layman, which hath not lands or tenements to the value of forty shillings . . . shall have or keep any greyhound, hound, nor other dog to hunt; nor shall use ferrets, hayes, nets, hare-pipes, nor cords, nor other engines for to take or destroy deer, hares, nor conies [rabbits], nor other gentlemen's game, upon pain of one year's imprisonment.[4]

The law didn't ban hunting, it *defined hunting as an exclusive privilege of the landed elite*—people for whom killing animals was a sport, not a necessity.

One need not be an animal rights advocate to be appalled by the animal-killing obsessions of the English rich. Hunting in deer parks could be particularly brutal. Deer so tame they would walk up to be petted were shot from shelters while gamekeepers drove them past. Others were coursed—chased by dogs and riders until they collapsed from exhaustion. Gamekeepers sometimes wounded the deer in advance so they ran slowly enough for nobles to kill. Some deer parks included grandstands that gave spectators a good view of the slaughter.

In the late 1700s, landowners began raising pheasants and partridges in captivity, for the "sport" called *battue*. Thousands of tame birds were driven toward a line of rich men, armed with rifles and shotguns, whose goal was to kill the largest possible number of flying birds in the shortest possible time. Thomas Coke, later Earl of Leicester, was admired for shooting eighty birds with just ninety shots. At a shooting party attended by the Duke of Wellington in 1823, eight people killed 1,088 birds in three days.

Even today, over 50 million factory-farmed pheasants and partridges are released annually in Britain, just to be shot. On some northern estates, "sportsmen" pay thousands of pounds to kill several hundred birds a day, in a kind of anti-ecotourism. The fee may include a luncheon attended by the local lord, but no one eats the game.

Class Law

The Game Laws criminalized traditional rights that, economic historian Michael Perelman writes, "were far from inconsequential for the rural poor. For them, hunting was an important means of providing for oneself and one's family, rather than pleasant recreation. The Game Laws, in this sense, became part of the larger movement to cut off large masses of the rural people from their traditional means of production."[5]

Precisely because hunting was so important to the lives of the great majority of people, the Forest and Game Laws were difficult to enforce. The poor continued to hunt in royal forests and on their lords' lands, and there were no police forces to stop them. In time most local authorities concluded that the cost and effort of capturing, convicting, and imprisoning the offenders was not worth the effort. As a 1603 act lamented, "The vulgar sort and men of small worth" who hunted illegally were "not of sufficiency to pay the said penalties," or to "answer the cost and charges of any that should inform and prosecute against them," so "few suits have been attempted upon the said laws."[6]

During the Civil War and Commonwealth, commoners and soldiers freely killed deer and other wildlife for food and the very notion of restricted hunting vanished. Well into the 1700s, "old people could still remember the outrageous freedoms taken in the Commonwealth days, when the deer had been slaughtered wholesale, the Great Park turned over to farms, and the foresters had enlarged their 'rights' beyond previous imagining."[7]

A new and more vicious era of game laws began with *An Act for the better preservation of Game* in 1671.[8] It established more restrictive property qualifications for hunters—freehold land worth £100 a year, or leased land worth £150 a year, amounts that were many times a laborer's wages—and set the penalty for unauthorized hunting at three times the value of the game, legal costs, and three months imprisonment. "*With* the property qualification, you could shoot hares with impunity even if you threw the carcasses away to rot; *without* it, you were deemed to be a criminal if you took one hare when your family was starving."[9]

The most far-reaching innovation in the 1671 act gave enforcement powers to gamekeepers employed by landowners. In addition to catching poachers, gamekeepers could search homes without a warrant, and confiscate and destroy any dogs, guns, nets, traps, or other equipment that might be used for hunting or fishing. An accused poacher could be convicted on the sworn testimony of one witness, often the gamekeeper who accused him. A subsequent act gave half of any fine collected to the witness, and allowed game-keepers and their assistants to use whatever force they deemed necessary to capture poachers.[10]

As a result, Peter Munsche points out, "in addition to their role as prosecutors, the gentry also commanded a corps of gamekeepers whose duty it was to prevent the unqualified from hunting or even possessing the means to hunt."[11]

> The gamekeeper, in short, was a policeman. Indeed, aside from excise officers, he was the closest thing to a professional law enforcement official to be found in rural England before the middle of the nineteenth century. What made the gamekeeper truly unique was that, unlike the exciseman, he was a private servant. He enforced the law, not in the service of the state, but rather for the lord of the manor.[12]

The rural poor hated gamekeepers with the same passion that later generations of working people would feel toward scabs and Pinkerton's union-busting thugs. They were known for demanding bribes, fabricating evidence, and violent assaults—and in many cases for poaching more game than the people they arrested. Even if the local gamekeeper was fair and honest, he was hated as the face of a system that denied them access to subsistence, a system in which many poor men and women were whipped, imprisoned, transported to Australia, or even executed, for trying to feed their families.

The Black Act

There was a curious omission in game laws—the lists of forbidden game did not include the two most hunted animals, deer and rabbits. By definition, game were animals that roamed free, but by the 1600s there were few wild deer and rabbits left in England. Every landed estate of any size included a deer park, a large fenced or walled area in which deer were raised, and in which only the owner, his friends, and the gamekeeper could hunt. Many estates also raised rabbits (then called coneys) for their meat and skins, in large protected warrens. The animals were *property*, so taking them without permission wasn't poaching, it was *theft*.

> Deer and rabbits were protected by statutes which forbade anyone, qualified or not, to hunt or take these animals without the permission of the person on whose land they were found. . . . As a result of enclosure, they had become a type of private property and were entitled to legal protection as such.[13]

The legal consequences for theft were much more serious than those for unlawfully hunting game. A poacher generally faced a £5 fine or three months in prison, while a deer-stealer could be transported overseas for seven years, or even executed.

In February 1723, a royal proclamation offered a £100 reward for information leading to the arrest of any of the "great number of disorderly and ill-designing people" who had stolen deer, attacked people, and "shot at them in their houses, maimed their horses and cattle, broke down their gates and fences, and cut down avenues, plantations, and heads of fish-ponds, and robbed them of the fish."[14] These offenders, known as "Blacks" because they disguised their faces with soot, operated primarily in royal forests south and west of London. Their actions provided the excuse for a new and uniquely punitive law.

As E. P. Thompson shows in *Whigs and Hunters*, official accounts exaggerated the extent and violence of the attacks and failed to mention that the Blacks were protesting the conversion of common land into deer parks. The leader of one group, calling himself King John, insisted that they were loyal to King George, and "had no other design than to do justice, and to see that the rich did not insult or oppress the poor; that they were determined not to leave a deer on the Chase, being well assured it was originally designed to feed cattle, and not fatten deer for the clergy."[15] As Thompson writes, the Blacks were less concerned with poaching deer than with "enforcing the definition of rights to which the 'country people' had become habituated, and also . . . resisting the private emparkments which encroached upon their tillage, their firing [firewood] and their grazing."[16]

This was not an emergency, but the government acted as if it was. In May 1723, *An Act for the more effectual discovery and punishment of deer-stealers* was rushed through Parliament without debate. Usually called the Waltham Black Act or simply the Black Act, it condemned to death anyone "armed with swords, firearms, or other offensive weapons, and having his or their faces blacked, or being otherwise disguised," who poached deer, rabbits or fish, or even just entered any place where deer or rabbits were kept—and that was just the start. The death penalty was also prescribed for wounding cattle, cutting down trees, setting fire to houses or haystacks, shooting at anyone, sending unsigned threatening letters, and more. Anyone formally accused of such crimes who failed to turn himself in would be declared guilty without trial.[17]

In a single stroke, Parliament had created at least fifty new capital crimes. Indeed, legal scholar Leon Radzinowicz points out that when all the variants were counted, over 350 new crimes were now punishable by hanging:

> It is very doubtful whether any other country possessed a criminal code with anything like so many capital provisions, as there were in this single statute. . . .
>
> There is hardly a criminal act which did not come within the provisions of the Black Act: offences against public order, against the administration of criminal justice, against property, against the person, malicious injuries to property of varying degree—all came under this statute and all were punishable by death.[18]

The Black Act was part of what came to be called the Bloody Code, a legal regime that prescribed the death penalty for a huge number of crimes, including, for example, the theft of goods worth more than 12 pence, about 5 percent of a skilled worker's weekly wage. Initially described as a temporary measure that would expire in three years, the Black Act was repeatedly extended and made permanent in 1758. It was finally repealed in 1823, and even then some members of the House of Lords voted to retain the death penalty for stealing deer.

At least three dozen other eighteenth-century laws set punishments ranging from fines to transportation for various forms of unlawful hunting, and it appears that prosecutors and judges only used the Black Act itself to make examples of particular offenders. When they did invoke it, juries were reluctant to convict poachers if the result would be hanging, and about half of all death sentences in the 1700s were commuted to transportation, so many of the hundreds of thousands of people sent to hard labor in the colonies had been convicted of no more than hunting rabbits.

(Transportation was considered a less severe sentence than hanging, but it was by no means a minor punishment. Many died during the long ocean voyage and in Australia they were subject to forced labor. Although the sentence was for a fixed number of years, few could afford passage home, so their exile was permanent.)

England's rulers truly believed that the poor were both inferior and dangerous: in a book that went through three editions between 1699 and 1708, a former bursar of Oxford's University College warned that many commoners were "very rough and savage in their dispositions, being of levelling principles, and refractory to government, insolent and tumultuous," and it would be easier to "teach a hog to play upon the bagpipes, than to soften such brutes by courtesy."

> The best way therefore will be to bridle them, and to make them feel the Spur too, when they begin to play their tricks, and kick.... Such men then are to be look'd upon as trashy weeds or nettles, growing usually upon dunghills, which if touch'd gently will sting, but being squeez'd hard will never hurt.[19]

Combine that with the conviction that property was sacred, and, in John Locke's words, that "government has no other end but the preservation of property,"[20] and you have justification for a law that treated poor people's lives as less valuable than deer and rabbits. The Black Act provided what E. P. Thompson calls "an armoury of sanctions to be used, in times of necessity, against disturbance."[21] Similarly, Douglas Hay describes its provisions as "the legal instruments which enforced the division of property by terror," but argues that the ruling elite knew that excessive use of those instruments would be counterproductive:

> If gentlemen in Parliament were willing to hang a proportion of offenders every year in order to stage the moral drama of the gallows, it is extremely doubtful that they ever believed that the capital statutes should be strictly enforced. The impact of sentencing and hanging could only be diminished if it became too common….
>
> The law made enough examples to inculcate fear, but not so many as to harden or repel a populace that had to assent, in some measure at least, to the rule of property.[22]

Nevertheless, the gentlemen in Parliament were determined to find some combination of precisely defined offenses and severe punishments that would stop poaching. To that end, they adopted "a long series of unprecedentedly harsh game laws, which steadily and purposefully extended the gentry's control over foodstuffs that had once been much more fairly shared by all."[23] Between 1703 and 1830, they passed forty-five separate statutes relating to deer, rabbits, and game. In addition to existing laws that forbade trespassing and hunting while poor, they outlawed night-hunting, buying, selling, or possessing game, hunting in disguise, owning or using hunting or fishing equipment, destroying walls and fences, stealing eggs, and much more. Depending on which law was used, for the same offense a convicted poacher might be fined, whipped, pilloried, imprisoned at hard labor, transported, or executed.[24]

The fact that so many laws were passed shows that Parliament failed to stop poaching. Like the anti-enclosure laws of the 1500s, the Bloody Code addressed only symptoms, leaving the causes untouched. For a large and growing number of people, the threat of punishment, even execution, was of less concern than hunger. Especially after 1750, enclosure deprived growing numbers of poor farmers and laborers of access to the common land that had been an important source of food. When the commons were converted to deer parks or rabbit warrens, the temptation to hunt there was strong. The poor viewed hunting for food as a right, not a crime: the real theft was the legal and physical enclosure of wild animals by the rich:

> The majority of country people, both farmers and labourers, never accepted the game laws and the exclusive nature of the rural sport of shooting. No armies of keepers, no statute book of laws, no mantraps, and certainly no titled gentleman, could dissuade them from their belief that poaching was not a crime. Game, in their opinion, was made for the poor as well as for the rich, a view justified in the Bible. God put man "in command of the fishes in the sea, and all that flies through the air. . . ." Thus to be caught poaching was considered "a hard case" to which no moral stigma was attached.[25]

As the poet and clergyman George Crabbe wrote in 1819:

> The poacher questions with perverted mind,
> Were not the gifts of heaven for all design'd?[26]

About the same time, a writer who described himself as "a country gentleman and proprietor of game" argued that the game laws actually encouraged poaching:

> It cannot be denied that three fourths of the legitimate consumers of game in the present day can only procure it by tempting others to a positive breach of the laws; for they can get it by no

other means except by purchase from those who employ the country poacher in almost every rural village in the kingdom, or corrupt the land-owner's gamekeeper, on half the extensive properties of England, to take it for them.[27]

Poaching for sale wasn't new—a seventeenth-century proverb declared that a polite guest should "never inquire whence venison comes"[28]—but in the eighteenth and nineteenth centuries it became an important source of income for working people who could not feed themselves solely by working in fields or factories.

Poaching Wars

In 1816, Parliament passed an act that added seven years of hard labor in Australia as a possible punishment for anyone caught with a net or stick with intent to take game or rabbits. A leaflet distributed to landowners near Bath showed that the poachers were defiant:

TAKE NOTICE! We have lately heard and seen that there is an Act passed that whatever poacher is caught destroying game is to be transported for seven years—*This is English liberty!*

Now we do swear to each other that the first of our company this law is inflicted on that there shall not be one gentleman's seat in our country escape the rage of fire! We are nine in number, and we will burn every gentleman's house of note. The first that impeaches shall be *shot*. We have sworn not to impeach. You may think it a threat, but they will find it a reality. The Game Laws were too severe before. The Lord of all men sent these animals for the peasants as well as for the Prince. God will not let the people be oppressed. He will assist us in our undertaking, and we will execute it with caution.[29]

In the next eleven years, some 1,700 men were convicted under that act, and about 10 percent of those were transported, but poaching continued to grow. In the 1840s there were close to 5,000 unlawful hunting convictions a year, accounting for between a quarter and a third of all male convictions in some rural counties in 1843. Even after the defeat of Chartism in 1848, when social unrest generally declined, poaching convictions continued to rise, peaking at close to 12,400 in 1877. These figures confirm John Archer's judgment that in the 1700s and 1800s, "poaching was the most constant and common method employed by the poor of snubbing the tenets of the wealthier classes."[30]

Organizationally, poaching took two forms—gangs and individual poachers.

Confrontations between gamekeepers and gangs of a dozen or more armed men were frequently the subject of sensational articles in the predecessors of today's tabloid newspapers. Although the reports were often exaggerated, poaching gangs did exist, servicing urban markets for game, especially in fast-growing London. By the late 1700s, new turnpike roads and regular coach services made it possible to deliver game to the metropolis from almost anywhere in the country in one or two days. Parliament's response—ever more severe punishments—only ensured that the gangs would fight to resist capture. Many raids led to armed battles in which gamekeepers and poachers were wounded or killed.

This was poaching for profit, and it was conducted with the violence that frequently characterizes capitalism's illegal side. As E. P. Thompson writes of the Blacks, the fact that the laws they broke were oppressive and unfair "does not make them instantly into good and worthy 'social' criminals, hermetically sealed off from other kinds of crime. Offenses which may command our sympathy—poaching or smuggling—were not conducted in especially gentlemanly ways."[31]

Nevertheless, the poaching laws were so unpopular that men who broke them were viewed as heroes. In 1844, for example, John Roberts, who admitted that he had killed during a raid, was publicly hanged in Manchester. Newspapers reported that 30,000 people "greeted Roberts with cheers, while they reserved their indignation for the executioner," who was pelted with stones. When Roberts was hung, "a tempest of execration burst from the vast assemblage." Forty policemen stood guard to keep order and protect the hangman.[32]

Although battles between poaching gangs and gamekeepers received widespread publicity, most poachers, including the great majority of those convicted, worked alone. A study of court records in East Anglia found that "they were invariably male, they hailed from the country in which they poached, and in 80 per cent of the cases they were agricultural labourers."[33]

In every village there were men who defied the law and the gamekeepers by catching small game, fish, or birds to feed their families, and who sometimes sold a few to their neighbors. Every villager knew who the local poachers were, respected their skill, and refused to inform or testify against them. In hard times, when crops failed or employers cut back, the number of nighttime hunters increased. More generally, poaching increased sharply in the years immediately before outbursts of social unrest. As Marxist historians Eric Hobsbawm and George Rudé comment, "If we require an index of the rising social tensions in the village, this is perhaps the best one we can get."[34]

HISTORIAN MICHAEL ŽMOLEK ARGUES that "the elaboration of the 'Bloody Code' was a logical extension of the process of declaring null and void the local, customary laws of the manor by asserting absolute property rights under common law, which was state law, effected through enclosure."

> The Code reflects a practical obsession on the part of the ruling landed elite with consolidating their private property. So long as there were still large numbers of rural dwellers who felt they had customary rights to walk upon the fields and enjoy access to the commons . . . [then] fences, hedges and legal title to a plot of land were not enough. That ownership had to be backed up

with a kind of legal closure, one which would severely punish the first wave of transgressors, thereby sending a clear signal to any would be future transgressors that the owner's property was inviolable.[35]

The very existence of the Bloody Code refutes the common claim that capitalism triumphed because it better reflected the dictates of human nature than previous social orders. The poor were not easily reconciled to a system that expelled them from the land. England's ruling class tried to terrorize them into submission, but widespread poaching continued for nearly two centuries after the Black Act was passed. Threats of torture, transportation, and death could not stop the working poor from hunting for food, because they firmly believed that the Earth ought to be a common treasury for all.

PART THREE

CONSEQUENCES

The Landlords' Revolution

Many millions of acres of land, which were virtually the property of the poor, have been converted into property for the rich. The idle have in this, as in every other instance, been benefited at the expense of the industrious.

—PERCY RAVENSTONE, 1821[1]

One of the great myths of English history is that destroying the commons caused an agricultural revolution that fed the industrial working class. In his classic history of English agriculture, for example, John Prothero (later Lord Ernle) described the eighteenth-century enclosures as a regrettable necessity.

The divorce of the peasantry from the soil, and the extinction of commoners, open-field farmers, and eventually small freeholders, were the heavy price which the nation ultimately paid for the supply of bread and meat to its manufacturing population.[2]

That claim has been repeated endlessly in textbooks, agricultural histories, and university lectures. In the 1960s J. D. Chambers and G. E. Mingay repeated it in their influential book, *The Agricultural Revolution, 1750–1880*.

This departure from traditional practice marks a new agricultural epoch, and its acceleration in the second half of the eighteenth century in the form of classical enclosure movement and the first unmistakable steps by the agricultural pioneers towards "high farming," mark the opening of the Agricultural Revolution just as surely as factory production marks the dawn of a new industrial age. From this time, the Agricultural Revolution reveals itself as an indispensable and integral part of the Industrial Revolution, sharing with it the social and scientific attributes that gave the latter its unique character of transition to the modern technological age of mass-production of food, as well as of manufactured goods.[3]

In historian Robert Allen's words, "few ideas have commanded as much assent amongst historians as the claim that enclosures and large farms were responsible for the growth in productivity."[4] Utsa and Prabhat Patnaik concur:

Almost every book on the Industrial Revolution in Britain in the eighteenth century contains a mandatory chapter titled "The Agricultural Revolution." Other chapters are variously headed "The Transport Revolution," "The Commercial Revolution," and so on. That an agricultural revolution took place in the eighteenth century as precondition to the transition to factory production in the last quarter of the century is widely accepted.[5]

Enclosures in the 1800s certainly created larger farms, but, contrary to the accepted wisdom, working people were not better fed as a result.

No Good Husbandry Without Enclosure?

The view that agricultural improvement required enclosure hinges on the claim that common field farming was inherently conservative, not to say backward. Because fields were shared and decisions were made by consensus, the argument goes, a single recalcitrant farmer could prevent the adoption of improved methods or new crops, so innovation and experimentation were impossible. Enclosure advocates promised that consolidating and privatizing the land would free progressive farmers to improve the land and use modern methods to increase productivity. England would prosper, and everyone would be better off.

Arthur Young, the most widely read agricultural writer of the 1700s, firmly believed that "without inclosures there can be no good husbandry; while a country is laid out in open field lands, every good farmer tied down to the husbandry of his slovenly neighbours, it is simply impossible that agriculture should flourish." Enclosure didn't just eliminate shared management (which he called barbarous), it created larger farms, which in his view were always more productive than small ones.

> A considerable farmer, with a greater proportional wealth than the smaller occupier, is able to work great improvements in his business, and experience tells us, that this is constantly the case; he can build, hedge, ditch, plant, plough, harrow, drain, manure, hoe, weed, and, in a word, execute every operation of his business, better and more effectually than a little farmer.

Because he had more resources, the large farmer excelled at "making the soil yield its utmost produce," and as a result "himself, his landlord, and the nation are the richer for the size of his farm."[6]

Young was the most effective of many eighteenth-century propagandists for enclosure and consolidation. Their arguments—that common-field agriculture was backward and unproductive, that common rights prevented modernization, that enclosure made improvement possible, and that large capital-intensive farms were more productive than small ones—were exactly what enclosing landlords and their parliamentary representatives wanted to hear. Enclosing wasn't greedy or sinful—it was action in the national interest.

Many an enclosing landlord thought only of the satisfaction of doubling or trebling his rent: that is unquestionable.... But there were many whose eyes glistened as they thought of the prosperity they were to bring to English agriculture, applying to a wider and wider domain the lessons that were to be learnt from the processes of scientific farming.[7]

Unquestioned belief in the superiority of large enclosed farms worked by landless proletarians was a central feature of classical political economy, consistent with Adam Smith's famous claim that "the private interests and passions of individuals naturally dispose them to turn their stocks towards the employments which in ordinary cases are most advantageous to the society." Of course, the individuals Smith meant were capitalists, not the poor, and he never explained just how the invisible hand would magically produce that "universal opulence which extends itself to the lowest ranks of the people," but his views were rarely questioned.[8]

The *Economist* magazine—the most influential voice of militant free market capitalism—described the idea that small farms could ever be as productive as large ones as a "fallacious notion ... everywhere contradicted by facts and experience. Usually petit-farming is a miserable affair." "The great secret of farming we think is this— the judicious application of a sufficient amount of capital to the soil."[9] The *Economist*'s editors and others like them believed that parliamentary enclosure had freed landlords and farmers to invest in improvements that increased food production, and that without enclosure the workers who left the land to work in factories could not have been fed.

Questioning the Revolution

In the 1970s, some historians stopped repeating the ideological claim that open field farming was backward and big farms were better than small ones, and began investigating what had actually happened before, during, and after enclosure. Their research has completely rewritten the "enclosures and agricultural revolution" narrative. Robert Allen, for example, reanalyzed Arthur Young's statistics comparing crop yields in enclosed and unenclosed farms. Young said the numbers proved that enclosure improved efficiency, but Allen found that they actually showed that "open and enclosed farms were equally efficient."[10]

Other researchers have shown that open field farmers did not, in fact, resist new agricultural practices. Many open field communities introduced new irrigation systems and switched to the four-field system of crop rotation in the 1600s. Indeed, agricultural historian Eric Kerridge has shown in detail that *all* of the major improvements in technique and technology that have been attributed to a supposed eighteenth-century agricultural revolution were actually in wide use "before 1720, most of them before 1673, and many of them much earlier still."[11] The claim that peasants resisted improved methods reflects anti-peasant prejudice, not the real activity of working farmers.

Gregory Clark finds "no evidence that common fields in England in the eighteenth century necessarily reduced the efficiency of agriculture by any amount." While larger farms may have been more profitable because they employed fewer workers per acre, Clark says, "the enclosure movement is a complete bust in explaining the growth of agricultural productivity."[12]

While some historians still hold to the old view,[13] the evidence is against them. An important study by Robert Allen shows that food production scarcely increased at all during the years of parliamentary enclosures. He identifies three distinct phases of growth:

1) 1520 to 1740: farm production doubled.
2) 1740 to 1800: farm production increased about 10 percent.
3) 1800 to 1850: farm production increased about 65 percent.[14]

The population of England and Wales about doubled between 1500 and 1740. It grew more than 50 percent between 1740 and 1800, and more than 200 percent in the next fifty years. So after two centuries of consistent availability, food production per person fell dramatically after 1740. Throughout the Industrial Revolution, "the output of English farms failed to keep pace with population growth."[15]

At a time that has been described as a golden age for the landed aristocracy, most people barely survived. An adult male engaged in hard physical work—that is, most men—required between 3,200 and 3,550 calories a day. All of the food produced in England or imported would have allowed an *average* (median) of 3,200 calories per person a day. By definition, half of the population ate less, and many ate much less.[16]

Most industrial workers and agricultural laborers were malnourished: they were less healthy and died younger than their ancestors a century earlier. "The average height of rural-born English women fell by more than 0.75 inches, and that of urban-born English women by 0.5 inches, between 1800 and 1815."[17] Even after food price inflation ended, official reports showed that "the diet of the great part of the families of the agricultural workers is below the minimum necessary 'to avoid starvation diseases.'"[18]

Over half of most laboring families' income was spent on flour and bread, so in years when the harvest was poor and prices spiked, actual consumption fell far below the long-term average. Historian Douglas Hay calculates that even at normal prices, 10 percent of the population would not have been able to buy enough bread to maintain their families' health. "In hard years perhaps 20 per cent of the population could not, unaided, have bought sufficient bread even if they had been able to eliminate all other expenditure . . . in a very hard year, 45 per cent of the entire population could be thrown into such destitution."[19]

On top of a long-term rise in the cost of bread after 1750, prices spiked in years of bad harvests, leading to widespread rioting in 1756–57, 1766–67, 1773, 1782, 1795, and 1800–1801. People whose rural grandparents had torn down fences and hedges to defend the right to *grow food* were now fighting in towns and cities for the right to *buy food*.

The rioters when they found themselves masters of the situation did not use their strength to plunder the shops: they organized distribution, selling the food they seized at what they considered fair rates, and handing over the proceeds to the owners. They did not rob: they fixed prices and when the owner of provisions was making for a dearer market they stopped his carts and made him sell on the spot.[20]

As E. P. Thompson writes, for working people, "it appeared to be 'unnatural' that any man should profit from the necessities of others. . . . In times of dearth, prices of "necessities" should remain at a customary level, even though there might be less all round." Food riots were attempts to impose that "moral economy" in a society that whose rulers were rejecting it. "The breakthrough of the new political economy of the free market was also the break-down of the old moral economy of provision."[21]

Robbing the World's Soil

Far from feeding the poor through increased domestic production, the British food system in the years of parliamentary enclosure experienced what food historian Chris Otter calls a "radical shift to outsourcing." In *Diet for a Large Planet*, Otter documents England's transition from a country that not only fed itself but exported food in the first half of the 1700s, to one that was heavily dependent on imported food, mainly from its colonies, in the 1800s:

[Britain's] precocious industrialization, urbanization, and population growth, combined with abundant fossil fuels, a vast empire, and liberal political economy, created the conditions under which the idea of using the entire planet as a food source became thinkable, viable, and systemically embedded. . . .

The volume of British food imports rose almost eightfold between 1850–52 and 1910–12, by which time they represented around two-fifths of all British imports by value. Over four-fifths of bread consumed in Britain came from imported grain by 1909.[22]

In his 1848 opus *Principles of Political Economy,* philosopher and economist John Stuart Mill wrote that "England . . . no longer depends on the fertility of her own soil to keep up her rate of profits, but on the soil of the whole world."[23] In other words, England avoided mass starvation during the Industrial Revolution by robbing the soil and starving the people in its imperial possessions.

> Britain came to command, operationalize, and metabolize tremendous quantities of animal and plant food. It could deny food to starving populations or supply it by dictating the terms on which it would be granted. Slow violence was the result in Ireland (1845–50) and India (1876–78, 1896–1902, 1943–45). Crisis was initially caused by phytopathological or climatic crises striking populations in states of extreme economic precariousness. The British used these crises as opportunities to further marketize, depeasantize, and depopulate such fracture zones and absorb them into their agro-food systems. . . .
>
> Famine was effectively outsourced. We can conservatively place the death toll in nineteenth-century Ireland and India at around 13 million people.[24]

The first major source of imported food was England's first colony, Ireland. England's rulers had confiscated more than three million acres of Ireland's food-producing land in the 1600s—Irish-Catholic landlords owned 59 percent of the farmland in 1641, 14 percent in 1703, and less than 5 percent by 1750.[25] More than half of the new landlords were English absentees who sold the land's produce to English merchants. As Marx pointed out, Ireland was "merely an agricultural district of England which happens to be divided by a wide stretch of water from the country for which it provides corn, wool, cattle and industrial and military recruits."[26]

While literally millions of Irish cottagers and laborers subsisted on potatoes and skimmed milk, grain, beef, pork, butter, and cheese from their landlords' farms was shipped across the Irish Sea. Food shipments to England increased 250 percent between 1760 and 1790, and by the 1840s three-fifths of Ireland's annual food production was being exported. The profits were not reinvested in Irish soil—they too went to England. In 1804 a parliamentary committee estimated that £2 million a year (equal to over 200 times that amount today) flowed from Irish estates to the English lords, gentry, and merchants who owned them.[27]

Food from tropical colonies also became an important part of British working-class diets. Tea from China, on which the East India Company had a monopoly, was the most widely consumed non-alcoholic drink, and sugar from the West Indies provided about 4 percent of calories in 1800. Kenneth Pomeranz estimates that it would have taken at least 1,300,000 acres to produce the same calories on English farmland.[28] By the end of the 1800s, Britain was importing most of the wheat grown on some 26 million acres of Indian farmland, and over four-fifths of the flour used to make bread in Britain was ground from imported grain.[29]

As we saw in chapter 6, Utsa Patnaik has carefully documented the mechanisms and extent of the drain of wealth from India to Britain over two centuries. That research is a vital part of her larger argument that debunks the myth of an agricultural revolution that fed the British poor and made the Industrial Revolution possible. She writes: "The first industrial nation, Britain suffered a food deficit by the 1790s even before the first phase of the Industrial Revolution had got underway, and only increasing food imports from its nearest colony, Ireland, and food and raw material imports from its tropical colonial possessions in the West Indies and India, allowed its industrial transition to proceed at all."[30]

Capitalist Failure?

A 10 percent increase in agricultural production over sixty years, from 1740 to 1800, is essentially zero annual growth. What happened? Why did food production stall? Why did enclosure not deliver as promised? Various explanations have been proposed, and it is likely that multiple factors were involved.

As we've seen, new technologies and techniques had been widely adopted, in both enclosed farms and open fields, before parliamentary enclosure took off. Yield improvements from those changes may have plateaued by the early 1700s, leaving little room for further gains until nitrogen and phosphate fertilizers were introduced in the 1840s.

Even on unimproved land, the prospect of estate consolidation or enclosure may have discouraged tenants from making expensive changes that would only benefit landlords. And the costs of enclosure—legal bills and building new walls, fences, hedges, roads, and farm buildings—likely diverted energy and investment away from changes that might have increased production.

After enclosure, the increased rents that landlords demanded reduced the surplus available for capitalist tenant farmers to reinvest. As Marx wrote, for the capitalist, the landlord was "a mere superfetation, a Sybarite excrescence, a parasite on capitalist production, the louse that sits upon him."[31]

All of those factors were likely involved, but the most important point is that despite the promises landlords and capitalist farmers made in enclosure petitions, what they wanted was not *more food*, but *more land and more revenue*. As Marx commented, "The more or less plausible legal pretexts for appropriation which the great landlords found" were really cover for "the opportunity that makes the thief."[32] Economic historian Davis Kedrosky points out that "since farm wages were relatively high and grain prices low, it paid (especially on heavy soils) to conserve labor costs and reap the superior profits of animal husbandry." Grain acreage did increase, about 30 percent, but "pasturage rose by 75 percent, becoming by far the largest single land use in the country at 17.5 million acres."[33]

Profit-focused farmers shifted away from wheat and other grains, the staple foods of the poor, toward beef, pork and wool, which required significantly less labour and commanded higher prices from rich consumers and textile manufacturers. "Output growth thus slowed to a creep, in spite of the expansion of Britain's land area and the intensive cultivation of existing arable."[34]

In short, capitalism worked as it always does, reducing its wage bill and increasing its profits. Profits took priority over people, producing "the total failure of domestic capitalist transformation of agriculture to meet basic food grain needs from internal production."[35]

Revolution, By and For the Landlords

The enclosure-driven "agricultural revolution" of the 1700s was supposedly made possible by the inventions of Jethro Tull, Charles Townsend, Thomas Coke and a few other innovative landowners. As historian Mark Overton writes, in the great man version of agricultural history, brilliant rich men forced progress on the poor and stupid masses. "These men are seen to have triumphed over a conservative mass of country bumpkins and single-handedly transformed English agriculture within a few years from a peasant subsistence economy into a thriving capitalist agricultural system capable of feeding the teeming millions in the new industrial cities."[36]

This fairy tale still appears in some textbooks, but it has been refuted by serious research. "Most historians now agree that many of the agricultural improvements ascribed to the 'Great Men' of the eighteenth century, including the innovation of new crops and structural changes like enclosure, had long antecedents and may be traced back into the seventeenth century if not earlier."[37]

The real agricultural innovators were not landlords who took credit after the fact, but the "country bumpkins" who actually worked the land. Contrary to the claims of enclosure promoters, "open field villages could and did adopt the fertility-enhancing techniques of the early modern period."[38]

Research continues, but it is now widely agreed that in the 1600s and early 1700s self-employed family farmers (yeomen) substantially increased production by introducing drainage, irrigation, better seeds, and other improvements. The most important change was the shift from the traditional three-field rotation (grain, beans, fallow) to a four-field rotation (wheat, turnips, barley, clover) that not only devoted more land to grain each year, but also provided year-round fodder for animals whose manure enriched the fields, *and*—although the peasant innovators could not have known why—increased yields by adding organic matter and nutrients to the soil.

As historian Martin Daunton writes, "The myth of the improving landowner, enlightening ignorant small farmers, has been dispelled."

> Rather than the heroic, pioneering example of a few publicists battling against the ignorance of farmers to disseminate new techniques . . . yields were raised by the tedious, back breaking seasonal labours of countless anonymous farmers and their workers . . . The small yeomen farmers become the agents of improvement rather than the custodians of inertia. . . .
>
> Farm size was probably not the crucial consideration, for there is little sign that large farms had higher yields, and neither was enclosure a necessary precondition, for yields in Oxfordshire also rose in the open fields. [39]

The English Revolution of 1642–1660 failed to break with the past in two vital respects: it didn't expropriate the great landowners and it refused to give peasants permanent rights to the land they had farmed for generations. Together, those failures opened the way to a radical shift in land ownership. After the restoration of the monarchy in 1660, landlords began buying out or evicting yeoman farmers, a process that culminated in the parliamentary enclosures, farm amalgamations, and concentration of land ownership in which the gentry and aristocracy appropriated the land that yeomen families had improved. By the early 1800s, the aristocracy and the gentry owned 80 percent of England's farmland, and the independent peasantry had all but disappeared.

While many landlords insisted that they had only the national interest in mind, ultimately their motives were financial: larger farms commanded higher rents, because they used fewer workers and fewer draught animals (oxen and horses) per acre. Rents doubled or tripled, but fertility gains were insignificant compared to the achievements of the yeomen's revolution.

The "agricultural revolution" was a revolution by and for the landlords. For the great majority it was a great reversal, a counter-revolution in which the people who best knew the land, and who had worked hard to make it more productive, were expropriated by a tiny class of rentiers whose primary interests were increased rents, political power and luxurious lifestyles. Some landlords invested in drainage and other improvements, but most treated their vast estates as sources of personal income and sites for conspicuous consumption. In the eighteenth and early nineteenth centuries, English landowners spent "enormous sums on country houses and their accompanying landscaped parks [that] rose to new levels of extravagance, astonishing observers."

> Nature was brought to serve a Promethean arrogance. Hillocks were levelled, streams dammed and diverted, lakes manufactured, and trees planted by the thousands. Great houses were built from incomes derived from vast landholdings or offices of state. The construction of two-hundred-room houses on parks stretching for thousands of acres testifies to a degree of wealth unknown since the days of Caesar and Crassus.[40]

Just think, Raymond Williams writes, of "how long and systematic the exploitation and seizure must have been to rear that many houses, on that scale." It was exploitation based on the seizure of land that generations of peasants and yeomen had worked and improved. "Much of the real profit of a more modern agriculture went not into productive investment but into that explicit social declaration: a mutually competitive but still uniform exposition, at every turn, of an established and commanding class power."[41]

Lavishly furnished mansions, the equivalents of today's private jets and superyachts, were financed by the labor of workers who lived on the edge of starvation. Farmers paid higher rents, yeomen lost their land, and laborers' wages fell while the price of food soared. All the benefits of enclosure went to the large landowners, who grew richer than ever. "The 'average' working man remained very close to subsistence level at a time when he was surrounded by the evidence of the increase of national wealth, much of it transparently the product of his own labour."[42]

The era of parliamentary enclosure powerfully confirmed Marx's view that there is an "intimate connection between the pangs of hunger suffered by the most industrious layers of the working class, and the extravagant consumption, coarse or refined, of the rich."[43] Enclosure radically changed Britain's class structure and physically reorganized millions of acres of land. For most people, the changes made life worse.

————⚘————

Did Capitalism End Extreme Poverty?

Closely related to the "agricultural revolution" myth is the claim that most of the world's population lived in extreme poverty, unable to access essential goods, until capitalism rescued them. In his book *Enlightenment Now* Stephen Pinker promotes that view, which he calls the Great Escape, using a graph that seems to show a decline in extreme poverty, from 90 percent of the world's population in 1820 to less than 10 percent in 2020.

That claim is exploded by Dylan Sullivan and Jason Hickel in a paper published in the journal *World Development* in January 2023. Examining data from Europe, Latin America, sub-Saharan Africa, South Asia and China, they show:

> The rise of capitalism coincided with a deterioration in human welfare. In every region studied here, incorporation into the capitalist world-system was associated with a decline in wages to below subsistence, a deterioration in human stature, and a marked upturn in premature mortality. In parts of Latin America, sub-Saharan Africa, and South Asia, key welfare metrics have still not recovered.

Living conditions only began improving in the 1880s in northwestern Europe, and in the mid-1900s in the Global South. Those turning points occurred long after capitalism was entrenched—they correspond to the rise of trade unions, socialist parties, anti-colonial struggles and other radical social movements that won significant reforms.

Pinker's graph shows an increase in GDP per capita, which is not a useful indicator for societies in which most production and consumption occurred outside the market. "GDP fails to adequately account for non-commodity forms of provisioning, such as subsistence farming, foraging, and access to commons, which are important sources of consumption for much of the world's population, particularly during historical periods."

Studies of actual consumption levels show that prior to the Industrial

Revolution most people were indeed poor, but "very few were living without access to basic food, clothing, fuel, and housing." Widespread extreme poverty generally occurred only in "periods of severe social dislocation, such as famines, wars, and institutionalized dispossession—particularly under colonialism." Sullivan and Hickel conclude:

> Contrary to claims about extreme poverty being a natural human condition, it is reasonable to assume that human communities are in fact innately capable of producing enough to meet their own basic needs (i.e., for food, clothing, and shelter), with their own labour and with the resources available to them in their environment or through exchange. Barring natural disasters, people will generally succeed in this objective. The main exception is under conditions where people are cut off from land and commons, or where their labour, resources and productive capacities are appropriated by a ruling class or an external imperial power. This explains the prevalence of extreme poverty under capitalism. . . .
>
> Capitalism is not unique in producing poverty; poverty may result from any system where an underclass lacks political and economic power. It is clear, however, that the expansion of the capitalist world-system caused a dramatic and prolonged process of impoverishment on a scale unparalleled in recorded history.

———— 11 ————

"Only Hunger Can Spur Them on to Labour"

We find on the market a set of buyers, possessed of land, machinery, raw material, and the means of subsistence, all of them, save land in its crude state, the *products of labour,* and on the other hand, a set of sellers who have nothing to sell except their labouring power, their working arms and brains.

—KARL MARX[1]

I n the *Communist Manifesto*, Marx and Engels scoffed at landowners and capitalists who were outraged at proposals to do away with private property. "In your existing society," they wrote, "private property is already done away with for nine-tenths of the population; its existence for the few is solely due to its nonexistence in the hands of those nine-tenths."

No official statistics on landownership existed at the time, but modern research shows that the communists' estimate was remarkably accurate. By 1803, only 13.5 percent of families in England owned any real estate at all, and most of those owned very little. The richest one percent of the population owned 49 percent of the land; the richest 5 percent owned 86 percent.[2]

By the nineteenth century, a unique rural society had emerged in England. This new society was characterized by exceptional inequality. English property ownership was unusually concentrated. Rents had risen, while wages stagnated. By the nineteenth century, the landlord's mansion was lavish, the farmer's house modest, the labourer's cottage a hovel.[3]

That gross inequality was the result of three centuries of expropriation, "the process which divorce[d] the worker from the ownership of the conditions of his own labor."[4]

The landowners who replaced tenants with sheep in the fifteenth century unintentionally began the creation of a class of people without an income and with little hope of getting one. The ruling class response, as we saw in chapter 3, was a combination of terrorism and charity—forced labor and extreme punishments for vagrancy, and laws that required each parish to aid the "deserving poor." The most effective, though unplanned, response was emigration: if Britain had not also been involved in the conquest and genocidal clearance of the New World, as historians Alexander Anievas and Kerem Nişancıoğlu write, "it is likely that capitalism would have been choked off by the limits of English agrarian capitalism."

> Where the internal market could not absorb them, the dispossessed were exported *en masse* to the colonies as settlers or indentured servants. In particular, those considered indebted, poor, dispossessed, criminal, vagrant or rebellious were targeted—what propagandists of the time described as the "rank multitude," those "who cannot live at home."[5]

Emigration was a safety valve during the long transition from feudalism to capitalism, but it wasn't sufficient to ensure anything close to full employment, let alone subsistence wages for all. As the cost of providing relief for the poor increased—total payments rose from £690,000 in 1748 to £1,900,000 in 1785 to £4,100,000 in 1803—a growing body of sentiment among industrialists and landowners favored eliminating both punishment and public relief, in favor of letting market forces decide who lived or died. A leading advocate of that view was Joseph Townsend, who, as Marx later commented, "glorified misery as a necessary condition of wealth in a thoroughly brutal way."[6] A Methodist minister whose Christianity apparently did not include the Golden Rule, Townsend argued that public relief violated natural laws by feeding the lazy and indigent:

> The poor know little of the motives which stimulate the higher ranks to action—pride, honour, and ambition. In general it is only hunger which can spur and goad them on to labour; yet our laws have said, they shall never hunger. The laws, it must be confessed, have likewise said that they shall be compelled to work. But then legal constraint is attended with too much trouble, violence, and noise; creates ill will, and never can be productive of good and acceptable service: whereas hunger is not only a peaceable, silent, unremitted pressure, but, as the most natural motive to industry and labour, it calls forth the most powerful exertions. . . .
>
> Hunger will tame the fiercest animals, it will teach decency and civility, obedience and subjection, to the most brutish, the most obstinate, and the most perverse.[7]

Townsend's views became influential through Thomas Malthus, who "borrowed" them (unattributed) in his 1798 *Essay on the Principle of Population*. In the second edition (1803) Malthus wrote:

> A man who is born into a world already possessed, if he cannot get subsistence from his parents on whom he has a just demand, and if the society do not want his labour, has no claim of right to the smallest portion of food, and, in fact, has no business to be where he is. At nature's mighty feast there is no vacant cover for him. She tells him to be gone, and will quickly execute her own orders.

These sentences were considered too inflammatory for subsequent editions, but they accurately summarized the basis of public policy toward the poor in the nineteenth century. As Michael Perelman writes, Malthus told the ruling class what they wanted to hear, that poverty was the fault of the poor:

> Malthus' ideas prevailed neither by virtue of their merit nor of their originality, but rather by their timeliness. The revolutionary changes in English agriculture and industry were eliminating traditional forms of employment faster than new industries could create alternative employment, producing an apparent "population surplus" and attendant poverty.... At the same time, the relative surplus population created a huge burden of poor relief. Because relief only seemed an unnecessary expense to the bourgeoisie and also appeared to reduce the necessity to accept employment in the "dark satanic mills" of the industrial revolution, the Poor Laws came in for considerable criticism. . . .
>
> Malthus proved to the satisfaction of the ruling classes that they had no responsibility for the existing state of affairs. They were not about to raise questions about subjects such as the effect of private property on the availability of resources: it was enough for them that Malthus showed that "the real cause of the continued depression and poverty of the lower classes of society was the growth of population."[8]

Malthusian ideology, combined with unbounded faith in the power of the market to solve all problems, was the official basis of British social policy throughout the 1800s. Practical results included prison-like workhouses for the unemployed in Britain and the death by starvation of millions in Ireland and India.

"The More They Work for Themselves, the Less They Will for Us."

Although faith in free markets and free choice was widely professed, landowners and capitalist farmers held another belief even more strongly, that the rural poor should be forced to work for them. It was one thing to insist that the poor should have to work, but quite another to allow them to work for themselves.

As we've seen, Arthur Young was the leading advocate of enclosure and large farms. He had little to say about poverty until the mid-1790s, when he became extremely religious following the death of two of his daughters. At the end of the decade, he returned from an extended tour of agricultural districts, "convinced that enclosure and 'an open war against cottages' were leading to deepening poverty in England." After 1800, "Young's views shift from a self-confident assertion of the profound and widespread benefits to be obtained from enclosure to one equally concerned with its effects on the poor and dismayed at many of the changes he perceived in rural England."[9] The extent of his change of heart is apparent in his statement that "I had rather that all the commons of England were sunk into the sea, than that the poor should in future be treated on enclosing as they have generally been hitherto."[10]

In his 1801 report to the Board of Agriculture, Young argued that millions had been deprived of the means to support themselves, forcing them to beg for support from the parish. He still believed that enclosure was essential for England's prosperity, but he now urged Parliament to purchase enough undeveloped land (waste) to give each commoner family a cottage and an acre of land, sufficient for growing potatoes and pasturing a cow. The cost would be less than the poor rates, and the change would "render this country as happy for the lower classes as it has long been for the higher ones."[11]

He admitted that his proposal "will be esteemed wild and visionary," and the Board apparently agreed, since they rejected it. Young published it himself, but, as he later wrote, "It never had the smallest effect except in exciting opposition and ridicule."[12]

Young thought that giving small plots of land to the poor would restore their independence and dignity—and that was exactly why landowners and farmers across England opposed his plan. In a report to the Board of Agriculture on conditions in Shropshire, John Bishton argued that when poor people own land, it "operates upon their minds as a sort of independence; this idea leads the man to lose many days work, by which he gets a habit of indolence. ... The surrounding farmers, by this means, have neither industrious labourers, or servants."[13]

Similarly John Middleton, reporting from Middlesex, urged the eviction of commoners who had settled on the commons, because the "trifling advantages" those plots provided "unfortunately gives their minds an improper bias, and inculcates a desire to live, from that time forward, without labour, or at least with as little as possible."[14]

John Arbuthnot, who was elected to the Royal Society for his contributions to husbandry, favored enclosing wastelands because the commoners who used them were too independent. "If you offer them work, they will tell you that they must go to lock up their sheep, cut furzes, get their cow out of the pound, or perhaps they must take their horse to be shod, that he may carry them to a horse-race or cricket-match."[15]

John Billingsley, who had enclosed over 13,000 acres in Somerset and invested heavily in canals and turnpike roads, argued that preventing cottagers from using common land had improved their attitudes "by exciting a spirit of activity and industry, whereby habits of sloth have been by degrees overcome, and supineness and inactivity have been exchanged for vigour and exertion." Use of the common, on the other hand, had "moral effects of an injurious tendency."

> The possession of a cow or two, with a hog, and a few geese, naturally exalts the peasant in his own conception, above his brethren in the same rank of society. It inspires some degree of confidence in a property, inadequate to his support. In sauntering after his cattle, he acquires a habit of indolence. Quarter, half, and occasionally whole days are imperceptibly lost. Day labour becomes disgusting.[16]

Even writers who conceded that giving land to labourers might reduce the poor rates warned against excessive generosity. The influential *Commercial Agricultural and Manufacturer's Magazine*, for example, said quarter-acre gardens would be enough, and no cows should be permitted: "When a labourer becomes possessed of more land than he and his family can cultivate in the evenings, or other leisure times, the farmer can no longer depend on him for constant work, and the hay-making and harvest (without very favourable weather) must suffer to a degree which (in extent) would sometimes prove a national inconvenience."[17]

These writers were expressing the strongly held view of their class, that labourers existed to work for them, and nothing should be allowed to prevent that. Their class bias is blatant and crude: no one ever suggested that owning thousands of acres made the gentry and aristocracy indolent and let them live without working, although of course it did. Their concern was *not* that laborers with land wouldn't work—it was that they wouldn't work *for capitalist farmers*. The success of capitalist farming required ensuring that agricultural labourers and their families were permanently hungry.

A particularly explicit statement of that position came in 1834, when agricultural reformer John Ellman explained to the Royal Commission on the Poor Laws why large farmers opposed any plan to give land to laborers, even if it would reduce the poor rates. "We can do little or nothing to prevent pauperism; the farmers will have it; they prefer that the labourers should be slaves; they object to their having gardens, saying, 'The more they work for themselves, the less they will for us.'"[18]

In their final report, the Poor Law Commissioners summarized the evidence they heard on the subject: "The employers of paupers are attached to a system which enables them to dismiss and resume their labourers according to their daily or even hourly want of them, to reduce wages to the minimum, or even below the minimum of what will support an unmarried man."[19]

And in 1844, a witness before Parliament's Select Committee on

Enclosures complained about the "disinclination on the part of the cottier [cottager] to be employed. He occupies himself by the care of any stock which he may be able to pasture on the common; it requires, of course, to be looked after, and his little portion of land, whatever it is, demands all his time and attention to cultivate it."[20]

It is hard to imagine clearer confirmations of Marx's assertion that "the process which divorces the worker from the ownership of the conditions of his own labor" was a key factor in the rise of capitalism.

Life Transformed

As the popular rural writer George Sturt wrote about the ways enclosure affected life in his parents' village, even cottagers who retained small gardens were pulled away from self-provisioning, into the commodity economy.

> When the cottager was left with nothing to depend upon save his garden alone, as a peasant he was a broken man—a peasant shut out from his countryside and cut off from his resources. True, he might still grow vegetables, and keep a pig or two, and provide himself with pork; but there was little else that he could do in the old way. It was out of the question to obtain most of his supplies by his own handiwork: they had to be procured, ready-made, from some other source. That source, I need hardly say, was a shop. So the once self-supporting cottager turned into a spender of money at the baker's, the coal-merchant's, the provision-dealer's; and, of course, needing to spend money, he needed first to get it.[21]

The change was even greater for those who had to leave the land entirely. All the necessities of life had to be purchased, and that meant working for wages, under unnatural conditions. Separation from the land was also separation from the cycles of the natural world: instead of being subject to the sun, seasons and soil, factory workers were ruled by clocks, time-sheets, and overseers. Farm work was never easy, but it involved many different tasks; factory workers had to do one thing, over and over, serving machines. As industrialist and utopian socialist Robert Owen wrote of the first generation of Scottish factory workers, "The regularly trained Scottish peasantry disdained the idea of working early and late, day after day."[22]

Under the spur of hunger, men and women who had largely controlled the pace and intensity of their work, who had worked collectively and convivially with their families and neighbors, were made subject to the dictates of profit. Economic historian Gregory Clark shows that capitalists used penalties "to *coerce* workers into doing more than they would have freely chosen if they had maintained control over their hours of work and work intensity."

> The employer dictated when workers worked, their conduct on the job, and that they steadily attend to their assigned tasks. Under discipline workers were rewarded not only according to their output, as in the workshop, but also—or even exclusively— based on their behavior in the workplace. Workers were heavily penalized for small deviations from the approved rules of conduct. . . .
>
> These included arriving a few minutes late in the morning, being absent from their machine, talking or eating at work, drinking beer, and whistling, singing, and engaging in other forms of horseplay.[23]

Under capitalism, Marx writes, "it is not the worker who employs the conditions of his work, but rather the reverse, the conditions of work employ the worker."[24] Today, we are so used to that order of things that it seems natural, but in fact it arrived recently in human history, and working people actively resisted the change. It was ultimately imposed by the implacable discipline of hunger, in a long and difficult transition.

Centuries are required before the "free" laborer, owing to the greater development of the capitalist mode of production, makes a voluntary agreement, i.e. is compelled by social conditions to sell the whole of his active life, his very capacity for labor, in return for the price of his customary means of subsistence, to sell his birth-right for a mess of pottage.[25]

12

"The Alpha and Omega of the Coming Revolution"

Expropriation is the starting-point of the capitalist mode of production, whose goal is to carry it through to completion, and even in the last instance to expropriate all individuals from the means of production.

—KARL MARX[1]

"Sweating blood and filth with every pore from head to toe" characterises not only the birth of capital but also its progress in the world at every step.

—ROSA LUXEMBURG[2]

The forced separation of the poor from the land was a much-hated feature of eighteenth- and nineteenth-century capitalism in Europe, so it is not surprising that the utopian socialists of that time sought to eliminate the division between rural and urban life. Charles Fourier in France and Robert Owen in Britain proposed to overcome capitalist exploitation and alienation by establishing self-sufficient cooperative communities that would engage in both manufactures and agriculture, in which women and men were equal, and all would share responsibilities. In the 1830s, the Grand National Consolidated Trades Union endorsed Owen's views, and at least ten Owenite socialist communities were established in various parts of England.

Land reform also played an important role in England's first mass working-class movement, Chartism. "The long pedigree of agrarian agitation—from opposition to enclosure, through Thomas Spence, to early 1830s interest in communal land-holding . . . ran like a red thread through English radicalism." In the 1840s, the Chartist newspaper *Northern Star* promoted "a vision for a model agricultural community, a 1,000-acre estate divided into 4-acre plots, with 100 acres set aside as common land and a village centre with a school, library and surgery."[3]

"A necessary condition of communist association"

Marx and Engels's approach to socialism and communism was not based on abstract ideas or morality, but on the real struggles of working people and real trends in existing capitalist society. Their response to working class support for land reform in the early 1800s is an example. As early as 1843, Engels condemned "the monopolisation of the land by a few, the exclusion of the rest from that which is the condition of their life."[4] In 1845–46, in *The German Ideology*, they declared that communism would not be possible so long as the separation of town and country continued:

The contradiction between town and country can only exist within the framework of private property. It is the most crass expression of the subjection of the individual under the division of labour, under a definite activity forced upon him—a subjection which makes one man into a restricted town-animal, the other into a restricted country-animal, and daily creates anew the conflict between their interests. . . . The abolition of the contradiction between town and country is one of the first conditions of communal life.[5]

In *Principles of Communism*, an early draft of *The Communist Manifesto*, Engels described elimination of the separation between city and country as "an essential condition of communist association." His list of immediate measures to be undertaken after a victorious proletarian revolution included "the erection of large palaces on national estates as common dwellings for communities of citizens engaged in industry as well as agriculture, and combining the advantages of both urban and rural life without the one-sidedness and disadvantages of either."[6]

In 1848, Marx and Engels wrote "the abolition of the distinction between town and country" into the first published communist program. The *Communist Manifesto*'s list of measures that proletarians should introduce to make "despotic inroads on the rights of property, and on the conditions of bourgeois production" included "combined operations in running agriculture and industry, making for the gradual elimination of the antithesis of town and country."[7]

And in 1851, Marx wrote: "The more I dig into this muck, the more I become convinced that reform of agriculture and the shitty property relations based on it, is the alpha and omega of the coming revolution."[8]

The strategic importance of agriculture in capitalist society was an important part of Marx's research for *Capital*. In the notebooks later published as the *Grundrisse*, he described how capitalism's need to grow turns the entire natural world into commodities:

The tendency to create the *world market* is directly given in the concept of capital itself. . . . *Commerce* no longer appears here as a function taking place between independent productions for the exchange of their excess, but rather as an essentially all-embracing presupposition and moment of production itself. . . .

Hence exploration of all of nature in order to discover new, useful qualities in things; universal exchange of the products of all alien climates and lands; new (artificial) preparation of natural objects, by which they are given new use values.[9]

The commodification of the land and its products broke the metabolic connection between humanity and nature, replacing it with capital and wage labor:

> It is not the unity of living and active humanity with the natural, inorganic conditions of their metabolic exchange with nature, and hence their appropriation of nature, which requires explanation or is the result of a historic process, but rather the separation between these inorganic conditions of human existence and this active existence, a separation which is completely posited only in the relation of wage labour and capital.[10]

In capitalist agriculture, dependence on markets and the cost of land are barriers to rational production. Instead of "a conscious and rational treatment of the land as permanent communal property, as the inalienable condition for the existence and reproduction of the chain of human generations, we have the exploitation and the squandering of the powers of the earth."[11]

> Large landed property reduces the agricultural population to an ever decreasing minimum and confronts it with an ever growing industrial population crammed together in large towns; in this way it produces conditions that provoke an irreparable rift in the interdependent process of social metabolism, a metabolism prescribed by the natural laws of life itself. The result of this is a squandering of the vitality of the soil, which is carried by trade far beyond the bounds of a single country.[12]

Capitalism "collects the population together in great centers, and causes the urban population to achieve an ever-growing preponderance." This simultaneously consolidates a potentially revolutionary working class and undermines the natural conditions that make life possible.

> Capitalist production . . . disturbs the metabolic interaction between man and the earth, i.e. it prevents the return to the soil of its constituent elements consumed by man in the form of food and clothing; hence it hinders the operation of the eternal natural condition for the lasting fertility of the soil. . . .
>
> All progress in capitalist agriculture is a progress in the art, not only of robbing the worker, but of robbing the soil; all progress in increasing the fertility of the soil for a given time is a progress towards ruining the more long-lasting sources of that fertility. . . . Capitalist production, therefore, only develops the techniques and the degree of combination of the social process of production by simultaneously undermining the original sources of all wealth—the soil and the worker.[13]

Capital's inexorable drive to expand extended the town-country antithesis beyond national boundaries:

> By constantly turning workers into "supernumeraries," large-scale industry, in all countries where it has taken root, spurs on rapid increases in emigration and the colonization of foreign lands, which are thereby converted into settlements for growing the raw material of the mother country. . . . A new and international division of labour springs up, one suited to the requirements of the main industrial countries, and it converts one part of the globe into a chiefly agricultural field of production for supplying the other part, which remains a pre-eminently industrial field.[14]

"More and More a Practical Demand"

For Marx and Engels, the town-country divide was not a theoretical abstraction—it was directly relevant to the political movements and strategies of their time. In the late 1860s and early 1870s, Germany experienced an economic boom, leading to rapid expansion of heavy industry, and rapid migration of rural workers to the cities. The resulting "acute housing shortage," Engels later wrote, "filled the press of the day with contributions on the 'housing question,' and gave rise to all sorts of social quackery."[15] In his view, a workers' government could end the immediate crisis easily:

> In the beginning . . . each social revolution will have to take things as it finds them and do its best to get rid of the most crying evils with the means at its disposal. . . . The housing shortage can be remedied immediately by expropriating a part of the luxury dwellings belonging to the propertied classes and by quartering workers in the remaining part.[16]

Whether the former owners would be reimbursed would depend on the circumstances at the time. "To attempt to answer such a question in advance and for all cases would be utopia-making, and I leave that to others."[17]

Describing the expropriation of bourgeois homes as *a transitional measure*, Engels insisted that a permanent solution to the housing question would only be possible "if the whole social order from which it springs is fundamentally refashioned."

> How a social revolution would solve this question depends not only on the circumstances which would exist in each case, but is also connected with still more far-reaching questions, among which one of the most fundamental is the abolition of the antithesis between town and country. . . .
>
> And with this we have arrived at the kernel of the problem. The housing question can only be solved when society has been sufficiently transformed for a start to be made towards abolishing the antithesis between town and country, which has been brought to an extreme point by present-day capitalist society.[18]

That transformation would not be possible so long as capitalism exists:

> Far from being able to abolish this antithesis, capitalist society on the contrary is compelled to intensify it day by day. . . . Only by the solution of the social question, that is, by the abolition of the capitalist mode of production, is the solution of the housing question made possible. To want to solve the housing question while at the same time desiring to maintain the modern big cities is an absurdity. The modern big cities, however, will be abolished only by the abolition of the capitalist mode of production.[19]

Responding to accusations that eliminating the town-country divide was utopian, Engels replied bluntly: "The abolition of the antithesis between town and country is no more and no less utopian than the abolition of the antithesis between capitalists and wage workers."[20] It was not an arbitrary proposal plucked from the air, but a social and ecological necessity.

"Not Merely Possible . . . a Direct Necessity"

Of all the works that Engels wrote to educate German socialists in the 1870s, none was more influential than *Herr Eugen Dühring's Revolution in Science*. Now better-known as *Anti-Dühring*, it replied to a then-influential philosophy professor who condemned Marxism and class struggle, and proposed a "socialitarian" system based on a "universal system of justice" as an alternative to socialism. Engels's reply included important discussions of the town-country divide:

> The utopians were already perfectly clear in their minds as to the effects of the division of labour, the stunting on the one hand of the labourer, and on the other of the labour function, which is restricted to the lifelong uniform mechanical repetition of one and the same operation. The abolition of the antithesis between

town and country was demanded by Fourier, as by Owen, as the first basic prerequisite for the abolition of the old division of labour altogether.[21]

Dühring viewed the separation between town and country as "in the nature of things inevitable," but hoped that "as a result of some inventions," some factories might move to the country.[22] Engels responded that simply moving factories would change nothing of importance. In fact, as happened in England, it would just create new factory towns. "Only the abolition of the capitalist character of modern industry can bring us out of this new vicious circle, can resolve this contradiction in modern industry, which is constantly reproducing itself."[23]

Unlike Dühring, and unlike some socialists today, Engels rejected the "idea that society can take possession of all means of production in the aggregate without revolutionizing from top to bottom the old method of production and first of all putting an end to the old division of labour."[24] To succeed, the socialist revolution would have to implement "the most equal distribution possible of modern industry over the whole country," and "do away with the old division of labour, along with the separation of town and country, and . . . revolutionize the whole of production."[25]

> It is true that in the huge towns civilization has bequeathed us a heritage which it will take much time and trouble to get rid of. But it must and will be got rid of, however protracted a process it may be.[26]

Four decades later, speaking at the founding conference of the German Communist Party, Rosa Luxemburg reasserted the central importance of ending the rift between industry and agriculture, town and country:

> It would be a folly to realize socialism while leaving the agricultural system unchanged. From the standpoint of socialist

economics in general, manufacturing industry cannot be remodeled unless it is amalgamated with a socialist reorganization of agriculture. The most important idea of the socialist economic order is the abolition of the opposition and the division between city and country. This division, this conflict, this contradiction, is a purely capitalist phenomenon which must be eliminated as soon as we place ourselves upon the socialist standpoint.[27]

THE MARXIST CRITIQUE OF THE division between town and country wasn't just about geographic balancing or breaking up unhealthy cities, though both were important. It was a call for healing the metabolic rift created by capitalism, by reestablishing humanity's direct connection with the soil on which life depends, unifying manufacturing with agriculture, and ending our separation from the natural world. It was a call for restoration of the commons on a higher level, as social property rationally regulated by the associated producers.

13

The Struggle Continues

Imperialism is a system of exploitation that occurs not only in the brutal form of those who come with guns to conquer territory. Imperialism often occurs in more subtle forms, a loan, food aid, blackmail. We are fighting this system that allows a handful of men on earth to rule all of humanity.

—THOMAS SANKARA

This book has focused on England and Scotland, but the long wars of expropriation have not been limited in space or time. As we saw in chapter 6, enclosures and clearances in Britain in the eighteenth and early nineteenth centuries were paralleled and reinforced by plunder in South Asia and the expropriation of African lives to work stolen land in the Caribbean. In the late 1800s, when enclosure was largely complete in England and Scotland, Europe's great powers divided up Africa and dispossessed hundreds of millions of people, creating the murderous Belgian regime in the Congo, Britain's apartheid colonies in southern Africa, and other instances of what Luxemburg aptly labeled "the blight of capitalist civilization."[1] By 1900, Europe's colonial empires covered half of Earth's land area—Britain alone ruled 25 percent of the world's people.

Under imperialist control, the natural wealth of colonies and formally independent countries flowed inexorably to the wealthy north. Eduardo Galeano described the process movingly:

Latin America is the region of open veins. The history of Latin America's underdevelopment is, as someone has said, an integral part of the history of world capitalism's development. Our defeat was always implicit in the victory of others; our wealth has always generated our poverty by nourishing the prosperity of others—the empires and their native overseers. In the colonial and neocolonial alchemy, gold changes into scrap metal and food into poison.[2]

Walter Rodney documented the same process in Africa:

Colonial Africa fell within that part of the international capitalist economy from which surplus was drawn to feed the metropolitan sector. Colonialism was not merely a system of exploitation, but one whose essential purpose was to repatriate the profits to the so-called mother country. From an African viewpoint, that amounted to consistent expatriation of surplus produced by African labor out of African resources. It meant the development of Europe as part of the same dialectical process in which Africa was underdeveloped.[3]

Galeano's *Open Veins of Latin America* and Rodney's *How Europe Underdeveloped Africa* are essential reading on imperialist expropriation. As both show, the enrichment of Northern corporations and states by plundering the South did not cease when the colonial era formally ended. Rather, as John Bellamy Foster and Brett Clark write, "Expropriation continued to define the external logic of the system, establishing, maintaining, and extending capitalism's boundaries through its relations to households, colonies, and elemental natural processes—all of which lay outside the circuit of capital."[4]

The imperialist bandits stole more than precious metals and tropical foods. As Marx said of Ireland, the colonial regimes also "exported the soil without even allowing its cultivators the means for replacing the constituents of the exhausted soil."[5] In *Dust Bowls of Empire*, sociologist Hannah Holleman shows that "the global problem of soil erosion emerged by the turn of the century, associated with the vigorous seizure of native lands and displacement of peoples, the imposition of racist land tenure policies, the spread of cash crops, and continuation of plantation-style agriculture."[6]

Later in the 1900s, dispossession and farm consolidation in the former colonies was accelerated by the so-called Green Revolution, which increased yields of corn and rice, but only for farmers who could afford significant investments in hybrid and genetically modified seeds, synthetic fertilizer, pesticides, and irrigation.

Larger farmers with capital or access to credit and better-endowed lands could afford the necessary inputs and irrigation costs and success with the new technologies encouraged expansion, allowing them to dispossess smaller farmers who were excluded from these technologies by lack of scale and capital, and who struggled to compete against the price pressures caused by productivity gains.

The Green revolution sowed the seeds, figuratively and materially, of growing corporate control over the agricultural system and the dramatic reduction of crop diversity.[7]

The damage done by the Green Revolution was exacerbated by the neoliberal policies, imposed on many southern countries by the World Bank, that slashed public support to small farmers and eliminated measures that protected them from global competition. In the 1900s, twenty to thirty million people a year in southern countries migrated from the countryside to cities, and by 2007, for the first time in history, more people worldwide lived in cities than in rural areas.

Land Grabbing

Since the late 1900s, capital's continuing war against the commons has dispossessed millions of peasant families in Africa, Latin America, and Asia. Early examples included Mexico, where millions lost their livelihoods after a 1992 constitutional amendment privatized the publicly owned and peasant-managed *ejidos* that included half of the country's farmland; and India after 2000, where the expropriation of peasants to create tax-free zones for export industries led to years of protests that successfully blocked some of the highest-profile projects.

The Mexican and Indian cases presaged a global land rush. Beginning about 2008, international investors responded en masse to the financial crisis and food price inflation by buying or leasing huge tracts of agricultural land in the Global South. Interviewed in 2012, multi-billionaire Warren Buffett explained why land was a better investment than gold:

> If you buy an ounce of gold today . . . 100 years from now you'll have one ounce of gold and it won't have done anything for you in between. If you buy 100 acres of farmland, it will produce for you every year. You can use that money to buy more farmland; you can do all kinds of things. For 100 years it'll produce things for you and you still have 100 acres of farmland.

He added: "With land you can get somebody else to do all the work, give them a percentage of the crop and you can sit back there for a hundred years."[8]

By 2022, the non-profit Land Matrix database included information on nearly 2,200 concluded land deals of 200 hectares or more, totalling some 65 million hectares.[9] So much of the acquired land was publicly or communally owned, especially in Africa, that it has been suggested that most should be called *commons grabs*.[10]

When the growth of land grabbing came to public attention

after 2008, there was speculation that the buyers were governments seeking to protect food supplies for their citizens. Other
analysts argued that the new mega-farms, some as large as 10,000
hectares, would produce more food, reducing world hunger and
creating secure employment for displaced peasants. Subsequent
developments and research have disproven those views. The land
grabs are profit-seeking, pure and simple, as recent research on
Large-Scale Land Acquisitions (LSLAs) reveals:

Food production: a large proportion of crops produced on LSLA
farms is for non-food purposes. Thus, the shift from smallholder farms to LSLAs often results in an effective loss of food
production relative to the food–non-food production ratios of
smallholder farms. Claims that LSLAs are a means to improve
food security in the host countries should therefore be taken
with caution.

Yields: despite the common argument that LSLA farms could
help to close the yield gap, the evidence available does not support the assumption that LSLA farms are generally able to obtain
higher yields per area than smallholder farms even though they
usually apply higher amounts of external inputs. Some studies
even showed that under the same agro-ecological conditions,
larger farms generally achieve lower productivity per hectare
than smaller farms.

Loss of commons: LSLAs target commons or so called public
land to a significant degree. Poor and marginalised groups (such
as pastoralists, indigenous people, women, and immigrants)
are often disproportionately affected by the loss of commons,
because of their greater dependence on communal assets.

Employment creation: although employment creation clearly
benefits some, its scope, its merely seasonal character (2–5
months of employment per year), and its low remuneration

are mostly insufficient to compensate for the loss of livelihoods from small-scale farming.[11]

The Agriculture at a Crossroads project drew similar conclusions in a survey of recent reports on land grabs.

Only 9% of the agricultural projects listed by the Land Matrix in November 2018 (total area 40.98 million hectares) were exclusively destined for food production. 38% of the area was intended for non-food crops and 15% for the cultivation of flex-crops that can be used for biofuels and animal feed, as well as food. The remaining land was intended for the cultivation of different crops at the same time.

Since the year 2000, foreign investors have acquired 26.7 million hectares of land around the globe for agriculture, according to a Land Matrix report that covers 1,004 concluded agricultural deals. Africa accounts for 42% of the deals, and 10 million hectares of land. Land acquisitions are concentrated along important rivers such as the Niger and the Senegal rivers, and in East Africa.

For the decade spanning 2007–2017, GRAIN has documented at least 135 farmland deals intended for food crop production that backfired. They represent a massive 17.5 million hectares, almost the size of Uruguay. These are not failed land grabs, since the land almost never goes back to the communities, but failed agribusiness projects. Failed land grabs for agricultural production peaked in 2010, but they are on the rise again since 2015.

Despite a history of customary use and ownership of over 50% of the world's land area, indigenous peoples and local communities—up to 2.5 billion women and men—possess ownership rights to just one-fifth of the land that is rightfully theirs. The remaining five billion hectares remain unprotected and vulnerable to land grabs from more powerful entities like governments and corporations. . . .

Land investors appear to be targeting countries with poor governance in order to maximize profit and minimize red tape.

Analysis by Oxfam shows that over three-quarters of the 56 countries where land deals were agreed between 2000 and 2011 scored below average on four World Bank governance indicators: Voice and Accountability, Regulatory Quality, Rule of Law and Control of Corruption.

A study of the economic impact of land grabbing on rural livelihoods estimates that the total income loss for local communities is $34 billion worldwide, a number comparable to the $35 billion loaned by the World Bank for development and aid in 2012. . . .

Behind the current scramble for land is a worldwide struggle for control over access to water. In recent years, Saudi Arabian companies have acquired millions of hectares of land overseas to produce food to ship back home. The country does not lack land for food production; what's missing is water for irrigation.[12]

As sociologist Farshad Araghi puts it, "Capital came to life via enclosures, and it continues to live through enclosures."[13]

The period of unprecedented economic growth and environmental devastation since the Second World War has been dubbed the Great Acceleration by Earth System scientists. It is also marked, John Bellamy Foster argues, by "a Great Expropriation of the global commons and the dispossession of humanity on a scale exceeding all previous human history."

The system of original expropriation, which was the basis of the creation of the industrial proletariat and the modern system of labor exploitation, has metamorphosed into a planetary juggernaut, a robbery system encompassing the entire earth, leading to a more universal dispossession and destruction. The result is the creation of a global environmental reserve army of the dispossessed, the product of capital's drive to monopolize the biogeochemical processes of the planet, at the expense of humanity as a whole.[14]

Resistance

On June 10, 2022, Tanzanian paramilitary forces opened fire on Maasai people in the Ngorongoro district on the eastern edge of the Serengeti National Park. At least thirty-one people were seriously injured, one died, and hundreds took refuge in Kenya. The Maasai, a semi-nomadic pastoral people, were removing the concrete posts that demarked 1,500 square kilometers of traditional grazing land that the government has defined as a Game Controlled Area and leased to a company that organizes private hunting safaris for the Dubai royal family. If the enclosure proceeds, 70,000 Maasai will be evicted from land their communities have shared for centuries.

In May 2022, on the other side of the globe, Indigenous organizations in the Peruvian Amazon region denounced "the expansion of oil palm monocultures, land grabbing and trafficking, illegal mining, an increase in narcotics trafficking which is causing violence, killings and threats in our own territory." They declared a 120-day emergency during which all outsiders were prohibited from entering their region, and demanded "the legal recognition of the ancestral territories of Indigenous Peoples through the granting and registration of land titles."[15]

Also in May 2022, in southern India, hundreds of members of the Tamil Nadu Farmers Association, an affiliate of La Via Campesina, marched to demand compensation for land that was stolen to build Bharathiar University. The courts have ruled in the farmers' favor, but the government has refused to pay. The protesters were met by over a hundred police who prevented them from entering the campus.

In July 2022, farmers in Kenya demanded that the Ondo state government cancel the 99-year leases it has signed giving 50,000 hectares of farmland to private companies. According to a member of the state assembly, "SAO Agro services Ltd., aided by eight vehicles loaded with personnel of Amotekun security corps and officers of the Nigerian Army, invaded Ofosu area with a bulldozer to begin the destruction of farm lands of over 20,000 farmers who are presently farming on the land."[16]

As these examples illustrate, protests against land expropriation are frequent and widespread. From pipeline battles and the Land Back movement in North America, to the mass action that ended water privatization in Bolivia, to occupations and protests by subsistence farmers throughout the Global South, capital's war against the commons is facing increasing opposition in the twenty-first century. The international peasants' movement La Via Campesina plays a leading role in organizing and coordinating the fight for a world "where we share our lands and territories peacefully and fairly among our peoples, be we peasants, Indigenous peoples, artisanal fishers, pastoralists, or others." (See Appendix 3.)

The fight for peasants' rights is intimately bound up with the fight against environmental destruction. João Pedro Stedile of Brazil's Landless Workers Movement (MST—Movimento dos Trabalhadores Rurais Sem Terra) writes:

Structural changes that prevent further damage to nature, climate change, and global warming will only be possible when we overcome the drive for profit that fuels greed over nature's gifts. In other words, there can be no private property over the gifts of nature. We cannot continue to treat food and basic energy sources for the population as commodities, but rather as rights of the people.

For this to happen, we need to envision a post-capitalist model of production. Capitalism does not represent a solution or progress for humanity, on the contrary, it is the source of all environmental and social problems, because profit and accumulation are incompatible with social equality. . . .

Above all, we need to contribute to organizing the working class, peasants, young people, women, students, religious people—in short, all working people—to carry out great mass mobilizations and fight in defense of our lives, the life of the planet, and the well-being of humanity.

Time is short. Without mass struggle, there will be no change.[17]

Indigenous peoples are playing a key role in global resistance to twenty-first century enclosures. As Nick Estes of the Lower Brule Sioux writes in *Our History Is the Future*, their struggles are vital to human liberation:

Indigenous peoples must lead the way. Our history and long traditions of Indigenous resistance provide possibilities for futures premised on justice. After all, Indigenous resistance is animated by our ancestors' refusal to be forgotten, and it is our resolute refusal to forget our ancestors and our history that animates our vision for liberation.

Whereas past revolutionary struggles have strived for the emancipation of labor from capital, we are challenged not just to imagine, but to demand the emancipation of the earth from capital. For the earth to live, capitalism must die.[18]

IN THE 1600s, AN UNKNOWN POET summarized the hypocrisy and brutality of expropriation in four brief lines:

> The law locks up the man or woman
> Who steals the goose from off the common
> But leaves the greater villain loose
> Who steals the common from the goose.

The seldom-quoted fourth verse sums up the lesson of this book:

> The law locks up the man or woman
> Who steals the goose from off the common

> And geese will still a common lack
> Till they go and steal it back.

In Marxist terms, we need to expropriate the expropriators. Today's movements of the oppressed and dispossessed to steal back the commons offer real hope that capitalism's five-century war against the commons can be defeated and reversed in our time. Supporting them is an elementary responsibility for all partisans of social justice.

Appendices

Notes

Bibliography

Index

The Meaning of "So-Called Primitive Accumulation"

In Part Eight of Capital, *titled "So-Called Primitive Accumulation," Marx describes the brutal processes that separated working people from the means of subsistence and concentrated wealth in the hands of landlords and capitalists. It's one of the most dramatic and readable parts of the book.*

It is also a continuing source of confusion and debate. Literally dozens of articles have tried to explain what "primitive accumulation" really meant. Did it occur only in the distant past, or does it continue today? Was "primitive" a mistranslation? Should the name be changed? What exactly was "Marx's theory of primitive accumulation"?

In this article, first published in Climate & Capitalism *in September 2022, I argue that Marx thought "primitive accumulation" was a misleading and erroneous concept. Understanding what he actually wrote shines light on two essential Marxist concepts: exploitation and expropriation.*

On June 20 and 27, 1865, Karl Marx gave a two-part lecture to members of the International Workingmen's Association (the First International) in London. In clear and direct English, he drew on insights that would appear in the nearly finished first volume of

Capital, to explain the labor theory of value, surplus value, class struggle, and the importance of trade unions as "centres of resistance against the encroachments of capital."[1] Since an English translation of *Capital* wasn't published until after his death, those talks were the only opportunity that English-speaking workers had to learn those ideas directly from their author.

While explaining how workers sell their ability to work, Marx asked rhetorically how it came about that there are two types of people in the market—capitalists who own the means of production, and workers who must sell their labor-power in order to survive.

> How does this strange phenomenon arise, that we find on the market a set of buyers, possessed of land, machinery, raw material, and the means of subsistence, all of them, save land in its crude state, the *products of labour*, and on the other hand, a set of sellers who have nothing to sell except their labouring power, their working arms and brains? That the one set buys continually in order to make a profit and enrich themselves, while the other set continually sells in order to earn their livelihood?[2]

A full answer was outside the scope of his lecture, he said, but "the inquiry into this question would be an inquiry into what the economists call '*Previous*, or *Original Accumulation*,' but which ought to be called *Original Expropriation*."

> We should find that this so-called *Original Accumulation* means nothing but a series of historical processes, resulting in a *Decomposition of the Original Union* existing between the Labouring Man and his Instruments of Labour. . . . The *Separation* between the Man of Labour and the Instruments of Labour once established, such a state of things will maintain itself and reproduce itself upon a constantly increasing scale, until a new and fundamental revolution in the mode of production should again overturn it, and restore the original union in a new historical form.[3]

Marx was always very careful in his use of words. He didn't replace *accumulation* with *expropriation* lightly. The switch is particularly important because this was the only time he discussed the issue in English—it wasn't filtered through a translation.[4]

In *Capital*, the subject occupies eight chapters in the part titled "*Die sogenannte ursprüngliche Akkumulation*"—later rendered in English translations as "So-Called Primitive Accumulation." Once again, Marx's careful use of words is important—he added "so-called" to make a point, that the historical processes were *not primitive* and *not accumulation*. Much of the confusion about Marx's meaning reflects failure to understand his ironic intent, here and elsewhere.

In the first paragraph he tells us that "*ursprüngliche*" *Akkumulation* is his translation of Adam Smith's words "previous accumulation." He put the word *ursprüngliche* (previous) in scare quotes, signaling that the word is inappropriate. For some reason the quote marks are omitted in the English translations, so his irony is lost.

In the 1800s, primitive was a synonym for original—for example, the Primitive Methodist Church claimed to follow the original teachings of Methodism. As a result, the French edition of *Capital*, which Marx edited in the 1870s, translated *ursprüngliche* as *primitive*, which carried over to the 1887 English translation, and we have been stuck with *primitive accumulation* ever since, even though the word's meaning has changed.

Marx explains why he used so-called and scare quotes by comparing the idea of previous accumulation to the Christian doctrine that we all suffer because Adam and Eve sinned in a distant mythical past. Proponents of previous accumulation tell an equivalent nursery tale:

> Long, long ago there were two sorts of people; one, the diligent, intelligent and above all frugal elite; the other, lazy rascals, spending their substance, and more, in riotous living. . . . Thus it came to pass that the former sort accumulated wealth, and the latter sort finally had nothing to sell except their own skins.

And from this original sin dates the poverty of the great majority who, despite all their labour, have up to now nothing to sell but themselves, and the wealth of the few that increases constantly, although they have long ceased to work.

"Such insipid childishness is every day preached to us in defense of property," but when we consider actual history, "it is a notorious fact that conquest, enslavement, robbery, murder, in short, force, play the greatest part." The chapters of So-Called Primitive Accumulation describe the actual processes by which "great masses of men [were] suddenly and forcibly torn from their means of subsistence, and hurled onto the labor-market as free, unprotected and rightless proletarians."

These newly freed men became sellers of themselves only after they had been robbed of all their own means of production, and all the guarantees of existence afforded by the old feudal arrangements. And this history, the history of their expropriation, is written in the annals of mankind in letters of blood and fire.

Marx's account focuses on expropriation in England, because the dispossession of working people was most complete there, but he also refers to the mass murder of Indigenous people in the Americas, the plundering of India, and the trade in African slaves—"these idyllic proceedings are the chief moments of primitive accumulation." That sentence, and others like it, illustrate Marx's consistently sarcastic take on primitive accumulation. He is not *describing* primitive accumulation, he is condemning those who use the concept to conceal the brutal reality of expropriation.

Failure to understand that Marx was polemicizing against the concept of "primitive accumulation" has led to another misconception—that Marx thought it occurred only in the distant past, when capitalism was being born. That was what pro-capitalist writers meant by previous accumulation, and as we've seen, Marx compared that view to the Garden of Eden myth. Marx's chapters on so-called primitive accumulation emphasized the violent expropriations that laid the basis for early capitalism because he was responding to the claim that capitalism evolved peacefully. But his account also includes the Opium Wars of the 1840s and 1850s, the Highland Clearances in capitalist Scotland, the colonial-created famine that killed a million people in Orissa in India in 1866, and plans for enclosing and privatizing land in Australia. All of these took place during Marx's lifetime and while he was writing *Capital*. None of them were part of capitalism's prehistory.

The expropriations that occurred in capitalism's first centuries were devastating, but far from complete. In Marx's view, capital could not rest there. Its ultimate goal was "to expropriate all individuals from the means of production."[5] Elsewhere he wrote of big capitalists "dispossessing the smaller capitalists and expropriating the final residue of direct producers who still have something left to expropriate."[6] In other words, expropriation continues well after capitalism matures.

We often use the word *accumulation* loosely, for gathering up or hoarding, but for Marx it had a specific meaning, the increase of capital by the addition of surplus value, a continuous process that results from the exploitation of wage-labor.[7] The examples he describes in "So-Called Primitive Accumulation" all refer to robbery, dispossession, and expropriation—discrete appropriations without equivalent exchange. *Expropriation, not accumulation.*

In the history of capitalism, we see a constant, dialectical interplay between the two forms of class robbery that Peter Linebaugh has dubbed X^2—*expropriation* and *exploitation*. "Expropriation is prior to exploitation, yet the two are interdependent. Expropriation not only prepares the ground, so to speak, it intensifies exploitation."[8]

Expropriation is *open* robbery. It includes forced enclosure, dispossession, slavery and other forms of theft, without equivalent exchange. Exploitation is *concealed* robbery. Workers appear to receive full payment for their labor in the form of wages, but in fact the employer receives more value than he pays for.

What political economists described as a gradual buildup of wealth by men who were more industrious and frugal than others was actually violent, forcible expropriation that created the original context for exploitation and has continued to expand it ever since. As John Bellamy Foster and Brett Clark write in *The Robbery of Nature*:

> Like any complex, dynamic system, capitalism has both an inner force that propels it and objective conditions outside itself that set its boundaries, the relations to which are forever changing. The inner dynamic of the system is governed by the process of exploitation of labor power, under the guise of equal exchange, while its primary relation to its external environment is one of expropriation.[9]

In short, Marx did not have a "theory of primitive accumulation." He devoted eight chapters of *Capital* to demonstrating that the political economists who promoted such a theory were wrong, that it was a "nursery tale" invented to whitewash capital's real history. That's why he preceded the words "primitive accumulation" by "so-called."

Marx's preference for "original expropriation" wasn't just playing with words. That expression captured his view that "the expropriation from the land of the direct producers—private ownership for some, involving non-ownership of the land for others—is *the basis of the capitalist mode of production*."[10]

The continuing separation of humanity from our direct relationship with the earth was not and is not a peaceful process: it is written in letters of blood and fire.

Marx and Engels and Russia's Peasant Communes

If Karl Marx were alive today, would he support corporate land grabs in the Global South as progressive measures? Did he believe that all societies must pass through a predetermined sequence of stages to fully developed capitalism, so resistance was futile or even reactionary? Rather than speculate in the abstract, consider how he and Engels responded to the assault on peasant communes in Russia during their lifetime. This article was first published in Monthly Review *in October 2022.*

> What is threatening the life of the Russian commune is neither historical inevitability nor a theory; it is oppression by the State and exploitation by capitalist intruders, who have been made powerful at the expense of the peasants by the very same State.
>
> —KARL MARX[1]

We live in a time of corporate global land grabs. Since the food price crisis of 2008, about 2,200 large-scale land acquisitions have been completed in developing nations, totaling 63 million hectares (131 million acres), an area the size of California and Mississippi combined. Most of the acquisitions affected farmland that was managed as common property by small farmers, leading some analysts to describe the process as "commons grabbing."[2]

In her 2018 book on these and other "new enclosures," feminist scholar Sylvia Federici argues that Marxism offers no guidance to opponents of commons-grabbing. Karl Marx and Frederick Engels, she writes, "fail at this moment of the new enclosures. The Marx of *Capital* would understand the new enclosures as he did the old, as a stage in the 'progressive nature' of capitalist development preparing the material conditions for a communist society."

In her view, "The enclosures were for Marx a historically positive event" because they were "a stage in the 'progressive nature' of capitalist development, preparing the material conditions for a communist society." Revolutionaries today, she writes, "must reject the idea—permeating most of Marx's published work—that capitalism is or has been a necessary stage in the history of human emancipation and a necessary precondition for the construction of a communist society."[3]

It is certainly true that some on the left, especially in the Soviet Union during and after Stalin's rule, promoted that view. It was stated explicitly in *Fundamentals of Marxism-Leninism*, an official textbook authored in 1960 by the Secretary of the Central Committee of the Communist Party of the Soviet Union:

> In spite of an immense variety of concrete details and particularities, all peoples travel what is basically the same path.... The development of society proceeds through the consecutive replacement, according to definite laws, of one socio-economic formation by another.[4]

Another influential book, written by members of the Moscow Institute of Social Philosophers, insisted that socialist governments must "purposefully influence the process of the disintegration of tribal and communal relations."

Countries that have freed themselves from colonial domination may study the experience of the Soviet Union in their efforts to overcome the historical backwardness of some regions, in particular those that still had communal relations at the time of the socialist revolution. The experience of the Soviet Union shows that in a society of social justice it is possible to transform tribal relations through the development of collective ownership.[5]

Statements like that, and the policies they reflected, justifiably alienated many peasant activists and their supporters. The question is: do they accurately reflect Marx's views?

In *Capital*, Marx describes enclosures in England as "the usurpation of the common lands," which led to "a degraded and almost servile condition of the mass of the people." He sharply condemned "the whole series of thefts, outrages and popular misery that accompanied the forcible expropriation of the people." And he devoted several pages to exposing and denouncing the process by which peasants in the Scottish Highlands "were systematically hunted and routed out," an outrage that was still going on while he was writing. Those words cannot possibly be read as endorsing the enclosure movement as historically positive.[6]

But the best account of Marx's views on the subject can be found in his real-world response to the destruction of commons-based peasant communities in Russia—*while it was actually happening.*

Until the 1860s, almost all Russian peasants held their land in a form of communal ownership known as *obshchina* or *mir*, which was similar, but not identical, to the commons-based communities in pre-industrial England. The communes were arranged in various ways, but typically each household farmed strips in open fields, and the land was periodically redistributed. Common lands and forests were managed by village assemblies.

In 1861, as part of a modernization program following Russia's humiliating defeat in the Crimean War, Tsar Alexander II abolished serfdom and promised that the freed serfs would receive land. In fact, landlords were given nearly half of the common land, while former serfs were only granted the right to *buy* land. The price, for plots that were often smaller than those they had worked as serfs, was two years of unpaid labor for the landlord, followed by "redemption payments" to the state for forty-nine years. This provoked protests and riots in many parts of the country. In the first year, more than half of the 111,000 peasant communities in Russia rejected official plans for breaking up their communal villages. As late as 1892, an estimated three-quarters of peasants were still working communally owned land.[7]

Peasant discontent was paralleled by a wave of student radicalism, inspired in particular by the writings of Nikolai Chernyshevsky, who supported a form of socialism based on the peasant communes. In the late 1860s, some Narodniks (populists) discovered Marx's works, and for several years the first edition of *Capital* was more widely read in Russia than anywhere else. A Russian translation—the first into any other language from the original German— was published in 1872.

Much Russian attention focused on Part Eight of *Capital*—"So-Called Primitive Accumulation"—which liberals and radicals read and reread as part of their debates about whether the peasant communes could provide a basis for socialism, or were doomed to be wiped away by ascendant capitalism. Inevitably, they turned to Marx himself for answers.

"The Finest Chance Ever Offered by History"

In the early 1860s Marx was undoubtedly aware of the peasant unrest and youth radicalization in Russia, but his long hours of research for what would become the first volume of *Capital*, coupled with his leadership role in the International Workingmen's Association (the First International), left no time to address those subjects. When *Capital* was finally published in 1867, it contained just a handful of passing references to Russia, and nothing about

Russian farming. Marx does not seem to have investigated social conditions in Russia before the late 1860s.

In October 1868, thirteen months after *Capital* was published, prominent Narodnik Nikolai Danielson wrote Marx proposing a Russian edition. Marx told Engels he was "naturally extraordinarily pleased,"[8] and immediately plunged into the project, corresponding extensively with Danielson, and teaching himself Russian, both to ensure the accuracy of the translation and in order to study economic and social conditions in the Russian empire.

In March 1870, a group of Russian exiles in Switzerland applied to join the International, naming Marx as their delegate on the General Council. Later that year, the group sent nineteen-year-old Elisabeth Dmitrieff, who subsequently played a leading role in the Paris Commune, to attend General Council meetings in London. While there, she became close friends with the Marx family, living with his daughters for three months and discussing Russian politics with him and Engels at length. In January 1871, at Marx's request, she wrote a summary of the issues as she and her comrades saw them, focusing on the communes. Referring to "the destinies of the peasant commune in Russia," she wrote:

> Its transformation into small individual ownership is, unhappily, more than probable. All government measures . . . have the singular goal of introducing private property, by the means of suppressing collective responsibility. A law passed last year has already abolished [collective ownership] in communes with fewer than forty souls (men's souls, because women, unhappily, do not have souls).[9]

Marx did not rush to judgment, or assume that what he had written about the commons elsewhere could simply be extended to Russia. Rather, as he later wrote, "In order to reach an informed judgment of the economic development of contemporary Russia, I learned Russian and then spent several long years studying official publications and others with a bearing on this subject."[10] Not until

1875 did he and Engels, who also knew Russian, feel qualified to address the subject publicly.

"On Social Relations in Russia," serialized under Engels's name in April 1875 in the newspaper *Der Volksstaat* and then published as a separate pamphlet, detailed the ruinous effects of breaking communes into individually owned farms. "The condition of the Russian peasants, since the emancipation from serfdom, has become intolerable and cannot be maintained much longer, and that for this reason alone, if for no other, a revolution is in the offing in Russia." Although communal agriculture was in decline, "the possibility undeniably exists of raising this form of society to a higher one . . . without it being necessary for the Russian peasants to go through the intermediate stage of bourgeois small holdings." To succeed, however, that transition would require material aid to modernize farming methods and overcome extreme poverty. "If anything can still save Russian communal ownership and give it a chance of growing into a new, really viable form, it is a proletarian revolution in Western Europe."[11]

In Russia, debates on the relevance of Marxism to Russian conditions and the peasant communes accelerated in the late 1870s. One of the sharpest criticisms of Marx came from Nikolai Mikhailovsky, the editor of the populist journal *Otechestvenniye Zapiski* (Notes from the Homeland). He charged that in *Capital*'s chapters on primitive accumulation, Marx had expounded a theory of universal progress under which Russia was doomed to follow Western Europe's brutal path to capitalism before socialism was possible.

All this "maiming of women and children" we still have before us, and from the point of view of Marx's historical theory, we should not protest them because it would mean acting to our own detriment; on the contrary, we should welcome them as the steep but necessary steps to the temple of happiness.

Nearly 150 years before Federici, Mikhailovsky wrote that Marxists were "pleased to see the producers being divorced from the means of production . . . as the first phase of the inevitable, and, in the final result, a beneficial process."[12] Marx's unfinished reply, written in 1878 but not published until 1886, reads like a direct response to some twenty-first-century critics.

Mikhailovsky's criticism, Marx wrote, incorrectly assumed that *Capital*'s chapters on primitive accumulation constituted a "theory of the general course fatally imposed on all peoples, whatever the historical circumstances in which they find themselves." In fact, "the chapter on primitive accumulation claims to do no more than to trace the path by which, in Western Europe, the capitalist economic order emerged from the womb of the feudal economic order."

The historical possibilities of Russian development could only be identified by empirical study—not "with the master-key of a general historico-philosophical theory whose supreme virtue consists in being supra-historical." After extensive study of Russian conditions, Marx wrote, "I have come to the conclusion that if Russia continues along the path it has followed since 1861, it will miss the finest chance ever offered by history to a people and undergo all the fateful vicissitudes of the capitalist regime."[13]

Marx wrote cautiously to evade tsarist censorship, but his meaning would have been crystal clear to anyone who had followed the debates: *if the Russian communes survive, they could provide a direct path to socialism.*

"The Fulcrum for Social Regeneration"

Marx developed his argument more fully in draft letters to Vera Zasulich, a populist who later became a member of Russia's first Marxist organization. In February 1881, she asked his opinion about the argument of some Russians who insisted that "the rural commune is an archaic form destined to perish by history," and attributed that view to Marx. Did he support "the theory that it is historically necessary for every country in the world to pass through all the phases of capitalist production"? She stressed that this was not simply a theoretical question. Whether the commune "is capable of developing in a socialist direction" or "is destined to perish" was "a life-and-death question above all for our social-ist party," because it would entirely determine their strategy and activity.[14]

Marx wrote four long drafts in response, but finally decided, on March 8, to send a short reply that included this very clear statement:

> The analysis provided in *Capital* . . . provides no reasons either for or against the vitality of the Russian commune, but the spe-cial study I have made of it, including a search for original source material, has convinced me that the commune is the fulcrum for social regeneration in Russia.[15]

That sentence, all by itself, undermines any claim that Marx saw the enclosure of Russian communes as "a historically positive event." But we can get a more complete view of his thinking from his drafts, which survived and were eventually published in 1924.

Once again, Marx insisted that he had "*expressly* restricted the 'historical inevitability' of this process to the countries of Western Europe" where specific conditions prevailed.

> But does this mean that the development of the "agricultural commune" must follow this route in every circumstance [in every historical context]? Not at all. Its constitutive form allows of the following alternative: either the element of private prop-erty which it implies gains the upper hand over the collective element, or the reverse takes place. Everything depends upon the historical context in which it is situated.[16]

The situation in Russia was different, so a different outcome was possible. The commune "occupies a unique situation without any precedent in history":

> Alone in Europe, it is still the organic, predominant form of rural life in a vast empire. Communal land ownership offers it

the natural basis for collective appropriation, and its historical context—the contemporaneity of capitalist production—provides it with the ready-made material conditions for largescale co-operative labour organised on a large scale. It may therefore incorporate the positive achievements developed by the capitalist system, without having to pass under its harsh tribute.[17]

"The very existence of the Russian commune is now threatened by a conspiracy of powerful interests," he noted, but if that threat is defeated, it "may become the *direct starting-point* of the economic system towards which modern society is tending; it may open a new chapter that does not begin with its own suicide."[18]

Marx and Engels repeated that argument the next year, in their Preface to the second Russian edition of the *Communist Manifesto*:

In Russia we find, face-to-face with the rapidly flowering capitalist swindle and bourgeois property, just beginning to develop, more than half the land owned in common by the peasants. Now the question is: can the Russian *obshchina*, though greatly undermined, yet a form of primeval common ownership of land, pass directly to the higher form of Communist common ownership? Or, on the contrary, must it first pass through the same process of dissolution such as constitutes the historical evolution of the West?

The only answer to that possible today is this: If the Russian Revolution becomes the signal for a proletarian revolution in the West, so that both complement each other, the present Russian common ownership of land may serve as the starting point for a communist development.[19]

"Our People in Russia"

Marx and Engels did not study Russian conditions out of academic curiosity. On the contrary, they believed that Russia, once the heartland of backwardness and reaction, had become "the vanguard of revolutionary action in Europe," so understanding it was a political necessity.[20] Based on what they learned, they consistently supported radical populists who took action against the tsarist regime, and distanced themselves from people who only analyzed and commented. Their approach was motivated, as Marx wrote in another context, by the conviction that "every step of real movement is more important than a dozen programs."[21]

After a period of decline in the late 1860s and early 1870s, the radical populist movement had been reborn, beginning in 1873, as "a chaotic mass pilgrimage of the intelligentsia to the people."

> Young men and women, most of them former students, numbering about a thousand in all, carried socialist propaganda to all corners of the country. . . . This movement, remarkable in scope and youthful idealism, the true cradle of the Russian revolution, was distinguished—as is proper to a cradle—by extreme naiveté. . . . What they wanted was a complete revolution, without abridgements or intermediate stages.[22]

The largely spontaneous movement "to the people" totally failed. The peasants did not respond, and over seven hundred young populists were arrested and sentenced to long terms in prison or Siberian exile. Still, the experience "awakened a burning desire to pass from words to action."[23]

On January 24, 1878, Vera Zasulich, acting on her own, shot and seriously wounded the governor of St. Petersburg, who had ordered the brutal beating of a political prisoner for refusing to doff his hat. She then used her widely publicized trial to expose the government's actions and policies, and on March 31 the jury found her not guilty, triggering widespread celebrations in Russia and across Western Europe. Although she didn't intend it, and took no part, her action inspired others to follow her example: in the following months some half a dozen government and police officials were assassinated.

Marx and Engels fully supported the new stage of populist struggle. In an article published just before Zasulich's trial, Engels wrote:

The government agents are committing incredible atrocities. Against such wild animals one must defend oneself as one can, with powder and lead. Political assassination in Russia is the only means which men of intelligence, dignity and character possess to defend themselves against the agents of an unprecedented despotism.[24]

In September he praised "our people in Russia" who "by their ruthless action, [had] put the fear of God into the Russian government."[25]

In October 1879, the largest populist organization, Zemlya i Volya (Land and Freedom), split in two. The majority, calling themselves Narodnaya Volya (People's Will), advocated "disorganizing" activity (terrorism) aimed at overthrowing the autocracy. The minority, whose members included future Marxists Georgi Plekhanov, Pavel Axelrod, and Vera Zasulich, favored a focus on propaganda and education directed to the peasantry—their group's name, Cherny Peredel (Black or General Redistribution), referred to expropriation of the landlords' estates. Marx ridiculed them for abstaining from the struggle, calling them "mere doctrinaires, confused anarchist socialists, [whose] influence upon the Russian 'theatre of war' is zero."[26]

Unlike the terrorists, who risk life and limb, these men—most of whom (but not all) left Russia *of their own accord* constitute the so-called Propaganda Party. (In order to disseminate *propaganda in Russia*—they remove *to Geneva*! What a *quid pro quo*!) These gentry are all of them opposed to politico-revolutionary action. Russia is to leap head-over-heels into the anarchist-communist-atheist millennium! Meanwhile they pave the way for that leap by tedious doctrinairism.[27]

On March 1, 1881, after several failed attempts, Narodnaya Volya assassinated Tsar Alexander II. One member died in the attack, but another was arrested and tortured into revealing the names and locations of his comrades. Six central leaders were arrested, and their trial became a *cause célèbre* across Europe. In a letter to Jenny Longuet, Marx praised the defendants' political seriousness:

> Have you been following the course of the legal proceedings against the assassins in Petersburg? They are sterling people through and through, *sans pose melodramatique* [without melodramatic posturing], simple, matter-of-fact, heroic…. [They] are at pains to teach Europe that their *modus operandi* is a specifically Russian and historically inevitable mode of action which no more lends itself to moralizing—for or against—than does the earthquake in Chios.[28]

Many prominent figures, including the novelist Victor Hugo, protested the trial, which was conducted by hand-picked judges, but the defendants were sentenced to death. Sophia Perovskaya, Andrei Zhelyabov, Nikolai Kibalchich, Nikolai Rysakov, and Timofei Mikhailov were publicly executed before a huge crowd on April 3. The execution of Gesia Gelman was delayed because she was pregnant, but she died in prison five days after her child was born.

The executions and the subsequent arrest of hundreds of Narodnaya Volya members and sympathizers effectively destroyed the radical populist movement. Marx and Engels befriended a few exiles who escaped to Western Europe, and hoped for a revival, but the regime headed by Alexander III was more entrenched and repressive than ever. The Russian left did not begin to recover until the 1890s.

"Real, Profane History"

With the benefit of hindsight, it is evident that Marx and Engels overestimated the strength of the revolutionary movement in Russia and underestimated the strength of the absolutist regime. Their writings on Russia must be read with that in mind.

But it is also essential to recognize that their approach to the peasant communes and Russian politics was very different from that attributed to them by critics past and present, and sometimes defended by Marxists in the twentieth century.

1. *They did not try to force fit the peasant communes into a predetermined historical model.* As Teodor Shanin writes, Marx "refused to deduce social reality from his own books."[29] He and Engels did not have a one-size-fits-all "historico-philosophical theory" that defined a particular path history must follow. The idea that history can take and has taken various paths runs through their work. Decades earlier, in *The German Ideology,* they had explicitly rejected, as "speculatively distorted," theories in which "later history is made the goal of earlier history."[30] And, as Eric Hobsbawm pointed out in his introduction Marx's mid-1850s notes on precapitalist societies, his account of historical stages was analytical, not chronological:

> The statement that the Asiatic, ancient, feudal and bourgeois formations are "progressive" does not therefore imply any simple unilinear view of history, nor a simple view that all history is progress. It merely states that each of these systems is in crucial respects further removed from the primitive state of man.[31]

Particularly important for Marx's response to Mikhailovsky, the account of "so-called primitive accumulation" in *Capital* said explicitly that "the history of this expropriation assumes different aspects in different countries, and runs through its various phases in different orders of succession and at different historical epochs. *Only in England, which we therefore take as our example, has it the classic form.*"[32] The historical chapters of *Capital* described and explained what had actually happened in Western Europe, particularly England, *not* what ought to or must happen in all cases, regardless of context. To understand what was possible in Russia it was necessary to "descend from pure theory to the Russian reality."[33]

Recognizing that the situation in Russia raised questions he had not yet considered, Marx undertook detailed research, reading literally hundreds of books and reports and discussing with Russians who visited London, before drawing any conclusions. Even then he did not try to define an inevitable historical path. Instead, he concluded that the communes *might* provide a direct path to socialism *if* their decay was halted in time, and *if* they received material support from the West, and *if* a successful revolution overthrew the Russian autocracy.

2. *They did not assume that their social and political outlook qualified them to dictate tactics from afar.* In 1885, Vera Zasulich asked Engels for advice on the tactics Marxists should adopt in Russia. His reply displayed a political modesty that is all too rare in the left today:

> To me the historic theory of Marx is the fundamental condition of all reasoned and consistent revolutionary tactics; to discover these tactics one has only to apply the theory to the economic and political conditions of the country in question.
>
> But to do this one must know these conditions; and so far as I am concerned I know too little about the actual situation in Russia to presume myself competent to judge the details of the tactics demanded by this situation at a given moment.[34]

During Narodnaya Volya's terrorist attacks on tsarism, Marx and Engels deferred to the tactical judgment of frontline revolutionaries, and praised them for insisting in court that their tactics were specific to the Russian situation.[35]

Their enthusiastic support for Narodnaya Volya in 1879–1881 goes against the conviction of many Marxists that assassination and terrorism are never appropriate. For them, an absolute prohibition of particular tactics was just as wrong as the idea that certain tactics are always appropriate. In one paragraph where he praised Narodnaya Volya's actions, Marx also condemned the

German anarchist Johann Most for supporting terrorism. The difference was that the anarchist promoted tyrannicide as a universal liberatory panacea, while Narodnaya Volya insisted their tactics were specific to Russia conditions.[36]

Similarly, in an 1885 article, Engels condemned a terrorist bombing in London while defending Narodnaya Volya's tactics in Russia:

> The means of struggle employed by the Russian revolutionaries are dictated to them by necessity, by the actions of their opponents themselves. They must answer to their people and to history for the means they employ. But the gentlemen who are needlessly parodying this struggle in Western Europe in schoolboy fashion . . . who do not even direct their weapons against real enemies but against the public in general, these gentlemen are in no way successors or allies of the Russian revolutionaries, but rather their worst enemies.[37]

Critics past and present routinely accuse Marx and Engels of economic determinism. As a recent article put it, their "fatal flaw" was believing that "because capitalism's development was inexorable, there was little point in thinking about the actual transition from capitalism to socialism or the role the left might play in actively creating a better world."[38] Marx and Engels's response to Russian developments in the 1870s and 1880s completely explodes that caricature. They viewed Russian capitalist development not as "inexorable" but as open to a range of possibilities, and they actively supported efforts to transform Russian politics by overthrowing the tsar.

Their approach, as Marx wrote in his critique of Proudhon, was not to invent universal models, but to study "the real, profane history of men in every century and to present these men as both the authors and the actors of their own drama."[39]

And that made all the difference.

The Declaration of Nyéléni

Adopted by a conference organized by La Via Campesina International Peasants Movement, in Mali on February 27, 2007.

We, more than 500 representatives from more than 80 countries, of organizations of peasants/family farmers, artisanal fisher-folk, Indigenous peoples, landless peoples, rural workers, migrants, pastoralists, forest communities, women, youth, consumers, environmental and urban movements have gathered together in the village of Nyéléni in Sélingué, Mali, to strengthen a global movement for food sovereignty. We are doing this, brick by brick, have been living in huts constructed by hand in the local tradition, and eating food that is being produced and prepared by the Sélingué community. We give our collective endeavour the name "Nyéléni" as a tribute to and inspiration from a legendary Malian peasant woman who farmed and fed her peoples well.

Most of us are food producers and are ready, able and willing to feed all the world's peoples. Our heritage as food producers is critical to the future of humanity. This is specially so in the case of women and Indigenous peoples who are historical creators of knowledge about food and agriculture and are devalued. But this heritage and our capacities to produce healthy, good and abundant food are being threatened and undermined by neo-liberalism and global capitalism. Food sovereignty gives us the hope and power to preserve, recover and build on our food producing knowledge and capacity.

Food sovereignty is the right of peoples to healthy and culturally appropriate food produced through ecologically sound and sustainable methods, and their right to define their own food and agriculture systems. It puts those who produce, distribute and consume food at the heart of food systems and policies rather than the demands of markets and corporations. It defends the interests and inclusion of the next generation. It offers a strategy to resist and dismantle the current corporate trade and food regime, and directions for food, farming, pastoral and fisheries systems determined by local producers. Food sovereignty prioritises local and national economies and markets and empowers peasant and family farmer-driven agriculture, artisanal—fishing, pastoralist-led grazing, and food production, distribution and consumption based on environmental, social and economic sustainability. Food sovereignty promotes transparent trade that guarantees just income to all peoples and the rights of consumers to control their food and nutrition. It ensures that the rights to use and manage our lands, territories, waters, seeds, livestock and biodiversity are in the hands of those of us who produce food. Food sovereignty implies new social relations free of oppression and inequality between men and women, peoples, racial groups, social classes and generations.

In Nyéléni, through numerous debates and interactions, we are deepening our collective understanding of food sovereignty and learning about the reality of the struggles of our respective movements to retain autonomy and regain our powers. We now understand better the tools we need to build our movement and advance our collective vision.

What Are We Fighting For?

A world where . . .

- all peoples, nations and states are able to determine their own food-producing systems and policies that provide every one of us with good-quality, adequate, affordable, healthy, and culturally appropriate food;
- recognition and respect of women's roles and rights in food production, and representation of women in all decision-making bodies;
- all peoples in each of our countries are able to live with dignity, earn a living wage for their labour and have the opportunity to remain in their homes;
- food sovereignty is considered a basic human right, recognised and implemented by communities, peoples, states and international bodies;
- we are able to conserve and rehabilitate rural environments, fish stocks, landscapes and food traditions based on ecologically sustainable management of land, soils, water, seas, seeds, livestock and other biodiversity;
- we value, recognize and respect our diversity of traditional knowledge, food, language and culture, and the way we organise and express ourselves;
- there is genuine and integral agrarian reform that guarantees peasants full rights to land, defends and recovers the territories of Indigenous peoples, ensures fishing communities' access and control over their fishing areas and eco-systems, honours access and control over pastoral lands and migratory routes, assures decent jobs with fair remuneration and labour rights for all, and a future for young people in the countryside;
- agrarian reform revitalises inter-dependence between producers and consumers, ensures community survival, social and economic justice and ecological sustainability, and respect for local autonomy and governance with equal rights for women and men;
- it guarantees the right to territory and self-determination for our peoples;
- we share our lands and territories peacefully and fairly among

our peoples, be we peasants, Indigenous peoples, artisanal fishers, pastoralists, or others;

- in the case of natural and human-created disasters and conflict-recovery situations, food sovereignty acts as a kind of "insurance" that strengthens local recovery efforts and mitigates negative impacts;
- we remember that affected communities are not helpless, and where strong local organization for self-help is the key to recovery;
- peoples' power to make decisions about their material, natural and spiritual heritage are defended;
- all peoples have the right to defend their territories from the actions of transnational corporations.

What Are We Fighting Against?

- Imperialism, neo-liberalism, neo-colonialism and patriarchy, and all systems that impoverish life, resources and eco-systems, and the agents that promote the above such as international financial institutions, the World Trade Organization, free trade agreements, transnational corporations, and governments that are antagonistic to their peoples;
- The dumping of food at prices below the cost of production in the global economy;
- The domination of our food and food-producing systems by corporations that place profits before people, health and the environment;
- Technologies and practices that undercut our future food-producing capacities, damage the environment and put our health at risk. Those include transgenic crops and animals, terminator technology, industrial aquaculture and destructive fishing practices, the so-called white revolution of industrial dairy practices, the so-called "old" and "new" Green Revolutions, and the "Green Deserts" of industrial bio-fuel monocultures and other plantations;

- The privatization and commodification of food, basic and public services, knowledge, land, water, seeds, livestock and our natural heritage;
- Development projects/models and extractive industry that displace people and destroy our environments and natural heritage;
- Wars, conflicts, occupations, economic blockades, famines, forced displacement of people and confiscation of their land, and all forces and governments that cause and support them; post disaster and conflict reconstruction programmes that destroy our environments and capacities;
- The criminalization of all those who struggle to protect and defend our rights;
- Food aid that disguises dumping, introduces GMOs into local environments and food systems and creates new colonialism patterns;
- The internationalization and globalization of paternalistic and patriarchal values that marginalise women, diverse agricultural, Indigenous, pastoral and fisher communities around the world.

What Can and Will We Do About It?

Just as we are working with the local community in Sélingué to create a meeting space at Nyéléni, we are committed to building our collective movement for food sovereignty by forging alliances, supporting each other's struggles and extending our solidarity, strengths, and creativity to peoples all over the world who are committed to food sovereignty. Every struggle, in any part of the world for food sovereignty, is our struggle.

We have arrived at a number of collective actions to share our vision of food sovereignty with all peoples of this world, which are elaborated in our synthesis document. We will implement these actions in our respective local areas and regions, in our own movements and jointly in solidarity with other movements. We will share our vision and action agenda for food sovereignty with others who are not able to be with us here in Nyéléni so that the spirit of Nyéléni permeates across the world and becomes a powerful force to make food sovereignty a reality for peoples all over the world.

Finally, we give our unconditional and unwavering support to the peasant movements of Mali and ROPPA in their demands that food sovereignty become a reality in Mali and by extension in all of Africa.

Now is the time for food sovereignty!

Chronology of Major Events

For reference, these are some of the key events discussed in this book. I have included the accession dates for monarchs and heads of state as markers.

> 1215: Magna Carta and Forest Charter
> 1381: Peasants' Revolt (Wat Tyler's rebellion)
> 1485: Wars of the Roses end

1485: Henry VII (House of Tudor)
> 1489: First of many anti-enclosure acts

1509: Henry VIII
> 1516: *Utopia*, by Thomas More
> 1524–1525: German peasant war
> 1536–1541: Dissolution of the monasteries

1547: Edward VI
> 1549: Norfolk (Kett's) Rebellion

1553: Jane Seymour

1553: Mary I (Bloody Mary)

1558: Elizabeth I
> 1563: Statute of Artificers imposes forced labor on unemployed
> 1597: Last anti-enclosure act

1603: James I (House of Stuart)

1607: Midland Revolt

ca.1620–1780: Fenland Resistance

1623: First English colonies established in Caribbean, beginning growth of slave plantations

1624: Most anti-enclosure statutes repealed

1625: Charles I

1626–1632: Western Rising

1642–1649: Civil War

1649: Trial and execution of Charles I

1649: Commonwealth (republic) declared

1649: Leveller movement crushed at Battle of Burford

1649–1650: Digger communities

1652: *The Law of Freedom*, by Gerrard Winstanley

1653: Oliver Cromwell (Lord Protector)

1658: Richard Cromwell (Lord Protector)

1660: Charles II

1660: Royal African Company given monopoly on slave trade

1671: Game Act

1685: James II

1688–1689: "Glorious Revolution" overthrows James II, consolidates Parliamentary precedence over monarchy

1689: William III and Mary II

1688: Slave trade opened to all merchants; slave trade expands rapidly

1702: Anne

1714: George I (House of Hanover)

1723: Black Act establishes death penalty for hundreds of economic crimes

1724: Galloway Levellers' uprising

1727: George II

1745: Jacobite rebellion defeated in Scotland; feudal rights abolished

ca.1750: Lowland clearances begin

1757: East India Company seizes Bengal

1760: George III

1760–1815: Parliamentary enclosures peak in two waves, 1760–1776 and 1792–1815

1770: Bengal famine kills between 7 and 10 million people

1776: *The Wealth of Nations*, by Adam Smith

ca.1790: Highland clearances begin

1792: The Year of the Sheep

1793–1815: England at war with France

1808: Parliament outlaws slave trade but not slavery

ca.1814–1820: Sutherland Clearances

1830: William IV

1832: Reform Act abolishes rotten boroughs (parliamentary constituencies with very few electors), gives vote to small property owners

1834: Parliament abolishes slavery, recompenses slave owners

1834: Parliament passes New Poor Law, imposing forced labor on unemployed

1837–1848: Chartist Movement

1837: Victoria

1846: Corn Laws repealed, eliminating tariffs on imported grain

1846–1850: Irish famine kills 1 million people, forces over 1.5 million to emigrate

1847: *The Communist Manifesto*, by Karl Marx and Frederick Engels

1865: *Value, Price, and Profit*, lecture by Marx to International Workingmen's Association

1867: *Capital*, Volume 1, by Karl Marx

Bibliography

Aitchison, Peter, and Andrew Cassell. *The Lowland Clearances: Scotland's Silent Revolution, 1760–1830*. Origin, 2019.

Alford, Stephen. *Kingship and Politics in the Reign of Edward VI*. Cambridge University Press, 2007.

Allen, Robert C. "The Efficiency and Distributional Consequences of Eighteenth Century Enclosures." *Economic Journal* 92, no. 368 (December 1982): 937–53.

———. "The Nitrogen Hypothesis and the English Agricultural Revolution: A Biological Analysis." 2004. http://www.nuffield.ox.ac.uk/users/allen/unpublished/nitrogen.pdf.

———. *Enclosure and the Yeoman: The Agricultural Development of the South Midlands, 1540–1850*. Clarendon Press, 1992.

———. "Tracking the Agricultural Revolution in England." *The Economic History Review* 52, no. 2 (May 1999): 209–35.

Anderson, Perry. *Lineages of the Absolutist State*. Verso, 1979.

Angus, Ian. "The Fishing Revolution and the Origins of Capitalism." *Monthly Review*. In press, 2023.

Anievas, Alexander, and Kerem Nişancıoğlu. *How the West Came to Rule: The Geopolitical Origins of Capitalism*. Pluto Press, 2015.

Anon. "The Twelve Articles of the Swabian Peasants." German History in Documents and Images, https://germanhistorydocs.ghi-dc.org.

Anon. *The Anti-Projector, or, The History of the Fen Project*. Oxford Text Archive, 2016. https://ota.bodleian.ox.ac.uk/repository/xmlui/

Anon. *Three Letters on the Game Laws*. London, 1818.

Apetrei, Sarah. "'The Evill Masculine Powers': Gender in the Thought of Gerrard Winstanley." *Prose Studies* 36, no. 1 (2014): 52–62.

Appell, G. N. "Hardin's Myth of the Commons: The Tragedy of Conceptual Confusions." Digital Library of the Commons, 1993.

Araghi, Farshad. "The Invisible Hand and the Visible Foot." In *Peasants and Globalization: Political Economy, Rural Transformation and the Agrarian Question*, ed. A. Haroon Akhram-Lodhi and Kay Cristóbal,. Taylor & Francis, 2009. 111–47.

Arbuthnot, John. *An Inquiry Into the Connection Between the Present Price of Provisions, and the Size of Farms*. London: T. Cadell, 1773.

Archer, John E. *By a Flash and a Scare: Arson, Animal Maiming, and Poaching in East Anglia 1815–1870*. Breviary Stuff Publications, 2020.

Baker, Philip, ed. *The Levellers: The Putney Debates*. Verso, 2018.

Barczewski, Stephanie. *Country Houses and the British Empire, 1700–1930*. Manchester University Press, 2014.

Beier, A. L. "Engine of Manufacture: The Trades of London." In *London 1500–1700: The Making of the Metropolis*, ed. Roger Finlay and A. L. Beier, 141–67. Longman, 1986.

Berens, Lewis H. *The Digger Movement in the Days of the Commonwealth*. Simpkin, Marshall, 1906.

Beresford, M. W. "The Lost Villages of Medieval England." *Geographical Journal* 117, no. 2 (June 1951): 129–47.

Berman, Sheri. "Marxism's Fatal Flaw." *Dissent*, May 5, 2018.

Bernstein, Eduard. *Cromwell and Communism: Socialism and Democracy in the Great English Revolution*. Trans. H. J. Stenning. Shocken Books, 1963.

Billingsley, John. *General View of the Agriculture of the County of Somerset*. London: R. Cruttwell, 1798.

Bishton, J. *General View of the Agriculture of the County of Salop*. Brentford: P. Norbury, 1794.

Blackburn, Robin. *The Making of New World Slavery: From the Baroque to the Modern, 1492–1800*. Verso, 2010.

Boulton, Jeremy. "The 'Meaner Sort': Labouring People and the Poor." In *A Social History of England, 1500–1750*, ed. Keith Wrightson, 310–29. Cambridge University Press, 2017.

Bowden, Peter J. *The Wool Trade in Tudor and Stuart England*. Routledge, 2010.

Bowden, Peter. "Agricultural Prices, Farm Profits, and Rents." In *The*

Agrarian History of England and Wales IV, ed. Joan Thirsk, 593–695. Cambridge University Press, 1967.

Boyce, James. *Imperial Mud: The Fight for the Fens.* Icon Books, 2021.

Brailsford, H. N. *The Levellers and the English Revolution*, ed. Christopher Hill. Stanford University Press, 1961.

Brecht, Bertolt. "A Worker Reads History." All Poetry. https://allpoetry.com/.

Bromley, Daniel W., and Michael M. Cernea. *The Management of Common Property Natural Resources: Some Conceptual Operation Fallacies.* World Bank, 1996.

Browne, Randy. *Surviving Slavery in the British Caribbean.* University of Pennsylvania Press, 2017.

Bush, Michael L. *The Government Policy of Protector Somerset.* Edward Arnold, 1975.

Carlin, Norah. *The Causes of the English Civil War.* Blackwell, 1999.

Chambers, J. D., and G. E. Mingay. *The Agricultural Revolution, 1750–1880.* Batsford, 1966.

Chase, Malcolm. *Chartism: A New History.* Manchester University Press, 2013.

Chernikov, G. P. *Fundamentals of Scientific Socialism.* Progress Publishers, 1988.

Clark, Gregory. "Factory Discipline." *Journal of Economic History* 54, no. 1 (March 1994): 128–63.

———. "Too Much Revolution: Agriculture in the Industrial Revolution, 1700–1860." In *The British Industrial Revolution: An Economic Perspective*, ed. Joel Mokyr, 206–40. Routledge, 1999.

Coster, Robert. "A Mite Cast Into the Common Treasury." Radical Pamphlets from the English Civil War, n.d. https://www.exclassics.com/pamphlets/pamph007.htm.

Cox, Susan Jane Buck. "No Tragedy of the Commons." *Environmental Ethics* 7, no. 1 (1985): 49–61.

Crabbe, George. *The Poetical Works of George Crabbe.* A. & W. Galignani, 1829.

Cranmer, Thomas. *The Works of Thomas Cranmer*, ed. John Edmund Cox. Cambridge University Press, 1846.

Crowley, Robert. *The Select Works of Robert Crowley*, ed. J. M. Cowper. Kegan Paul Trench Trubner & Co., 1872.

Cunningham, Timothy. *A New and Complete Law Dictionary.* 3rd ed. Vol. 2. Rivington, Longman, 1783.

Dalrymple, William. *The Anarchy: The East India Company, Corporate Violence, and the Pillage of an Empire.* Bloomsbury, 2021.

Daniels, Stephen, and Briony Mcdonagh. "Enclosure Stories: Narratives from Northamptonshire." *Cultural Geographies* 19, no. 1 (January 2012): 107–21.

Dasgupta, Kalyan. "Uneven Development, the Russian Question and Marxian Paradigm." *Social Scientist* 13, no. 5 (May 1985): 3–18.

Daunton, M. J. *Progress and Poverty: An Economic and Social History of Britain 1700–1850*. Oxford University Press, 1995.

Davidson, Neil. "The Scottish Path to Capitalist Agriculture 1: From the Crisis of Feudalism to the Origins of Agrarian Transformation (1688–1746)." *Journal of Agrarian Change* 4, no. 3 (July 2004): 227–68.

———. "The Scottish Path to Capitalist Agriculture 2: The Capitalist Offensive (1747–1815)." *Journal of Agrarian Change* (August 2004): 411–60.

———. *Discovering the Scottish Revolution, 1692–1746*. Pluto Press, 2003.

Davies, C. S. L. "Slavery and Protector Somerset: The Vagrancy Act of 1547." *Economic History Review* 19, no. 3 (1966): 533.

Davies, Catharine. *A Religion of the Word: The Defence of the Reformation in the Reign of Edward VI*. Manchester University Press, 2002.

Davis, Mike. *Late Victorian Holocausts: El Niño Famines and the Making of the Third World*. Verso, 2002.

Dell'Angelo, Jampel, Grettel Navas, Marga Witteman, Giacomo D'Alisa, Arnim Scheidel, and Leah Temper. "Commons Grabbing and Agribusiness: Violence, Resistance and Social Mobilization." *Ecological Economics* 184 (June 2021).

Devine, T. M. *Scotland's Empire: The Origins of the Global Diaspora*. Penguin, 2004.

———. *The Scottish Clearances: A History of the Dispossessed, 1600–1900*. Penguin, 2019.

Dietz, Brian. "Overseas Trade and Metropolitan Growth." In *London 1500–1700: The Making of the Metropolis*, ed. A. L. Beier and Roger Finlay, 115–40. Longman Group, 1986.

Dimmock, Spencer. "Expropriation and the Political Origins of Agrarian Capitalism in England." In *Case Studies in the Origins of Capitalism*, ed. Xavier Lafrance and Charles Post. Palgrave Macmillan, 2019.

Dobb, Maurice. *Studies in the Development of Capitalism*. Rev. ed. International Publishers, 1963.

Dobson, R. B., ed. *The Peasants' Revolt of 1381*. Macmillan, 1986.

Dow, Alexander. "State of Bengal Under the East India Company." In *History of Hindostan*, 3:lxxi–cxiv. T. Beckett, 1772.

Dyer, Christopher. *An Age of Transition?: Economy and Society in England in the Later Middle Ages*. Clarendon Press, 2005.

Eichner, Carolyn J. *Surmounting the Barricades: Women in the Paris Commune*. Indiana University Press, 2004.

Elton, G. R. *England Under the Tudors*. Methuen, 1962.

Empson, Martin. *Kill All the Gentlemen: Class Struggle and Change in the English Countryside*. Bookmarks, 2018.

Engels, Friedrich. *The Condition of the Working Class in England*. Penguin, 2009.

Estes, Nick. *Our History Is the Future: Standing Rock versus the Dakota Access Pipeline, and the Long Tradition of Indigenous Resistance*. Verso, 2021.

Federici, Silvia. *Re-Enchanting the World: Feminism and the Politics of the Commons*. PM Press, 2018.

Ferguson, Arthur B. *The Articulate Citizen and the English Renaissance*. Duke University Press, 1965.

Finlay, Roger, and Beatrice Shearer. "Population Growth and Urban Expansion." In *London 1500–1700: The Making of the Metropolis*, ed. A. L. Beier and Roger Finlay. Longman, 1986.

Foster, John Bellamy, and Brett Clark. *The Robbery of Nature: Capitalism and the Ecological Rift*. Monthly Review Press, 2020.

Foster, John Bellamy. "The Defense of Nature: Resisting the Financializaton of the Earth." *Monthly Review* 73, no. 11 (April 2022): 1–22.

Foster, John Bellamy, Brett Clark, and Hannah Holleman. "Marx and the Commons." *Social Research* 88, no. 1 (2021): 1–30.

Fowler, Corinne. *Green Unpleasant Land: Creative Responses to Rural Britain's Colonial Connections*. Peepal Tree Press, 2020.

Galeano, Eduardo. *Open Veins of Latin America: Five Centuries of the Pillage of a Continent*. Trans. Cedric Belfrage. Monthly Review Press, 1974.

Gay, Edwin F. "Inclosures in England in the Sixteenth Century." *Quarterly Journal of Economics* 17, no. 4 (August 1903): 576–97.

Gay, Edwin F. "The Inclosure Movement in England." *Publications of the American Economic Association* 6, no. 2 (May 1905): 146–59.

Gay, Edwin F. "The Midland Revolt and the Inquisitions of Depopulation of 1607." *Transactions of the Royal Historical Society* 18 (1904): 195–244.

Hammond, J. L., and Barbara Hammond. *The Village Labourer* (1911). Longmans, 1966.

Handy, Jim. "'Almost Idiotic Wretchedness': A Long History of Blaming Peasants." *Journal of Peasant Studies* 36, no. 2 (April 2009): 325–44.

Handy, Jim. *Apostles of Inequality: Rural Poverty, Political Economy, and The Economist, 1760–1860*. University of Toronto Press, 2022.

Hardin, Garrett. "The Tragedy of the Commons." *Science* 62, no. 3859 (December 13, 1968): 1243–48.

———. *Biology: Its Principles and Implications*. W. H. Freeman, 1978.

Harrison, William. *The Description of England: The Classic Contemporary Account of Tudor Social Life*, ed. Georges Edelen. Washington, DC: Folger Shakespeare Library, 1994.

Hart, David, ed. "An Anthology of Leveller Tracts." Online Library of Liberty, July 14, 2016. https://oll.libertyfund.org/page/leveller-anthology-agreements.

Hatcher, John. *The History of the British Coal Industry*. Vol. 1. Oxford: Clarendon Press, 1993.

Hay, Douglas, Peter Linebaugh, John G. Rule, E. P. Thompson, and Cal Winslow, *Albion's Fatal Tree: Crime and Society in Eighteenth-Century England*. Verso, 2011.

Hay, Douglas. "War, Dearth and Theft in the Eighteenth Century: The Record of the English Courts." *Past and Present* 95, no. 1 (May 1982): 117–60.

Heller, Henry. *The Birth of Capitalism: A Twenty-First Century Perspective*. London: Pluto Press, 2011.

Hickel, Jason. *The Divide: Global Inequality from Conquest to Free Markets*. W. W. Norton, 2017.

Hill, Christopher, and Edmund Dell, eds. *The Good Old Cause: The English Revolution of 1640–1660*. 2nd ed. Routledge, 2012.

Hill, Christopher, ed. *Winstanley: 'The Law of Freedom' and Other Writings*. Cambridge University Press, 1983.

Hill, Christopher. *Change and Continuity in Seventeenth Century England*. London: Weidenfeld and Nicolson, 1974.

Hill, Christopher. *God's Englishman: Oliver Cromwell and the English Revolution*. Harper, 1972.

———. *Liberty Against the Law: Some Seventeenth-Century Controversies*. Verso, 2020.

———. *Puritanism and Revolution: Studies in Interpretation of the English Revolution of the 17th Century*. Schocken Books, 1964.

———. *Reformation to Industrial Revolution: A Social and Economic History of Britain, 1530–1780.* Weidenfeld & Nicolson, 1968.

———. *The Religion of Gerrard Winstanley.* Past and Present Society, 1978.

———. *The World Turned Upside Down: Radical Ideas During the English Revolution.* Pelican Books, 1975.

Hilton, Rodney. *Bond Men Made Free: Medieval Peasant Movements and the English Rising of 1381.* Routledge, 2003.

———. *Class Conflict and the Crisis of Feudalism: Essays in Medieval Social History.* Hambledon Press, 1985.

Hindle, Steve. "Imagining Insurrection in Seventeenth-Century England: Representations of the Midland Rising of 1607." *History Workshop Journal* 66, no. 1 (January 2008): 21–61.

Hobsbawm, E. J., and George Rudé. *Captain Swing.* Verso, 2014.

Hobsbawm, E. J., and Chris Wrigley. *Industry and Empire: The Birth of the Industrial Revolution.* New Press, 1999.

Holleman, Hannah. *Dust Bowls of Empire: Imperialism, Environmental Politics, and the Injustice of "Green" Capitalism.* Yale University Press, 2018.

Holstun, James. *Ehud's Dagger: Class Struggle in the English Revolution.* Verso, 2002.

Holstun, Jim. "Utopia Pre-Empted: Ketts Rebellion, Commoning, and the Hysterical Sublime." *Historical Materialism* 16, no. 3 (2008): 3–53.

Hoskins, W. G. *The Age of Plunder: the England of Henry VIII 1500–1547.* Kindleed, Sapere Books, 2020.

———. *The Midland Peasant: The Economic and Social History of a Leicestershire Village.* Macmillan, 1965.

Humphries, Jane. "Enclosures, Common Rights, and Women: The Proletarianization of Families in the Late Eighteenth and Early Nineteenth Centuries." *Journal of Economic History* (March 1990): 17–42.

Hunter, James. *The Making of the Crofting Community.* John Donald, 1976.

Huxtable, Sally-Anne. "Wealth, Power and the Global Country House." In *Interim Report on the Connections between Colonialism and Properties Now in the Care of the National Trust, Including Links with Historic Slavery,* ed. Sally-Anne Huxtable, Corinne Fowler, Christo Kefalas, and Emma Slocombe, 7–14. National Trust, 2020.

Inikori, Joseph E. "Market Structure and the Profits of the British African Trade in the Late Eighteenth Century." *Journal of Economic History*, December 1981, 745–76.

Kedrosky, Davis. "Allen's Pause: The British Agricultural Revolution at Bay, 1740–1800." Great Transformations, August 2, 2021. https://daviskedrosky.substack.com/p/allens–pause.

Kerridge, Eric. *The Agricultural Revolution*. Routledge, 2005.

Kinealy, Christine. *A New History of Ireland*. History Press, 2008.

Kussmaul, Ann. *Servants in Husbandry in Early Modern England*. Cambridge University Press, 1981.

Kuusinen, Otto. *Fundamentals of Marxism-Leninism Manual*. Foreign Languages Publishing House, 1961.

Latimer, Hugh. *Sermons by Hugh Latimer*. Christian Classics Ethereal Library, n.d. https://ccel.org/ccel/latimer/sermons/sermons.ii.ii.html.

Lindert, Peter H. "Who Owned Victorian England? The Debate over Landed Wealth and Inequality." *Agricultural History* 61, no. 4 (1987): 25–51.

Lindley, Keith. *Fenland Riots and the English Revolution*. Heinemann, 1982.

Linebaugh, Peter, and Marcus Rediker. *The Many-Headed Hydra: Sailors, Slaves, Commoners, and the Hidden History of the Revolutionary Atlantic*. Beacon Press, 2013.

Linebaugh, Peter. *Stop, Thief! The Commons, Enclosures and Resistance*. PM Press, 2014.

Linebaugh, Peter. *The Magna Carta Manifesto: Liberties and Commons for All*. University of California Press, 2008.

Livingston, Alistair. Thesis. "The Galloway Levellers—A Study of the Origins, Events and Consequences of Their Actions." University of Glasgow, 2009.

Locke, John. "Second Treatise of Government." Project Gutenberg, December 25, 2021. https://www.gutenberg.org/.

Loewenstein, David. "Afterword: Why Winstanley Still Matters." *Prose Studies* 36, no. 1 (2014): 90–96.

Luxemburg, Rosa. *The Accumulation of Capital*. Trans. Agnes Schwarzchild. Routledge, 2003.

———. *The Rosa Luxemburg Reader*. Ed. Peter Hudis and Kevin B. Anderson. Monthly Review Press, 2004.

MacCulloch, Diarmaid, and Anthony Fletcher. *Tudor Rebellions*. 6th ed. Routledge, 2016.

MacKinnnon, Iain, and Andrew Mackillop. *Plantation Slavery and*

Landownership in the West Highlands and Islands: Legacies and Lessons. Community Land Scotland, 2020.

Macpherson, C. B. *The Political Theory of Possessive Individualism: Hobbes to Locke.* Oxford University Press, 1962.

Malm, Andreas. *Fossil Capital: The Rise of Steam Power and the Roots of Global Warming.* Verso, 2016.

Mandel, Ernest. *Marxist Economic Theory.* Vol. 2. Trans. Brian Pearce. Monthly Review Press, 1968.

Manning, Brian. "A Voice for the Poor." *International Socialism*, no. 72 (September 1996).

———. *1649: The Crisis of the English Revolution.* Bookmarks, 1992.

———. *Aristocrats, Plebeians and Revolution in England 1640–1660.* Pluto Press, 1996.

Manning, Brian. *The English People and the English Revolution.* Bookmarks, 1991.

———. *The Far Left in the English Revolution, 1640 to 1660.* Bookmarks, 1999.

Manning, Roger B. *Village Revolts: Social Protest and Popular Disturbances in England, 1509–1640.* Oxford: Clarendon Press, 1988.

Marshall, P. J. *East Indian Fortunes: The British in Bengal in the Eighteenth Century.* Clarendon Press, 1976.

Martin, John E. *Feudalism to Capitalism: Peasant and Landlord in English Agrarian Development.* Macmillan, 1986.

Marx, Karl, and Frederick Engels. *Collected Works (MECW).* 50 vols. International Publishers, 1975–2004.

Marx, Karl. *Capital: A Critique of Political Economy.* Vol. 1. Trans. Ben Fowkes. Penguin Books, 1976.

———. *Capital: A Critique of Political Economy.* Vol. 3. Trans. David Fernbach. Penguin, 1981.

———. *Grundrisse: Introduction to the Critique of Political Economy.* Trans. Martin Nicolaus. Penguin, 1973.

———. *Pre-Capitalist Economic Formations.* International Publishers, 1965.

McDonagh, Briony, and Stephen Daniels. "Enclosure Stories: Narratives from Northamptonshire." *Cultural Geographies* 19, no. 1 (2012): 107–21.

McLeod, Donald. *Gloomy Memories in the Highlands of Scotland.* Archibald Sinclair, 1892.

McLynn, Frank. *Crime and Punishment in Eighteenth-Century England.* Routledge, 1989.

Meredith, David, and Deborah Oxley. "Nutrition and Health, 1700–1870." In *The Cambridge Economic History of Modern Britain* 1, ed. Roderick Floud, Jane Humphries, and Paul Johnson, 1:118–48. Cambridge University Press, 2014.

Middleton, John. *View of the Agriculture of Middlesex.* Macmillan, 1798.

Mill, John Stuart. *Principles of Political Economy.* Longmans, Green, Reader and Dyer, 1867.

Mokyr, Joel. *Why Ireland Starved: A Quantitative and Analytical History of the Irish Economy, 1800–1850.* Allen & Unwin, 1983.

More, Thomas. *Utopia.* Ed. George M. Logan. Trans. Robert M. Adams. 3rd ed. Cambridge University Press, 2016.

Muldew, Craig. "'Th'Ancient Distaff' and 'Whirling Spindle': Measuring the Contribution of Spinning to Household Earnings and the National Economy in England, 1550–1770." *Economic History Review* 65, no. 2 (2012): 498–526.

Munsche, P. B. *Gentlemen and Poachers: The English Game Laws, 1671–1831.* Cambridge University Press, 2008.

———. "The Gamekeeper and English Rural Society, 1660–1830." *Journal of British Studies* 20, no. 2 (1981): 82–105.

Neeson, J. M. *Commoners: Common Right, Enclosure and Social Change in England, 1700–1820.* Cambridge University Press, 1993.

Nef, J. U. "The Progress of Technology and the Growth of Large-Scale Industry in Great Britain, 1540–1640." *Economic History Review* 5, no. 1 (October 1934): 3–24.

Nef, John U. *The Rise of the British Coal Industry.* Vol. 1. Frank Cass, 1966.

Nelson, Louis P. *Architecture and Empire in Jamaica.* Yale University Press, 2016.

Neudert, Regina, and Lieske Voget-Kleschin. *What Are the Effects of Large-Scale Land Acquisitions in Africa on Selected Economic and Social Indicators?* Bischöfliches Hilfswerk MISEREOR, 2021.

Nicholas, Stephen, and Deborah Oxley. "The Living Standards of Women during the Industrial Revolution, 1795–1820." *Economic History Review* 46, no. 4 (November 1993): 723–49.

Nourse, Timothy. *Campania Foelix [1699].* University of Illinois: Text Creation Partnership, n.d. http://name.umdl.umich.edu/A52534.0001.001.

Oswald, John. *Review of the Constitution of Great Britain.* 3rd ed. London, 1792.

Otter, Chris. *Diet for a Large Planet: Industrial Britain, Food Systems, and World Ecology.* University of Chicago Press, 2020.

Overton, Mark. "Re-Establishing the English Agricultural Revolution." *Agricultural History Review* 44, no. 1 (1996): 1–20.

———. *Agricultural Revolution in England: The Transformation of the Agrarian Economy, 1500–1850.* Cambridge University Press, 1996.

Owen, Robert. *The Life of Robert Owen, Written by Himself.* Vol. 1. Effingham Wilson, 1857.

Patnaik, Utsa, and Prabhat Patnaik. "The Drain of Wealth." *Monthly Review* (February 2021).

———. *Capital and Imperialism: Theory, History, and the Present.* Monthly Review Press, 2021.

Patnaik, Utsa, Sam Moyo, and Issa G. Shivji. *The Agrarian Question in the Neoliberal Era: Primitive Accumulation and the Peasantry.* Pambazuka Press, 2011.

Patnaik, Utsa. "New Estimates of 18th-Century British Trade and Their Relation to Transfers from Tropical Colonies." In *The Making of History*, ed. K. N. Panikkar, Terence J. Byres, and Utsa Patnaik, 359–402. Anthem South Asian Studies, 2002.

Perelman, Michael. "Marx, Malthus, and the Concept of Natural Resource Scarcity." *Antipode* (September 1979): 80–91.

———. *The Invention of Capitalism: Classical Political Economy and the Secret History of Primitive Accumulation.* Duke University Press, 2000.

Polanyi, Karl. *The Great Transformation: The Political and Economic Origins of Our Time.* Beacon Press, 2001.

Pomeranz, Kenneth. *The Great Divergence: China, Europe, and the Making of the Modern World Economy.* Princeton University Press, 2000.

Poor Law Commissioners. *The First Report of the Commissioners for Inquiring Into the Administration and Operation of the Poor Laws in 1834.* HMSO, 1894.

Prebble, John. *Culloden.* Penguin, 1967.

Prothero, John. *English Farming, Past and Present.* Longmans, Green, 1912.

Radzinowicz, L. "The Waltham Black Act: A Study of the Legislative Attitude towards Crime in the Eighteenth Century." *Cambridge Law Journal* 9, no. 1 (1945): 56–81.

Ravenstone, Piercy. *A Few Doubts as to the Correctness of Some Opinions*

Generally Entertained on the Subjects of Population and Political Economy. J. Andrews, 1821.

Rediker, Marcus. *Between the Devil and the Deep Blue Sea: Merchant Seamen, Pirates and the Anglo-American Maritime World, 1700–1750.* Cambridge University Press, 1987.

Richards, Eric. *The Highland Clearances: People, Landlords and Rural Turmoil.* Edinburgh: Birlinn, 2016.

Robins, Nick. *The Corporation That Changed the World.* Pluto Press, 2006.

Rodney, Walter. *How Europe Underdeveloped Africa.* Pambazuka Press, 2012.

Rogers, Pat. "The Waltham Blacks and the Black Act." *Historical Journal* 17, no. 3 (1974): 465–86.

Rogers, Thorold. *A History of Agriculture and Prices in England, from the Year After the Oxford Parliament (1259) to the Commencement of the Continental War (1793).* Vol. 5. Clarendon Press, 1887.

Rusticus. "Sketch of a General Inclosure Bill." *Commercial Agricultural and Manufacturer's Magazine,* September 1800.

Sabine, George H., ed. *The Works of Gerrard Winstanley.* Cornell University Press, 1941.

Schofield, R. S., and E. A. Wrigley. *The Population History of England 1541–1871: A Reconstruction.* Edward Arnold, 1981.

Scruton, Thomas Edward. *Commons and Common Fields.* Batoche Books, 2003.

Shanin, Teodor, ed. *Late Marx and the Russian Road: Marx and "The Peripheries of Capitalism."* Monthly Review Press, 1983.

Sharp, Buchanan. *In Contempt of All Authority: Rural Artisans and Riot in the West of England, 1586–1660.* University of California Press, 1980.

Smith, Adam. *The Wealth of Nations.* Modern Library, 2000.

Smout, T. C. "The Landowner and the Planned Village in Scotland, 1730–1830." In *Scotland in the Age of Improvement,* ed. N. T. Phillipson and Rosalind Mitchison, 73–102. Edinburgh University Press, 1970.

Snell, Keith D. M. *Annals of the Labouring Poor: Social Change and Agrarian England: 1660–1900.* Cambridge University Press, 1985.

Somers, Robert. *Letters from the Highlands; or, The Famine of 1847.* Simpkin, Marshall, & Co., 1848.

Stedile, João Pedro. "We Only Have One Planet—Defending It Will

Require Collective Measures." *Monthly Review* (July, 2022): 86–91.

Stone, Lawrence. *The Crisis of the Aristocracy, 1558–1641*. Oxford University Press, 1965.

Sturt, George. *Change in the Village*. Doran, 1912.

Sullivan, Dylan, and Jason Hickel. "Capitalism and Extreme Poverty: A Global Analysis of Real Wages, Human Height, and Mortality since the Long 16th Century." *World Development* 161 (January 2023).

Tawney, R. H. "Introduction." In *Fenland Farming in the Sixteenth Century*, ed. Joan Thirsk, 3–6. Leicester University Press, 1965.

——. *Religion and the Rise of Capitalism: A Historical Study*. Angelico Press, 2021.

——. *The Agrarian Problem in the Sixteenth Century*. Lector House, 2021.

Tawney, R. H., and E. E. Power, eds. *Tudor Economic Documents*. Vol. 3. London: Longmans, Green, 1924.

Tharoor, Shashi. *An Age of Darkness: The British Empire in India*. Aleph, 2016.

Thirsk, Joan, ed. *Agricultural Change: Policy and Practice, 1500–1750*. Cambridge University Press, 1990.

Thompson, E. P. *Customs in Common*. New Press, 1991.

——. *The Making of the English Working Class*. Penguin, 1991.

——. *The Poverty of Theory, qnd Other Essays*. Merlin Press, 1978.

—— *Whigs and Hunters: The Origin of the Black Act*. Breviary Stuff Publications, 2013.

Tilley, Morris Palmer. *A Dictionary of the Proverbs in England in the Sixteenth and Seventeenth Centuries*. University of Michigan Press, 1950.

Townsend, Joseph. "A Dissertation on the Poor Laws (1786)." https://socialsciences.mcmaster.ca/econ/ugcm/3ll3/townsend/poorlaw.html.

Trotsky, Leon. *The History of the Russian Revolution*. Trans. Max Eastman. 3 vols. Sphere, 1967.

——. *The Young Lenin*. Trans. Max Eastman. Doubleday, 1972.

Walpole, Horace. *The Letters of Horace Walpole*. Vol. 8. Ed. P. Toynbee. Oxford University Press, 1905.

Walvin, James. *Making the Black Atlantic: Britain and the African Diaspora*. Bloomsbury, 2018.

Watters, Frances M. "The Peasant and the Village Commune." In *The*

Peasant in Nineteenth-Century Russia, ed. Wayne S. Vucinich, 133–57. Stanford University Press, 1988.

Webb, Darren. "The Bitter Product of Defeat? Reflections on Winstanley's Law of Freedom." *Political Studies* 52, no. 2 (2004): 199–215.

Weis, Tony. *The Global Food Economy: The Battle for the Future of Farming*. Zed Books, 2007.

Whatley, Christopher A. *The Industrial Revolution in Scotland*. Cambridge University Press, 1997.

Williams, Eric. *Capitalism and Slavery*. Penguin, 2022.

Williams, Raymond. *The Country and the City*. Vintage, 2016.

Winstanley, Gerrard. *The Law of Freedom, and Other Writings*. Ed. Christopher Hill. Penguin, 1973.

———. *The Complete Works of Gerrard Winstanley*. Ed. Thomas N. Corns, Ann Hughes, and David Loewenstein. Vol. 1. Oxford University Press, 2009.

Wood, Andy. *Riot, Rebellion and Popular Politics in Early Modern England*. Palgrave, 2002.

———. *The 1549 Rebellions and the Making of Early Modern England*. Cambridge University Press, 2007.

Wrightson, Keith. *Earthly Necessities: Economic Lives in Early Modern Britain*. Yale University Press, 2000.

Wrigley, Edward A., and Roger S. Schofield. *The Population History of England: 1541–1871; a Reconstruction*. Cambridge University Press, 2002.

Yerby, George. *The Economic Causes of the English Civil War: Freedom of Trade and the English Revolution*. New York: Routledge, 2020.

Young, Arthur, ed. *Annals of Agriculture and Other Useful Arts* xxxvi, 1801.

Young, Arthur. *An Inquiry into the Propriety of Applying Wastes to the Better Maintenance and Support of the Poor*. J. Rackham, 1801.

———. *The Autobiography of Arthur Young*. London: Smith, Elder, 1898.

Žmolek Michael Andrew. *Rethinking the Industrial Revolution: Five Centuries of Transition from Agrarian to Industrial Capitalism in England*. Haymarket, 2014.

Notes

REFERENCES

Abbreviations used for frequently cited works:

Capital 1 Marx, Karl. *Capital: A Critique of Political Economy*. Translated by Ben Fowkes. Vol. 1. Penguin Books, 1976.

Capital 3 Marx, Karl. *Capital: A Critique of Political Economy*. Translated by David Fernbach. Vol. 3. Penguin, 1981.

MECW Marx, Karl, and Frederick Engels. *Collected Works*. 50 vols. International Publishers, 1975–2004.

CWGW Winstanley, Gerrard. *The Complete Works of Gerrard Winstanley*. Edited by Thomas N. Corns, Ann Hughes, and David Loewenstein. Vol. 1. Oxford University Press, 2009.

LFOW Winstanley, Gerrard. *The Law of Freedom, and Other Writings* Edited by Christopher Hill. Penguin, 1973.

1. Introduction

1. *Capital 1*, 273.
2. *Capital 1*, 928.
3. *Capital 1*, 875–76.
4. *Capital 1*, 874.

1. "Systematic Theft of Communal Property"

1. Harrison, *The Description of England*, 217.
2. Holstun, "Utopia Pre-Empted," 5.
3. Quoted in Empson, *Kill All the Gentlemen*, 162.
4. MacCulloch and Fletcher, *Tudor Rebellions*, 70.

5. Wood, *Riot, Rebellion and Popular Politics*, 66–67.
6. *Capital 1*, 886.
7. Foster, Clark, and Holleman, "Marx and the Commons," 2–3.
8. Linebaugh, *The Magna Carta Manifesto*, 21–45.
9. Neeson, *Commoners*, 158–59.
10. Hilton, *Class Conflict and the Crisis of Feudalism*, 139–51.
11. Hilton, *Bond Men Made Free*, 32.
12. Hilton, *Bond Men Made Free*, 34.
13. Hardin, "The Tragedy of the Commons," *Science*, December 13, 1968.
14. Hardin, *Biology: Its Principles and Implications*, 707.
15. Bromley and Cernea, "Management of Common Property Natural Resources," 6.
16. Appell, "Hardin's Myth of the Commons."
17. Cox, "No Tragedy of the Commons," 60.
18. Neeson, *Commoners*, 112–13.
19. Neeson, *Commoners*, 117.
20. Neeson, *Commoners*, 118–20.
21. Neeson, *Commoners*, 132.
22. Neeson, *Commoners*, 157.
23. *Capital 3*, 959.
24. For an insightful summary and critique of the major positions in those debates, see Heller, *The Birth of Capitalism*.
25. Marx, *Grundrisse*, 510.
26. Hoskins, *Midland Peasant*, 141.
27. Overton, *Agricultural Revolution in England*, 8, 21.
28. More, *Utopia*, 19.
29. Myers, ed., *English Historical Documents, 1327–1485*, vol. 4, 1031. "Emparking" meant converting farmland into private forests or parks, where landlords could hunt.
30. Myers, ed., *English Historical Documents, 1327–1485*, vol. 4, 1029.
31. More, *Utopia*, 19–20.
32. Tawney, *Agrarian Problem*, 7.
33. Tawney, *Agrarian Problem*, 110.
34. Tawney and Power, eds., *Tudor Economic Documents*, vol. 1, 39, 41.
35. Tawney, *Agrarian Problem*, 124, 175.
36. Quoted in Beresford, "The Lost Villages," 132.
37. Dimmock, "Expropriation," 52.
38. Martin, *Feudalism to Capitalism*, 131.
39. Martin, *Feudalism to Capitalism*, 133.
40. Tawney, *Agrarian Problem*, 272–73.
41. *Capital 1*, 883.
42. Anderson, *Lineages of the Absolutist State*, 124–25.

43. Linebaugh, *The Magna Carta Manifesto*, 49.
44. Hill, *Reformation to Industrial Revolution*, 47–48.
45. Thirsk, *Agricultural Change*, 69.
46. Quoted in Scruton, *Commons and Common Fields*, 73.
47. Gay, "Inclosures in England in the Sixteenth Century," 576–97; "The Inclosure Movement in England," 146–59.
48. Gay, "Midland Revolt," 234, 237.
49. Elton, *England under the Tudors*, 78–80.
50. Tawney, *Agrarian Problem*, 166.
51. Martin, *Feudalism to Capitalism*, 132–38.
52. Hoskins, *Age of Plunder*, loc. 1256.
53. Yerby, *Economic Causes of the English Civil War*, 48.
54. Dyer, *An Age of Transition?*, 66.
55. Hill, *Reformation to Industrial Revolution*, 51.
56. Proceedings in the Commons, 1601: November 2–5.
57. Hill, *Reformation to Industrial Revolution*, 51.
58. Wrightson, *Earthly Necessities*, 162.
59. Peter Bowden, "Agricultural Prices, Farm Profits, and Rents," in Thirsk, ed., *Agrarian History of England and Wales*, vol. 4, 695, 690, 621.

2. "Cormorants and Greedy Gulls"

1. Cranmer, "A Sermon on Rebellion," *Works*, 196. The date 1550 is approximate.
2. Isaiah 5:8–9. English Standard Version.
3. Polanyi, *The Great Transformation*, 178.
4. Ferguson, *The Articulate Citizen*, xiii.
5. Tawney, *Religion and the Rise of Capitalism*, 140–41.
6. Latimer, "First Sermon Preached before King Edward, March 8, 1549," *Sermons*.
7. Quoted in Scruton, *Commons and Common Fields*, 81–82.
8. Crowley, "The Way to Wealth," *Select Works*, 132–33.
9. Crowley, "An information and petition," *Select Works*, 162, 157.
10. Davies, *A Religion of the Word*, 159.
11. Cranmer, "A Sermon on Rebellion," *Works*, 192, 193.
12. Latimer, "Fourth Sermon upon the Lord's Prayer (1552)," *Sermons*.
13. *MECW*, vol. 6, 494, 355.
14. Bush, *Government Policy of Protector Somerset*, 61.
15. Ferguson, *The Articulate Citizen*, 248.
16. Tawney, *Religion and the Rise of Capitalism*, 135.
17. Tawney, *Religion and the Rise of Capitalism*, 146–47.
18. Wrightson, *Earthly Necessities*, 202.
19. Stone, *Crisis of the Aristocracy*, 188, 189–90.

20. Macpherson, *Political Theory of Possessive Individualism*, passim.

3. Vagabonds, Migrants, and Wage Labor

1. Brecht, "A Worker Reads History" *All Poetry*, https://allpoetry. com/A–Worker–Reads–History.
2. *Capital 1*, 272–73.
3. *Capital 1*, 273.
4. Hill, *Liberty Against the Law*, 66.
5. Hill, *Change and Continuity*, 221, 237.
6. Kussmaul, *Servants in Husbandry*, 3, 4.
7. Kussmaul, *Servants in Husbandry*, 9.
8. Wood, *Riot, Rebellion and Popular Politics*, 83.
9. Humphries, "Enclosures, Common Rights, and Women," 21. Humphries's research focused on the 1700s, but her remarks apply with equal force to earlier years.
10. Boulton, "The 'Meaner Sort,'" in Wrightson, ed., *A Social History of England, 1500–1750*, 310–30.
11. Dobb, *Studies in the Development of Capitalism*, 233.
12. Rogers, *A History of Agriculture and Prices in England*, vol. 5, 628.
13. Tawney, *Agrarian Problem*, 33.
14. Quoted in Davies, "Slavery and Protector Somerset," 534.
15. *Capital 1*, 899.
16. Manning, *English People and the English Revolution*, 187–88. By-employment was occasional work.
17. No one knows exactly how many people immigrated and emigrated, because no one kept records. These figures are from Wrigley and Schofield, *Population History of England*, 219–28.
18. Finlay and Shearer, "Population Growth and Suburban Expansion," in Beier and Finlay, eds., *London 1500–1700*, 38. Other estimates of London's 1700 population range as high as 575,000.
19. Dietz, "Overseas Trade and Metropolitan Growth," in Beier and Finlay, eds., *London 1500–1700*, 129.
20. Beier, "Engine of Manufacture," in Beier and Finlay, eds., *London 1500–1700*, 163.
21. Ibid, 148.
22. Wrightson, *Earthly Necessities*, 313.
23. Manning, *Aristocrats, Plebeians and Revolution*, 62.
24. Ian Angus, "Fishing Revolution," *Monthly Review*, in press.
25. Linebaugh and Rediker, *Many-Headed Hydra*, 150.
26. Rediker, *Between the Devil and the Deep Blue Sea*, 290.
27. Wrightson, *Earthly Necessities*, 172.
28. Malm, *Fossil Capital*, 48.

29. Wrightson, *Earthly Necessities,* 170–71. A "staithe" was a wharf built specifically for transshipping coal.
30. Nef, "Progress of Technology," 14.
31. Hatcher, *History of the British Coal Industry,* 350.
32. Bowden, *Wool Trade in Tudor and Stuart England,* xv; Supple, *Commercial Crisis and Change in England,* 6.
33. Muldew, "'Th'ancient Distaff' and 'Whirling Spindle,'" 518, 523.
34. Manning, *Aristocrats, Plebeians and Revolution,* 62.
35. Manning, *1649,* 71–72.
36. *Capital 1,* 876.

4. "Here Were We Born and Here We Will Die"
1. Quoted in Alford, *Kingship and Politics,* 60.
2. Quotations in Wood, *1549 Rebellions,* 49.
3. Engels, "Peasant War in Germany" (1850) in *MECW,* vol. 10, 410.
4. Anon., "Twelve Articles of the Swabian Peasants, 1525."
5. Manning, *Village Revolts,* 3.
6. Mcdonagh and Daniels, "Enclosure Stories," 113.
7. Carlin, *Causes of the English Civil War,* 129.
8. Tawney, *Agrarian Problem,* 76.
9. Nef, *Rise of the British Coal Industry,* vol. 1, 342–43, 310.
10. Nef, *Rise of the British Coal Industry,* vol. 1, 312, 316–17, 291–92. See also Malm, *Fossil Capital,* 320–24.
11. Sharp, *In Contempt of All Authority,* 264.
12. Hindle, "Imagining Insurrection," 31.
13. Such figures appeared frequently in rural uprisings in England; later examples included Lady Skimmington, Ned Ludd, and Captain Swing.
14. Empson, *"Kill All the Gentlemen,"* 165.
15. Martin, *Feudalism to Capitalism,* 173.
16. Sharp, *In Contempt of All Authority,* 84–85.
17. Sharp, *In Contempt of All Authority,* 86.
18. Sharp, *In Contempt of All Authority,* 144.
19. Tawney, "Introduction," in Thirsk, *Fenland Farming in the Sixteenth Century,* 4.
20. Anon., *The Anti-Projector, or, The History of the Fen Project.*
21. Boyce, *Imperial Mud,* Kindle ed., loc. 840.
22. Manning, *English People and the English Revolution,* 194.
23. Lindley, *Fenland Riots,* 147.
24. Boyce, *Imperial Mud,* Kindle ed., loc. 1631–61.
25. Quoted in Boyce, *Imperial Mud,* Kindle ed., loc. 2243.
26. Boyce, *Imperial Mud,* Kindle ed., loc. 3036.

5. Diggers: "A Common Treasury for All"

1.   "The New Law of Righteousness," *CWGW*, 55–56.
2.   Manning, *Aristocrats, Plebeians and Revolution*, 1.
3.   Manning, *English People*, 195.
4.   "General Order for Possessions, to Secure Them from Riots and Tumults," *House of Lords Journal*, vol. 4, July 13, 1641.
5.   Lindley, *Fenland Riots*, 68.
6.   Sharp, *In Contempt of All Authority*, 228.
7.   Quoted in Lindley, *Fenland Riots*, 149.
8.   Manning, *Far Left in the English Revolution*, 130.
9.   Hill and Dell, eds., *Good Old Cause*, 424.
10. Hill, *Puritanism and Revolution*, 191.
11. Hart, ed., *Anthology of Leveller Tracts*.
12. *Tracts on Liberty by the Levellers and their Critics*, vol. 5 (1648).
13. Brailsford, *Levellers and the English Revolution*, 449–50.
14. "The True Levellers Standard Advanced," *WLOF*, 84.
15. Loewenstein, "Afterword: Why Winstanley Still Matters," 90.
16. Manning, *1649*, 79–80.
17. Quoted in Berens, *Digger Movement*, 151.
18. Bernstein, *Cromwell and Communism*, 131–32.
19. "The New Law of Righteousness," *GWCW*, 567.
20. "Fire in the Bush," *WLOF*, 214.
21. "The New Law of Righteousness," *GWCW*, 519.
22. "The New Law of Righteousness," *GWCW*, 506–7.
23. "A Watchword to the City of London and the Armie," *WLOF*, 127.
24. "A Watchword to the City of London and the Armie," *WLOF*, 127–8.
25. "An Appeal to the House of Commons," *WLOF*, 115, 116.
26. "The New Law of Righteousness," *GWCW*, 516–17.
27. Hill, *Change and Continuity*, 233.
28. Manning, *1649*, 119–20.
29. Coster, "A Mite Cast Into the Common Treasury."
30. "A New-Yeers Gift for the Parliament and Armie," *WLOF*, 173.
31. "The Law of Freedom in a Platform," *WLOF*, 285.
32. "The Law of Freedom in a Platform," *WLOF*, 312. Emphasis added.
33. Hill, *The World Turned Upside Down*, 97.
34. Hill, *The Religion of Gerrard Winstanley*, 40.
35. "The Law of Freedom in a Platform," *WLOF*, 285.
36. "An Appeal to the House of Commons," *WLOF*, 115. "Norman" refers to the view that the English had been free until the Norman Conquest in 1066, and that landlords were descendants of the Normans.
37. Webb, "The Bitter Product of Defeat?" 203.

38. "The Law of Freedom in a Platform," *WLOF*, 275–76.
39. "A New-Yeers Gift Sent to the Parliament and Armie," *WLOF,* 108, 112.
40. "The Law of Freedom in a Platform," *WLOF*, 276–77.
41. "The Law of Freedom in a Platform," *WLOF*, 276.
42. "The Law of Freedom in a Platform," *WLOF*, 282.
43. "The Law of Freedom in a Platform," *WLOF*, 287.
44. "The Law of Freedom in a Platform," *WLOF*, 295.
45. "The Law of Freedom in a Platform," *WLOF*, 295.
46. Macpherson, *Political Theory of Possessive Individualism,* 157.
47. "The Law of Freedom in a Platform," *WLOF*, 278.
48. "The Law of Freedom in a Platform," *WLOF*, 338–41, passim.
49. "The Law of Freedom in a Platform," *WLOF*, 295.
50. "The Law of Freedom in a Platform," *WLOF*, 320.
51. "The Law of Freedom in a Platform," *WLOF*, 368–69.
52. "The Law of Freedom in a Platform," *WLOF*, 381, 388.
53. "The Law of Freedom in a Platform," *WLOF*. 334.
54. "The Law of Freedom in a Platform," *WLOF*, 388.
55. Apetrei, "'The Evill Masculine Powers,'" 53.
56. Holstun, *Ehud's Dagger*, 377, 389. Emphasis added.
57. Empson, *Kill All the Gentlemen,* 196.
58. Baker, ed., *Levellers: The Putney Debates*, 73.
59. Manning, *1649*, 11.
60. Hill, *God's Englishman,* 260.

6. Empire and Expropriation

1. *Capital 1*, 915.
2. *Capital 1*, 918.
3. Hickel, *The Divide*, 94.
4. Williams, *Capitalism and Slavery*, 48.
5. Inikori, "Market Structure and the Profits of the British African Trade," 745.
6. Nelson, *Architecture and Empire in Jamaica*, 105.
7. Browne, *Surviving Slavery,* 3.
8. Smith, *Wealth of Nations*, 418.
9. See http://rowanwilliams.archbishopofcanterbury.org/articles.php/1432/slavery–is–gods–grief–sermon–at–westminster–abbey.html.
10. Blackburn, *Making of New World Slavery,* 542.
11. Huxtable et al., *Interim Report*, 13.
12. Davis, *Late Victorian Holocausts*, 311.
13. Walpole, *Letters*, 157.
14. Robins, *Corporation That Changed the World*, 3.
15. Ibid., 176.

16. Dow, *History of Hindostan*, vol. 3, lxx, lxxi.
17. Dalrymple, *The Anarchy*, 220–21.
18. Dalrymple, *The Anarchy*, 219–220.
19. Dalrymple, *The Anarchy*, 222.
20. U. Patnaik and P. Patnaik, "The Drain of Wealth," 3.
21. Quoted in Tharoor, *An Age of Darkness*, 11.
22. Fowler, *Green Unpleasant Land*, 44.
23. Mandel, *Marxist Economic Theory*, vol. 2, 443–44.
24. U. Patnaik, "New Estimates of 18th-Century British Trade and Their Relation to Transfers from Tropical Colonies," in *The Making of History*, ed. K. N. Panikkar et al., Table 5, 389.
25. Barczewski, *Country Houses and the British Empire*, 71, 15, 69–89.
26. Williams, *Capitalism and Slavery*, 86.
27. Marshall, *East Indian Fortunes*, 256.
28. Williams, *The Country and the City*, 150.
29. Walvin, *Making the Black Atlantic*, 106.
30. Huxtable et al., *Interim Report*.
31. MacKinnnon and Mackillop, *Plantation Slavery and Landownership in the West Highlands and Islands*, 7, 10, 18–19.
32. *Capital 1*, 925.

7. "A Plain Enough Case of Class Robbery"

1.   *Capital 1*, 889.
2.   Thompson, *Poverty of Theory*, 48.
3.   Thompson, *Whigs and Hunters*, 1.
4.   Hobsbawm and Wrigley, *Industry and Empire*, 7.
5.   *Capital 1*, 885.
6.   Oswald, *Review of the Constitution*, 20.
7.   Hammond and Hammond, *The Village Labourer*, 43.
8.   Hammond and Hammond, *The Village Labourer*, 38.
9.   Hammond and Hammond, *The Village Labourer*, 45.
10. Neeson, *Commoners*, 257.
11. Thompson, *Making of the English Working Class*, 237–38.
12. Hobsbawm and Wrigley, *Industry and Empire*, 7.
13. 9 George III, ca. 29.
14. Neeson, *Commoners*, 321–22.
15. Neeson, *Commoners*, 278–79.
16. *Capital 1*, 885.
17. Thompson, *Whigs and Hunters*, 88.

8. "The Lords and Lairds May Drive Us Out"

1.   Marx, *The Poverty of Philosophy*, *MECW*, vol. 6, 173.

2. Trotsky, *The History of the Russian Revolution*, vol. 1, 22.
3. Davidson, "Scottish Path 2," 415.
4. Davidson, "Scottish Path 1," 227.
5. Davidson, "How was this kingdom united?"
6. Davidson, "Scottish Path 2," 419.
7. Davidson, "Scottish Path 2," 416.
8. Davidson, "Scottish Path 1," 227.
9. Symson, *Large Description of Galloway*, quoted in Livingston, *Galloway Levellers*, 29.
10. Clerk, *A Journie to Galloway in 1721*, quoted in Livingston, *Galloway Levellers*, 53.
11. "Letter to the Right Hon. Augustus Du Cary," quoted in Davidson, *Discovering the Scottish Revolution 1*, 216.
12. Clerk, quoted in Devine, *Scottish Clearances*, 106.
13. Quoted in Livingston, *Galloway Levellers*, 61.
14. Devine, *Scottish Clearances*, 100–101. "Mailings" were small cottages or crofts.
15. Quoted in Livingston, *Galloway Levellers*, 79.
16. Devine, *Scottish Clearances*, 63. Common land was usually called *commonty* in Scotland.
17. Devine, *Scottish Clearances*, 78.
18. Aitchison and Cassell, *Lowland Clearances*, 56.
19. Davidson, "Scottish Path 2," 439.
20. Devine, *Scottish Clearances*, 150.
21. Devine, *Scottish Clearances*, 150.
22. Devine, *Scottish Clearances*, 193.
23. Smout, "The Landowner and the Planned Village," in Phillipson and Mitchison, eds., *Scotland in the Age of Improvement*, 79.
24. Whatley, *Industrial Revolution in Scotland*, 26.
25. Whatley, *Industrial Revolution in Scotland*, 25.
26. Malm, *Fossil Capital*, 45.
27. This account is mostly based on Richards, *Highland Clearances*, 86–104.
28. Richards, *Highland Clearances*, 86.
29. Quoted in Richards, *Highland Clearances*, 101.
30. Richards, *Highland Clearances*, 111.
31. Davidson, "Scottish Path 1," 244.
32. Devine, *Scotland's Empire*, 325.
33. John Prebble, *Culloden*, 314.
34. McLeod, *Gloomy Memories*, 6–8.
35. Somers, *Letters from the Highlands*, 26, 28. Marx quoted Somers in chapter 27 of *Capital 1*.
36. Devine, *Scottish Clearances*, 320–21.

37.   Robert Southey, *Journal of a Tour in Scotland in 1819*, 269.
38.   James Hunter, *Making of the Crofting Community*, 13.
39.   Richards, *Highland Clearances*, 320.

9. Poaching and the Bloody Code

1.   Manning, "A Voice for the Poor," 96.
2.   Engels, *Condition of the Working Class in England*, 266–67.
3.   Henry Knighton, quoted in Dobson, ed., *Peasants' Revolt of 1381*, 186.
4.   Cunningham, *A New and Complete Law Dictionary*, 5. A *haye* (or *haia*) was an enclosure for trapping deer.
5.   Perelman, *Invention of Capitalism*, 39.
6.   1 James I, chap. 27.
7.   Thompson, *Whigs and Hunters*, 16.
8.   22 & 23 Charles II, chap. 25.
9.   McLynn, *Crime and Punishment in Eighteenth-Century England*, 216.
10.   4 & 5 William & Mary, chap. 23.
11.   Munsche, *Gentlemen and Poachers*, 27.
12.   Munsche, "The Gamekeeper and English Rural Society," 83.
13.   Munsche, *Gentlemen and Poachers*, 5.
14.   Rogers, "The Waltham Blacks and the Black Act," 468; Thompson, *Whigs and Hunters*, 7.
15.   Quoted in Thompson, *Whigs and Hunters*, 99.
16.   Thompson, *Whigs and Hunters*, 36.
17.   For the full text of the Black Act, see Thompson, *Whigs and Hunters*, 213–20.
18.   Radzinowicz, "The Waltham Black Act," 72, 74.
19.   Nourse, *Campania Foelix* [1699], 15–16.
20.   Locke, *Second Treatise of Government*, sec. 94.
21.   Thompson, *Whigs and Hunters*. 152.
22.   Hay, "Property, Authority and the Criminal Law," in Hay et al., eds., *Albion's Fatal Tree*, 21, 56–57.
23.   Thirsk, "Agricultural Policy," in *Agricultural Change*, 195.
24.   For a summary of game-related statutes passed between 1660 and 1831, see Munsche, *Gentlemen and Poachers*, 169–86,
25.   Archer, *By a Flash and a Scare*, 211.
26.   Crabbe, *Poetical Works*, 311.
27.   Anon., *Three Letters on the Game Laws*, 331.
28.   Tilley, *Dictionary of the Proverbs in England*, 696.
29.   Quoted in Anon., *Three Letters on the Game Laws*, 357.
30.   Archer, *By a Flash and a Scare*, 211.
31.   Thompson, *Whigs and Hunters*, 149.
32.   *Morning Advertiser*, 23 January 1844; *Preston Chronicle*, 27 January 1844.

33. Archer, *By a Flash and a Scare*, 217.
34. Hobsbawm and Rudé, *Captain Swing*, 79–81, 285–86.
35. Žmolek, *Rethinking the Industrial Revolution*, 819.

10. The Landlords' Revolution

1.   Piercy Ravenstone, *A Few Doubts*, 263.
2.   Prothero, *English Farming, Past and Present*, 149.
3.   Chambers and Mingay, *Agricultural Revolution*, 4–5.
4.   Allen, *Enclosure and the Yeoman*, 2.
5.   Patnaik and Patnaik, *Capital and Imperialism*, 101.
6.   Allen, *Enclosure and the Yeoman*, 191.
7.   Hammond and Hammond, *Village Labourer*, 29.
8.   Smith, *Wealth of Nations*, 680, 12.
9.   Quoted in Jim Handy, "'Almost Idiotic Wretchedness.'" 329.
10. Allen, "The Efficiency and Distributional Consequences of Eighteenth-Century Enclosures," 850.
11. Kerridge, *Agricultural Revolution*, 328.
12. Clark, "Too Much Revolution," in Mokyr, ed., *The British Industrial Revolution*, 222, 224.
13. Overton, "Re-Establishing the English Agricultural Revolution," 6–7.
14. Allen, "Tracking the Agricultural Revolution in England," 215–16.
15. Allen, "Tracking the Agricultural Revolution in England," 217.
16. Meredith and Oxley, "Nutrition and Health, 1700–1870," in Floud et al., eds., *The Cambridge Economic History of Modern Britain*, 119–21.
17. Nicholas and Oxley, "Living Standards of Women," 746.
18. *Capital 1*, 835.
19. Hay, "War, Dearth and Theft in the Eighteenth Century," 132.
20. Hammond and Hammond, *Village Labourer*, 117.
21. Thompson, *Customs in Common*, 252, 258.
22. Otter, *Diet for a Large Planet*, 2, 6.
23. Mill, *Principles of Political Economy*, 447.
24. Otter, *Diet for a Large Planet*, 15.
25. Kinealy, *New History of Ireland*, 102, 120.
26. *Capital 1*, 860.
27. Mokyr, *Why Ireland Starved*, 198.
28. Pomeranz, *Great Divergence*, 275.
29. Otter, *Diet for a Large Planet*, 50, 48.
30. Patnaik, Moyo, and Shivji, *Agrarian Question*, 26. See also Patnaik and Patnaik, *Capital and Imperialism*, 101–114.
31. *MECW*, vol. 31, 539.
32. *Capital 3*, 905.
33. Kedrosky, "Allen's Pause."

34. Kedrosky, "Allen's Pause."
35. Patnaik, Moyo, and Shivji, *Agrarian Question*, 26.
36. Overton, *Agricultural Revolution*, 3–4.
37. Overton, *Agricultural Revolution*, 4.
38. Allen, "Nitrogen Hypothesis," 20.
39. Daunton, *Progress and Poverty*, 39, 37–8.
40. Žmolek, *Rethinking the Industrial Revolution*, 203.
41. Williams, *The Country and the City*, 151.
42. Thompson, *Making of the English Working Class*, 350.
43. *Capital 1*, 811.

11. "Only Hunger Can Spur Them on to Labour"

1.   Marx, "Value, Price and Profit," *MECW*, vol. 20, 128.
2.   Lindert, "Who Owned Victorian England?" 25–51.
3.   Allen, *Enclosure and the Yeoman*, 1.
4.   *Capital 1*, 874.
5.   Anievas and Nişancıoğlu, *How the West Came to Rule*, 151–52.
6.   *Capital 1*, 800.
7.   Townsend, "A Dissertation on the Poor Laws" (1786).
8.   Perelman, "Marx, Malthus, and the Concept of Natural Resource Scarcity," 81.
9.   Handy, *Apostles of Inequality*, 36, 55.
10. Young, *Annals of Agriculture 1801*, 214.
11. Young, *An Inquiry into the Propriety*.
12. Young, *Autobiography*, 433.
13. Bishton, *General View of the Agriculture of the County of Salop*, 24–25.
14. Middleton, *View of the Agriculture of Middlesex*, 103.
15. Arbuthnot, *An Inquiry Into the Connection*, 81.
16. Billingsley, *General View of the Agriculture of the County of Somerset*, 50, 52.
17. Rusticus, "Sketch of a General Inclosure Bill," 165.
18. Poor Law Commissioners, *First Report*, 51.
19. Ibid., 59.
20. Cited in Snell, *Annals of the Labouring Poor*, 170.
21. Sturt, *Change in the Village*, 127, 130, 133.
22. Owen, *The Life of Robert Owen*, 276.
23. Clark, "Factory Discipline," 128, 132.
24. *Capital 1*, 548.
25. *Capital 1*, 382.

12. "The Alpha and Omega of the Coming Revolution"

1.   *Capital 3*, 571.

2.   Luxemburg, *Accumulation of Capital*, 433. Luxemburg is quoting Marx. In a more recent translation, the phrase is "dripping from head to toe, from every pore, with blood and dirt." *Capital 1*, 926.
3.   Chase, *Chartism*, 167, 249.
4.   Engels, "Outlines of a Critique of Political Economy," *MECW*, vol. 3, 429.
5.   Marx and Engels, "German Ideology," *MECW*, vol. 5, 64.
6.   Engels, "Principles of Communism," *MECW*, vol. 6, 351, 354.
7.   *MECW*, vol. 6, 513, 504, 505. The final sentence is translated directly from the 1848 German edition. The 1888 English edition, which is reproduced in the *MECW*, omitted the phrase "making for," and added "by a more equable distribution of the populace over the country." Draper, *Adventures of The Communist Manifesto*, 163.
8.   Marx to Engels, August 14, 1851. My translation, from *Karl Marx Friedrich Engels Gesamtausgabe* (MEGA), Band 4, 183. The translation in *MECW*, vol. 38, 425, entirely omits Marx's earthy language.
9.   Marx, *Grundrisse*, 408–10.
10. Marx, *Grundrisse*, 489.
11. *Capital 3*, 948–49.
12. Ibid., 949.
13. *Capital 1*, 637, 638
14. *Capital 1*, 579–80.
15. Engels, "1887 Preface," 425.
16. Engels, "Housing Question," *MECW*, vol. 23, 348.
17. Engels, "Housing Question," *MECW*, vol. 23, 389, 386.
18. Engels, "Housing Question," *MECW*, vol. 23, 330, 347.
19. Engels, "Housing Question," *MECW*, vol. 23, 347–48.
20. Engels, "Housing Question," *MECW*, vol. 23, 384.
21. Engels, *Anti–Dühring*, *MECW*, vol. 25, 278.
22. Quoted in Engels, *Anti–Dühring*, *MECW*, vol. 25, 276.
23. Engels, *Anti–Dühring*, *MECW*, vol. 25, 282.
24. Engels, *Anti–Dühring*, *MECW*, vol. 25, 283.
25. Engels, *Anti–Dühring*, *MECW*, vol. 25, 284.
26. Engels, *Anti–Dühring*, *MECW*, vol. 25, 283.
27. Luxemburg, *The Rosa Luxemburg Reader*, 370.

13. The Struggle Continues

1.   Luxemburg, *Accumulation of Capital*, 352.
2.   Galeano, *Open Veins of Latin America*, 2. Emphasis in original.
3.   Rodney, *How Europe Underdeveloped Africa*, 149.
4.   Foster and Clark, *The Robbery of Nature*, 37.
5.   *Capital 1*, 860n.

6.   Holleman, *Dust Bowls of Empire*, 64.
7.   Weis, *Global Food Economy,* 108–9.
8.   https://www.cnbc.com/id/47322740.
9.   https://landmatrix.org/observatory/global/.
10. Dell'Angelo et al., "Commons Grabbing and Agribusiness."
11. Neudert and Voget-Kleschin, *What Are the Effects of Large-Scale Land Acquisitions in Africa?*, 5, 6.
12. "Land Grabbing," https://www.globalagriculture.org/report-topics/land-grabbing.html.
13. Araghi, "The Invisible Hand and the Visible Foot," 120.
14. Foster, "The Defense of Nature," 5, 17.
15. https://climateandcapitalism.com/2022/06/24/peruvian-indigenous-organizations-declare-state-of-emergency/.
16. https://www.vanguardngr.com/2022/07/ondo-farmers-lawmaker-kick-as-govt-allegedly-ceed-50000-hectares-of-land-to-private-companies/.
17. Stedile, "We Only Have One Planet," 90–91.
18. Estes, *Our History Is the Future,* 256–57.

Appendix 1: The Meaning of "So-Called Primitive Accumulation"

1.   Marx, "Value, Price and Profit," *MECW,* vol. 20, 149.
2.   "Value, Price and Profit," *MECW,* vol. 20, 128.
3.   "Value, Price and Profit," *MECW,* vol. 20, 128–29.
4.   Except where noted, the following quotations are from Marx, "So-Called Primitive Accumulation," *Capital 1*, 873–940.
5.   *Capital 3,* 571.
6.   *Capital 3,* 349.
7.   See chapters 24 and 25 of *Capital 1.*
8.   Linebaugh, *Stop Thief!,* 73.
9.   Foster and Clark, *Robbery of Nature,* 36.
10. *Capital 3,* 948. Emphasis added.

Appendix 2: Marx and Engels and Russia's Peasant Communes

1.   *MECW,* vol. 24, 362–63.
2.   The Land Matrix 2022, landmatrix.org/observatory/global/; Dell'Angelo et al., "Commons Grabbing and Agribusiness."
3.   Federici, *Re-Enchanting the World*, 38, 31, 154.
4.   Kuusinen, *Fundamentals of Marxism-Leninism Manual*, 163. The second sentence is similar to one in *Capital,* but it omits text that shows Marx was referring to capitalist societies that were already industrializing.
5.   Chernikov, *Fundamentals of Scientific Socialism*, 36–37. Emphasis added.

6. *Capital 1*, 888, 861, 889, 891.

7. Watters, "The Peasant and the Village Commune," 147.

8. *MECW*, vol. 43, 121.

9. Eichner, *Surmounting the Barricades*, 64.

10. *MECW*, vol. 24, 199.

11. *MECW*, vol. 24, 43, 48.

12. Quoted in Dasgupta, "Uneven Development, the Russian Question and Marxian Paradigm," 8–9.

13. "Marx: A letter to the Editorial Board of *Otechestvenniye Zapiski*," in Shanin, ed., *Late Marx*, 134–37.

14. "Zasulich: A letter to Marx," in Shanin, ed., *Late Marx*, 98–99.

15. "Karl Marx: The reply to Zasulich," in Shanin, ed., *Late Marx*, 123–24.

16. "Karl Marx: The reply to Zasulich," in Shanin, ed., *Late Marx*, 109.

17. "Karl Marx: The reply to Zasulich," in Shanin, ed., *Late Marx*, 121.

18. "Karl Marx: The reply to Zasulich," in Shanin, ed., *Late Marx*, 104, 121.

19. *MECW*, vol. 24, 426.

20. *MECW*, vol. 24, 426.

21. *MECW*, vol. 46, 69.

22. Trotsky, *The Young Lenin*, 28.

23. Trotsky, *The Young Lenin*, 31.

24. *MECW*, vol. 24, 252.

25. *MECW*, vol. 45, 384.

26. *MECW*, vol. 46, 83.

27. *MECW*, vol. 46, 45–46.

28. *MECW*, vol. 46, 83. An earthquake on the Greek island of Chios on April 3, 1881 killed nearly 8,000 people.

29. Shanin, ed., *Late Marx and the Russian Road*, 275.

30. *MECW*, vol. 5, 50.

31. Hobsbawm, "Introduction," in Marx, *Pre-Capitalist Economic Formations*, 38.

32. *Capital 1*, 876. Emphasis added.

33. *MECW*, vol. 24, 354.

34. MECW, vol. 47, 280.

35. *MECW*, vol. 46, 83.

36. *MECW*, vol. 46, 83.

37. *MECW*, vol. 26, 294.

38. Berman, "Marxism's Fatal Flaw."

39. *MECW*, vol. 6, 170.

Index